D0883466

UNA DESTINATIO VIAE DIVERSAE

·A·D·1852·

MILLS COLLEGE

LIBRARY

From the
Keller Educational
and Charitable
Fund

The Art
and Archaeology
of Pashash

The Art
and Archaeology
of Pashash

By Terence Grieder

University of Texas Press/Austin & London

The publication of this book was assisted by a grant from the Andrew W. Mellon Foundation.

Library of Congress Cataloging in Publication Data
Grieder, Terence.
The art and archaeology of Pashash.
Bibliography: p.
1. Pashash site, Peru. 2. Indians of South America—Peru—Art. I. Title.
F3429.1.A45G74   985'.1   77-8445
ISBN 0-292-70328-7
Copyright © 1978 by the University of Texas Press
All Rights Reserved
Printed in the United States of America

All photographs and drawings are by the author unless otherwise mentioned.
Design/Eje Wray
Typesetting/G&S Typesetters
Printing/University of Texas Printing Division
Binding/Universal Bookbindery

Contents

985
G824a

MILLS COLLEGE
LIBRARY

Mills College Library
Withdrawn

Acknowledgments

The Pashash project began in July and August 1969 with a season of reconnaissance in which Dr. Hermilio Rosas La Noire and I were in the field under the aegis of the National Museum of Anthropology and Archaeology in Lima. With the narrowing of the study to Pashash itself, the 1971 field season was authorized by Peruvian national Supreme Resolution no. 156, of March 9, 1971, signed by Arrisueño Cornejo, minister of education. The third season in the field, July and August 1973, was authorized by Supreme Resolution no. 1,728, of May 23, 1973, signed by Alfredo Carpio Becerra, general of division of the Peruvian Army, minister of education. Those immediately responsible for the project were, in 1971, archaeologist Alberto Bueno Mendoza and, in 1973, architect Frederick Cooper Llosa, the director of the Center of Investigation and Restoration of Monuments, both of the National Institute of Culture.

The United States Embassy was of indispensable aid in securing these authorizations. I am indebted to Edward T. Purcell and his successor, Frances E. Coughlin, cultural affairs officers of the embassy, and in particular to Jackelyne Portal Purdy, cultural affairs adviser, for her attention to and assistance with the problems of the project.

The professional staff in 1971 consisted of John Williamson Smith III, then a doctoral student in archaeology at the University of Texas at Austin, and myself. In 1973 the professional staff consisted of archaeologist Alberto Bueno Mendoza, conservator of Pachacamac, and myself, assisted by Dagmar Janiel Grieder.

The University of Texas has provided continual support. I am grateful to the late Chancellor Harry Huntt Ransom for personally authorizing the initial grant in 1969 and to Dr. William Glade, director of the Institute of Latin American Studies, for the support of the institute during this extended period. During the final season in Peru in 1975, which was devoted to laboratory analysis of the excavation collections, additional support came from the Latin American Archaeology Committee of the institute, chaired by Dr. James Neely, which provided grants to two Texas students—Janet Eager and Jerold Johnson—and to two Peruvian students—Carlos Farfán and Ponciano Paredes—to assist in the work. Alberto Bueno consulted in the work and kindly provided laboratory space at

Pachacamac, and Dagmar Grieder and I completed the crew. A project of this type is inevitably a group effort, and I wish to express my gratitude to all these colleagues for their enthusiastic and intelligent cooperation.

I wish to thank especially Holly Carver, for the editorial clarity she brought to many complex problems, and Eje Wray, for her artist's understanding of the design of this book.

Francisco Malpartida acted as foreman of the excavation crews during three seasons in the field. Julio Velázquez, Dionisio Rafaeli, Cirilo Paredes, Flavio Malpartida, Juan Herrera, Ernesto Manrique, Levente Canchis, Eloy Contreras, Marcelino Reyes, Marcos Pérez, Manuel Campos, Eleuterio Vivar, Juan Castañeda and his sons, all of Cabana, and the English traveler David Owen were members of the excavation crews at various times. I am grateful to these men for their efficiency in this heavy labor.

I am indebted to many friendly people in Cabana for their help and hospitality, in particular to Professor Nestor Ascencios G. of the Artisans' Center and to Javier Figueroa F., subprefect of the province of Pallasca. To Riva Alvarez Vázquez, director of the Artisans' Center, the whole project owes a special debt of gratitude for her kindness and continual assistance. Her breadth of understanding and willing collaboration were essential to the success of the project.

The Art
and Archaeology
of Pashash

1

2

3

6

4

7

5

Plate 1. *Lapis lazuli whorl from the burial offering. 4.9 cm. diameter, with a hole 1.8 cm. diameter through it. 12/7.46.*

Plate 2. *Spout-handled vessel in Cabana Cream Resist from the doorway offering. The celestial deity is depicted. 23.5 cm. high. 10/4.64.*

Plate 3. *Effigy head with spout in the turban. This fragment was part of the offering of broken vessels in the fill below the floor of the burial chamber. 9 cm. high. 12/3.4.*

Plate 4. *Red stone pedestal cup with representation of a crowned god. The eyes and crown have green stone inlays, and there are traces of iron red paint. This vessel was the center of the doorway offering. 7.3 cm. high. 10/4.1.*

Plate 5. *Feline-serpent effigy vessel from the doorway offering. 9.5 cm. high. 10/4.56.*

Plate 6. *Four cups from the burial offering. Back: 12/7.96; left:12/7.56; right: 12/7.61; front: 12/7.84, with red pigment powder.*

Plate 7. *Gold jewelry from the burial offering. Lower left: a hollow human head (12/7.32) and the top of a shaft with spiraling feline serpents (12/7.30). Also shown are the heads of pins 12/7.15, with an owl with green stone eyes; 12/7.10, with green stone inlays in the eye of the feline; and 12/7.7, a solid head; as well as 12/7.9, the top of a pin.*

Introduction

Leonardo da Vinci has said: "Two weaknesses leaning against one another add up to one strength." The halves of an arch cannot even stand upright; the whole arch supports a weight. Similarly, archaeological research is blind and empty without aesthetic re-creation, and aesthetic re-creation is irrational and often misguided without archaeological research. But, "leaning against one another," these two can support the "system that makes sense," that is, an historical synopsis.—Erwin Panofsky 1957: 19

This study of the archaeology of Pashash has been made from the standpoint of the history of art. During the past century, art history has developed as a dependency of two broader fields of study: history and archaeology. That is to say, the history of art depends for its chronology and its cultural context on the literary documents retained from the past or on the material remains recovered by archaeology. History and archaeology are more inclusive fields because they contain evidence of more aspects of life than can be discovered in art.

On the other hand, it would be difficult to sustain the argument that one could understand the intellectual life of any society without reference to its visual arts. Rudolf Arnheim has shown that perception is cognition (1969) and that "genuine art work requires organization which involves many, and perhaps all, of the cognitive operations known from theoretical thinking" (p. 263). "A work of art must do more than be itself: it must fulfill a semantic function . . ." (Arnheim 1957: 419–420). There is abundant evidence that perception and its expression in the visual arts are important at the primary inventive level and that verbal and theoretical expressions derive from them. The most famous example of the primacy of perception in cognition and the power of style over theory is Galileo's rejection of Kepler's elliptical planetary orbits in favor of perfect circles (Panofsky 1954). The case is not unique but, rather, typical.

Since art is in itself a functioning semantic system, it is possible to study it from two different points of view: analysis of the system and analysis of the content. Arnheim (1964) has demonstrated that the system itself has inherent meanings. Methods for the analysis of both the system and the content have been particularly developed in the study of Pre-Columbian art (Grieder 1975). George Kubler's "configurational" method, developed in the study of the art of Teotihuacan, is a good example of an analysis of the system which suggests conclusions about the content (Kubler 1967). Since conscious understanding requires the confirmation of society, we define "understanding content" by our ability to translate it into a verbal form. The art of Pashash is so consistent and repetitious in its imagery and symbols that we may assume that its content was consciously verbalized by its makers and its audience, but that is not always true of art. We are often confronted by art which has no accompanying verbal form; the latest avant-garde art in our own culture is the best example. The critic or the historian who wishes to translate the content into a verbal form must depend on what has been called the "ethnological" method in Pre-Columbian studies. That is, one seeks out informants within the culture, which is to say within the original audience of the art in question. Some special things, but by no means everything, can be learned if the informant is also the artist. If no informant from the original audience can be found, the historian is reduced to looking for informants among people who can be considered reasonably knowledgeable, who share some cultural trait which qualifies them to understand and translate the conventional meaning carried by the system. In general, the farther the informants are in time and space from the original audience, the more doubtful their translations.

The ethnological method has been the subject of controversy, but it must be stressed that a work of art means what its audience thinks it means; the audience discards objects if finds meaningless. In the case of the art of Pashash, for which the original audience is extinct and for which no translations of its visual symbols survive, we are forced to seek verbalizations in societies which share some cultural traits. Burial offerings containing, among other things, small pieces of rock crystal, a mirror, red pigment, and perhaps a sacrificed companion are found in many societies, and their symbolic meanings have been explained. The symbolic system which these societies share has been studied under the rubric of shamanism, a system of thought characteristic of hunting

societies, but one whose cosmology and social forms survived in complex agricultural societies in both Asia and America (Eliade 1964: chaps. 9, 11). (For shamanism in the Andean region, see the articles by Furst and Sharon in Furst 1972 and by Métraux in Steward 1963: vol. 5, pp. 588–599; also see Tschopik 1951.)

But it is the art, not the society, which is the special concern of this study. Taking the symbols and cosmology of shamanism as a model, Pashash art and burial practices become a coherent and meaningful system. Both archaeologists and art historians recognize the obligation to draw conclusions from their data. We will never know for certain whether the interpretation offered in chapter 10 coincides exactly with the ideas of the people of ancient Pashash, but with the material now available it seems to be the most complete, coherent, and economical interpretation possible.

From the viewpoint of art history, the principal weakness of the interpretation of Pashash art in terms of shamanic cosmology is that the interpretation remains very general. Implicit in the study of history is a belief in the importance of particular people and events. History may reveal the common experiences of typical people, but it is distinguished by its interest in the range of human experience, a range in which the unique experiences of individuals find their places. Historical studies begin with a generalization founded on previous research, which serves as an initial hypothesis. The generalization is useful as a point of departure, but it is always clear to the historian that it is a gross oversimplification of the complexities of the historical events. In this respect history is different from the social sciences and is complementary to them. As history proceeds from the general to the particular, the sciences proceed from the observation of particular phenomena to general principles or laws. As history emphasizes the range of individual experience, the sciences emphasize the norms and mean levels of experience. The narrative method of history finds its best expression in samples too small to be treated by the statistical methods required to reach the general laws of the sciences, but the validity of the narrative method as part of the range of human experience is undoubted.

Although history is in some respects the opposite of science, its method is nevertheless "scientific." The historian formulates a question, gathers evidence which bears on the question, and draws a conclusion based on the evidence.

With the exception of mathematics, which may use a truly deductive method, no science operates with a method inherently more rigorous than that of history (Reichenbach 1951). Yet even the inductive method carries historians only a short distance into their problems, for it, like deduction, is both based on and produces generalizations. Historians, and art historians in particular, are nominalists at heart. History is full of surprises. If it is not, then the investigation may have been a waste of time. Historical data are full of answers to questions one could not have asked until one saw the data. It is important that the value of history lies in its production of new knowledge that could not have been subsumed under a premise and that, in its conclusions, still resists reduction to generalizations.

To the historian the word "proof" is not very useful, since it implies some faith in the validity of an initial premise. For art historians, and especially for specialists in the art of nonliterate societies, the existence of the material object is the elementary evidence. They may need proof of the authenticity of the object as an ancient work, but its existence as an object is authenticated by their own senses.

This study is in large part a catalog of historical material, but it is also occupied at several points with inductive generalizations: defining the sequence of periods and phases, defining the styles, the relations between styles, and the meaning of symbols. These problems must be solved at an early stage of an art historical investigation, and their prominence here is an indication of the incompleteness of the study. The history of Andean art, and of Pre-Columbian art generally, is still in its infancy, as evidenced by the preoccupation with the formulation of generalizations which have sufficient validity to serve as initial hypotheses. The identification of ceramic workshop traditions and individual styles is a step toward the aesthetic re-creation which is one of the fundamentals of historical synopsis.

1. *Head of a warrior. Tenoned stone. National Museum of Anthropology and Archaeology, Lima.*

The Pashash project grew out of studies of the Chavín style which I had undertaken earlier. Those studies had provided a plausible picture of artistic development through the long Chavín period down to about 500 B.C., but the end of that style and the transition to later styles were obscure. In 1969 I was seeking a site which might reveal the "decline and fall" of the Chavín style and the rise of its principal successor, the Recuay style.

A stone head with a tenon for insertion in a masonry wall is a characteristic Chavín sculptural form. It appears also in some later styles, where it may be an indication of near or remote Chavín derivation. The head of a warrior wearing a helmet with a transverse crest (fig. 1), now in the collection of the National Museum in Lima, was attributed by the great Peruvian archaeologist Julio Tello (1929: fig. 46) to the ancient site of Pashash. This tenoned head in a non-Chavín style from a site just about 160 air kilometers from Chavín de Huantar, the major center of the Chavín style, hinted at the existence of exactly the historical evidence I was seeking. The hypothesis on which this project was based is that Pashash grew up as an important center at the end of the Chavín period and into the Recuay and would provide evidence of that transition.

Although the hypothesis can be considered correct, three seasons of excavation have not given us much evidence of Chavín culture at Pashash. The ceramic sequence begins with Chavinoid types and shows the transitions fairly clearly, but the architectural history of the site remains a major mystery. The effect of the hypothesis has been to direct our excavations toward test pits and cuts related to buildings, rather than toward broad clearing of living surfaces within single levels, which would give more social information. The advantage of beginning with small stratified excavations is their provision of information on the historical sequence with minimum destruction of the site, leaving an opportunity for future investigations.

At this point the project has been swamped with evidence of the Recuay style, and it has seemed wisest to deal with the material which has presented itself and hold the original question in abeyance. Art is a language—a universally human language in its fundamental structure. Taking that assumption as a working hypothesis, the problem of reading the form and content of the Recuay style at Pashash has emerged as the central question at this point. This study is intended to present the material which has come to light and to make the beginnings of an interpretive historical analysis.

2. *Opposite: the northern highlands of Peru. Pashash is located at 78°3' west longitude, 8°24' south latitude, in Pallasca Province of the department of Ancash. The map covers the region from the Pacific Ocean on the west over the high ranges of the Cordillera Blanca, just east of the Callejón de Huaylas, to the deep valley of the Marañon River, which flows northward into the Amazon, on the east.*
Following page: the region around Pashash, showing ancient sites.

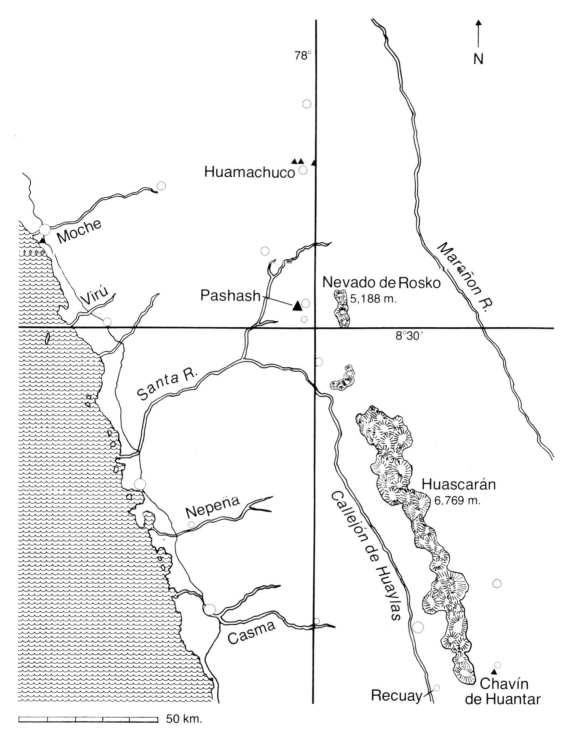

78°

N

Huamachuco

Moche

Virú

Pashash

Nevado de Rosko
5,188 m.

8°30′

Marañón R.

Santa R.

Nepeña

Callejón de Huaylas

Huascarán
6,769 m.

Casma

Recuay

Chavín
de Huantar

50 km.

▲ ancient sites mentioned in the text
○ modern towns and cities

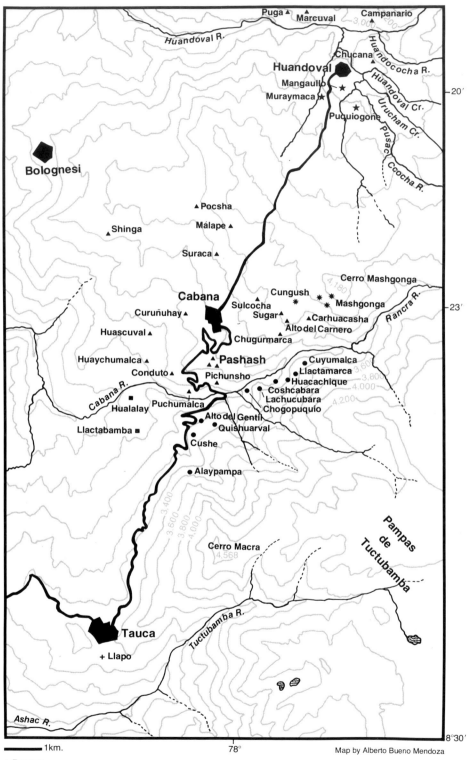

Puga ▲   ▲ Marcuval   □ Campanario

Huandoval R.   3.000

                                    Chucana ▲
                     Huandoval ⬟
                   Mangaullo
         Muraymaca ★   ★   Puquiogone ★

                                                    — 20'

Bolognesi ⬟

                     ▲ Pocsha
         Shinga ▲   Málape ▲

                     Suraca ▲

                                        Cerro Mashgonga
                                               4.180
                              Cungush ✳   ✳   ✳ Mashgonga
         Cabana ⬟   Sulcocha ▲
                   Curuñuhay ▲   Sugar ▲   ▲ Carhuacasha
         Huascuval ▲   Alto del Carnero ▲

                              Chugurmarca ▲

         Huaychumalca ▲   ▲ Pashash   ● Cuyumalca
                   Conduto ▲   ▲▲   ● Llactamarca
                         Pichunsho ▲   ● Huacachique
                                         ● Coshcabara
         Hualalay ■ Puchumalca ▲   ● Lachucubara
                                         ● Chogopuquio

         Llactabamba ■   ● Alto del Gentil
                              ● Quishuarval

                   ● Cushe

                   ● Alaypampa

                                        Pampas
                                          de
                                        Tuctubamba

                              Cerro Macra
                                 4.568

                   Tauca ⬟
                   + Llapo

         Ashac R.

━━━━ 1km.   78°   Map by Alberto Bueno Mendoza

▲ Recuay
■ post-Recuay
● probable post-Recuay
★ unknown culture
+ Chimu
✳ Inca

I.
The Site

The ruins of the ancient town now called
Pashash lie at an altitude of about 3,255 meters
on the Pacific slope of the Andes in northern
Peru. The ruins are strung along the crest of a
steep ridge for about 550 meters (fig. 3). Maximum width of the ruins as they are known is
about 250 meters. On the south, the ridge drops
precipitously to the Cabana River. On the north
the drop is more gradual to the small Pallasca
River, and most of the principal constructions are
located on this side. The first inhabitants of the
site had a late Chavín culture, to judge by the
remains of their pottery, but it is difficult to rec-
oncile the location of Pashash with the idea of
peaceful religious peasant villages once postulated for the Chavín period. The location is in-
convenient for farming or for the management
of water resources; its sole advantages are as a
lookout and as a refuge from attack. There is no
spot in the region more defensible than that
chosen by the inhabitants of Pashash.

Although the particular spot may have been
chosen for reasons of defense, the region is an
advantageous one for an agricultural people and
remains well populated today. Numerous ancient sites testify to the area's appeal to peoples
of successive cultures.

The Andean region offers limited areas for
permanent habitation. Occupation of the coastal
desert is limited to oasislike river valleys found
at intervals throughout its 3,000-kilometer
length. At the other extreme lie the snowfields
and tundras of the high mountains, which are
equally inhospitable to permanent settlement.
Between these zones lies a temperate strip, wa-
tered by seasonal rains and by runoff from the
high ranges. Lying roughly between an altitude
of 2,000 and 4,000 meters, this temperate zone
forms a continuous strip around the mountain
ranges, widening at times into highland basins
or narrowing into precipices. This zone must
always have been relatively attractive to people
who lived by subsistence farming. The eastern
slopes of the Andes, which are covered by dense
forest, with soil leached by the Amazonian rains,
require a different way of life, one dependent on
shifting agriculture and hunting. Thus, the
highland temperate zone was a refuge for settled agricultural people between the extremes of
the desert, the tundra, and the jungle.

An important effect of the continuity of this
temperate strip is the ease of communication it
provides. Although the people of the desert coast
were in communication from valley to valley,

which only the bases remain, or which are largely covered by alluvium. An ancient entrance through these walls was at a spot locally called "La Portada," an opening only 1.54 meters wide between two upright squared stones standing just 1.4 meters high. The irregular plan of the walls and the locations of modern paths suggest that other entrances may have existed, but none are evident.

Many of the walls at Pashash are retaining walls for earth platforms. The South Wall, closing the depression leading to the Cabana River, is over 12 meters high and is the largest of the remaining revetment walls, but others of more modest scale stood throughout the site.

The most spectacular existing construction is the platform called "El Caserón," which measures over 15 meters high and 30 meters across. The wall was built of very large stones cut and smoothed on just one face and chinked with spalls. Only the corners were constructed entirely of squared blocks. The handsome pattern

of block and spall was clearly intentional. The platform was built in three campaigns, evident in the horizontal levels, the upper one being set back a few centimeters. The stones are laid in mud mortar, but the whole structure is very solid; the few places where stones have fallen have not caused a general collapse. In the top surface at the west edge, there is a narrow rectangular opening of a shaft which may have served as a ventilator of the sort found in the Chavín period temples at Chavín de Huantar and Pacopampa. Surface clearing of the top by Alberto Bueno in 1973 revealed rectangular constructions but no obvious entrance. The great platform may have some interior passages, but it appears to be mainly solid rock and earth fill. Excavations at the base in 1969, by Hermilio Rosas, and 1971, by John W. Smith (Cuts 2, 3, and 8), revealed later walls of smaller stones set against the walls of El Caserón, but the deeply buried foundations of the great walls were not reached. The subsequent constructions appear

from their scale to have been domestic. It is clear that El Caserón merits more study.

As one penetrates deeper into the ruins, moving westward, one reaches the saddle between the ridge proper and La Capilla Hill (fig. 4). At the saddle, where a modern farmhouse is located, there is a large rock outcrop with crude petroglyphs, mostly simple pits and lines. The saddle was widened and fortified by the colossal South Wall on one side and by smaller walls, standing about 6 meters high, of which scarcely a trace remains, on the other.

La Capilla Hill, named for a modern chapel formerly on its top, rises at the end of the ridge (fig. 5). Its steep sides were further fortified by a series of walls which form platforms. Excavations into these platforms (Cut 6) have shown that the upper levels of the hill are largely composed of rock fill brought in to widen and level the hilltop. One climbs from the saddle onto the wide north terrace of the hill, which has the remains of numerous small stone chambers, probably houses (fig. 13). From this terrace one ascends onto the top platform by a stairway built parallel to the retaining wall. The top platform had small domestic structures along its western edge and a small two-room funerary temple on its eastern side. The burial and its offerings, which are the main subjects of this book, were discovered in the foundations of this structure. On the south the hill drops to a lower terrace, where there are remains of houses similar to those on the top and on the north terrace.

The huge stone walls of Pashash must always have been a landmark for succeeding peoples. When the Italian geographer, Antonio Raimondi, traveled through the region in April 1868, he was taken to see the ruins, "which consist of some double walls, in the form of quadrangular fortresses and which are known in the town [of Cabana] by the name of Great Walls of the Pagans [*Paredones de los Gentiles*]" (Raimondi 1874: 316; my translation).

On Raimondi's advice, the site was visited just a few years later by Charles Wiener, who was more impressed than Raimondi had been by the ruins and by the numerous and varied stone reliefs which he found in the village of Cabana, where they had been taken, supposedly, from the ruins of Pashash. He found "nearly thirty" reliefs built into modern house walls and plastered over. He took the trouble to clean the reliefs of their plaster coatings, drew them, and later had fourteen of them engraved, rather inaccurately, for inclusion in the account of his travels (1880: 165–172). (Three of the sculptures, either casts or originals evidently collected by Wiener, are in the collection of the Musée Ethnographique [Musée de l'Homme], Paris, and were reproduced in Means 1931: figs. 73–75.)

The stone sculptures continued to be the principal focus of scholarly interest. Richard Schaedel visited the site in 1948 and cataloged sixty-three stone sculptures in Cabana which evidently originated in the Pashash ruins. He wrote a brief description of the architecture and analyzed a five-hundred-sherd sample of the pottery, concluding that the site "pertains principally to the Recuay period." He found no evidence of direct influence of Tiahuanacoid or later cultures at Pashash (1952: 208, 210). On the other hand, in his cultural geography of Ancash, Félix Alvarez-Brun suggests that Pashash may have been the famous center of the Inca period cult of Catequilla mentioned in the sixteenth-century chronicles of Arriaga and Calancha (1970: 100). Pallasca style stone sculpture has also been assigned a date of A.D. 700–1000 (Emmerich 1968: no. 56). Schaedel's opinion that the site, at least as presently known, does not show a major occupation of the Wari period or of any later period is supported by the evidence gathered in this study.

It is clear that the assignment of the numerous ancient occupation sites in the province of Pallasca to their proper historical periods still presents us with many fascinating problems.

There is some evidence that at its greatest extension the ancient town covered the slopes of the hill where the modern town of Cabana now sits (fig. 6). In 1973 a tenoned head was found in a construction excavation on the north side of the church in the center of town. Local people have also mentioned other sculptures discovered in building foundations in the town. There

4. *El Caserón with La Capilla Hill in the distance.*
An old photograph, taken in the 1940s by Abraham Guillén.

5. *Opposite: La Capilla Hill from the east.*
The South Wall, over 12 m. high, is in the center
of the picture.

6. *The ruins of Pashash seen from Cabana,*
looking south.
The point in the middle distance is La Capilla
Hill.

are no recorded descriptions of these discoveries, but from the present ownership of stone carvings it would appear that the center of modern Cabana lies on an ancient area which included buildings with sculptural ornament. The relationship between what seem to have been two sectors of the site—one now town, the other ruins—has not been determined, but the ruins definitely contained both domestic and funerary constructions. It is conceivable that an administrative district might have been located where the town now stands, since the stone sculptures suggest military themes which would be appropriate in a secular area. It seems unlikely that any parts of the site which may lie beneath the modern town will ever be recorded. More than four centuries of occupation have no doubt eliminated or distorted any earlier remains, and the dense occupation gives few opportunities for archaeological sampling. Our

search in the ruins for possible locations of the tenoned heads has been fruitless, and it appears that it may be a mistake to imagine them as having ornamented the extant walls of, for example, El Caserón. The original setting of the sculptures is still a mystery. The map (fig. 3), which does not include the town, very likely does not show the buildings or even the area in which those stones were set, and the sculptures assigned by Schaedel to Pashash may all or partly originate in the heretofore undefined sector of the site now covered by the town of Cabana. Ancient Pashash was certainly larger than the area currently set aside. The excavations bear on the Cabana sculptures only to the extent that art motifs found in the ruins, many of them on materials other than stone, help define the period of the sculptures and their approximate dates.

2.
The Excavations

A series of five assumptions underlies the rationale of the excavations. The more general assumptions usually go without saying, but it may be worthwhile to record them very briefly. (1) It is important for us to know as much as we can about human history. (2) Experiences and attitudes very different from our own are especially worth seeking out. These two assumptions are widely shared, but they are difficult to defend logically. Other assumptions, which led to the particular emphasis of this project, are logically defensible. (3) The record of a people's experiences and attitudes remains in the things they made or built. (4) Material things are a more reliable record than performance expressions (e.g., oral traditions and musical and dance arts), which may be reinterpreted and revised by the performer as well as by the audience. My attention was directed to a particular region and a particular site by the fact that (5) the general absence of contextual data on art objects from highland Ancash of the periods after Chavín makes the understanding of Andean history impossible. Until some contextual data had been obtained and evaluated, this remained an assumption. Context—meaning both synchronic and diachronic relationships be-

tween material things—could be examined only by excavation. Extant walls, the most noticeable ancient things, provide a beginning for contextual studies, to which other materials can be related, and they tend to retain intact deposits which are naturally dispersed in an open site.

The locations of all the excavations were determined by the general desire to find stratified ceramic debris in relation to architecture. The pits were in other respects exploratory in the sense that they were scattered in order to reveal different kinds of occupation or different periods. They actually revealed uniformity, the same ceramic types appearing in the same sequence in all parts of the site which were tested.

The crews were recruited locally and were inexperienced in archaeology, but they ordinarily consisted of only three or four men for each cut, working under the close supervision of at least one member of the professional staff. Since all the excavated material was to be retained in Peru, fieldwork proceeded slowly to permit complete recording. Actual excavation was usually done from about 8:30 A.M. until about 2:00 P.M., the afternoon and evening being reserved for laboratory work and recording. Exceptions to this system occurred only when the burial offerings were encountered, since it was deemed unsafe to leave valuable material in the ground when our excavations, for which we were unable to obtain a guard, had been looted or disrupted several times at night. When the offerings were discovered, excavation continued until dark or until an appearance of sterility could be managed and the ground left clear.

It was our intention to make all the excavations by natural levels. If no natural level had been reached after 30 centimeters, or less in some cases, the excavated material was segregated and a new level was designated arbitrarily. In a few cases, such as Cut 1, no natural levels could be precisely determined, so the arbitrary levels were retained. There was no case in which a level used in the field was divided after analysis; the arbitrary field levels were always shallower than subsequent analysis showed to have been required.

Terrain and soil conditions influenced our work in certain ways. The steep hillsides and narrow ridges of the site make everything roll downhill. Therefore, we always had to assume that much of what we found may have been redeposited by sliding or washing down from above. This was clearly the case in Cut 3, in which some reversing of chronological levels seems certain. We particularly sought level spots for several cuts (Cuts 1, 4, 6, and 9) or places where slumping material might have settled or been trapped (Cuts 2 and 7). The hilly terrain also prevented the setting of a single datum point. The map (fig. 3), which was made with a Brunton compass and a tape, does not record topographic levels. Each excavation was measured independently, ordinarily taking the current ground surface or an extant architectural feature as the datum point.

The soil conditions affected our work in other ways. The soil in general is gray black and sets in hard lumps. To reduce it to a consistency which could be sifted through a screen was impractical, and the screening process was done by hand, with the supervisor frequently helping. Every cut had some stone in it, which made it hard to obtain sharp profiles and clean levels. Only Cut 3, which sectioned a deposit of alluvium, was largely free of stone. Cuts 2, 5, and 6, which ran into layers of massive stones which we interpret as construction fill, were abandoned when it became impossible to remove the stones without completely redesigning the cuts

and revising our intentions. Profiles in the excavations were constantly being cleaned, but they rarely gained a tailored appearance, due to large rocks which either projected or left gaps. The main concern of the supervisors in this regard was to prevent material from falling from higher levels into the level being cleared.

The character of this site is determined by constructed walls, by the fill and floors which were laid, and by the accumulations of living debris and erosion materials. These processes result in a gross stratigraphy in which most of the levels were produced by conscious human action, either constructive or destructive, with only the accumulation of debris being unintended by the inhabitants. The character of the site requires excavation mainly by construction units which can be considered to have been placed at a precise time; only debris represents slow accumulation. Thus, in most cases, the important distinctions are between levels. Higher or lower vertical location of materials within the levels is usually not significant.

The excavations were spread over a period of five years, during three of which fieldwork was done. Cuts 1 through 6 were done during the month of August 1969; Cuts 7 through 10 were done during July and August 1971; and Cuts 11 and 12 were done during July and August 1973. They are described here in groups pertaining to the two sectors of the site, without regard to the order in which they were done. The excavations in the northeastern part of the site (Cuts 1–3 and 7–8) will be described together, while those on La Capilla Hill (Cuts 4–6 and 9–12) will be described together.

All the excavated material is the property of the government of Peru and is in storage in government facilities. The material from Cuts 1 through 6 is stored at the National Museum of Anthropology and Archaeology in Lima. The material from Cuts 7 through 12 is stored at the Museum of Pachacamac.

Tables 1 through 9 summarize the ceramics from Cuts 1 through 9. Material from Cuts 10 through 12 is listed in appendix 2. Ceramic types are described in chapter 5. References to the excavations are abbreviated to the cut number, followed by a slash and the number of the level. Cataloged items are numbered following a period. For example, 12/7.57 refers to cataloged item 57 from Level 7 of Cut 12.

Excavations in the Northeastern Sector

Cut 1

The excavation was located in a nearly level area at the top of the ridge between two platform constructions (fig. 7). The location was chosen because natural erosion could not have contributed to the deposit. The strata had to have accumulated directly by human deposition, and natural erosion could only have reduced the deposit. I was the supervisor of the excavation.

The cut measured 2 by 5 meters in Level 1 but was reduced to 2 by 2.6 meters in Level 2. The digging was done in arbitrary levels of 20 centimeters each.

Level 1: 0–20 centimeters. Sod and brownish black soil.

Level 2: 20–40 centimeters. Irregular rocks in brownish black soil. The rocks are unworked and made no discernible pattern, but they appear to define an earlier surface.

Level 3: 40–60 centimeters. Brownish black soil on a sterile stone and shale base. Sherds were most abundant in this level, suggesting an accumulation of various periods in a very shallow soil. I have not been able to define meaningful natural strata in this cut. Sterile soil was reached at a depth of about 50 centimeters.

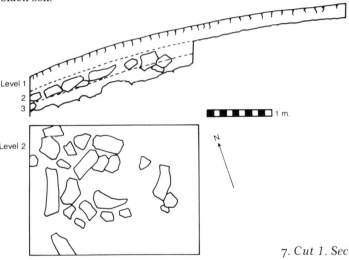

7. *Cut 1. Section and plan.*

Table 1.
Summary of the Ceramics from Cut 1

	Level 1	Level 2	Level 3	Total
Sherds	275	664	1,247	2,186
Rims	24	56	212	292
Pashash Orange & Vista Brown	218	614	1,073	1,905
Caserón Orange & Cabana Cream	56	50	174	280
Resist	1	0	1	2
Figurines	1	4	1	6

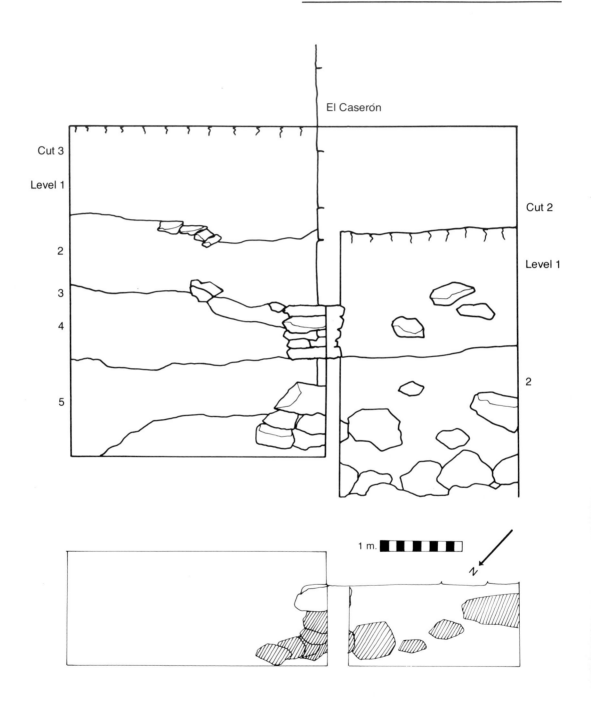

8. Cuts 2 and 3. Section and plan.
Hatching in the plan indicates Level 5;
unhatched indicates Level 4.

Cuts 2 and 3

These two excavations were located at the northeastern corner of El Caserón, at the lower end of the steep slope that flanks the building on the northeast (figs. 8, 9). Cut 2 was on the front, or western, face of the corner and was intended to reveal the foundation of El Caserón, but that proved to be beyond our resources. Cut 2 was abandoned at a depth of 420 centimeters in the stone fill which held few sherds. The most significant natural level was discernible at 260 centimeters, at the base of a stone wall which now stands just 60 centimeters high and divides Cut 2 from Cut 3. The fill above that level is defined culturally by the presence of Usú period potsherds, which are absent below the level of the

wall's base. Cut 2, which lies in an area shielded by El Caserón from slumping from above, seems to have a primary deposit. The sherd material from Cut 2 provides some evidence for the interpretation of the architecture. Both Cut 2 and Cut 3 were supervised by Hermilio Rosas.

Cut 3 extended 2.8 meters toward the northeast from the corner of El Caserón. It was excavated in five levels, all of them mainly alluvial soil which had been washed down along the side of El Caserón. Two of the levels contain the remains of stone walls, both of them of later date than El Caserón itself and both of very modest scale. The later is the late Recuay wall in Level 4, its period defined by the sherd material in Cut

9. *Cut 3 during excavation.*
El Caserón is in the background.

2. The earlier is a small curving wall in Level 5, which must be closer to the date of most of the potsherds in Cut 3. The large sample of pottery from Cut 3 did not reveal secure chronology, since it appeared that all the sherds had been redeposited by washing down and slumping from primary deposits farther up the hill. The radiocarbon measurements from this cut give further indications of mixing by redeposition. Nevertheless, the rich ceramic sample provides material for comparisons with the stratigraphically more reliable samples from other cuts.

The depth measurements of Cut 2 were taken from the higher surface level of the adjoining Cut 3. The upper 120 centimeters in Cut 2 are above the ground level.

Level 1: 120–260 centimeters. Gray soil and rock with little cultural material. Usú period plastically ornamented pottery appeared in this level.

Level 2: 260–420 centimeters. Gray soil and many rocks. The upper surface of this level seems to have been a ground surface when the wall between Cuts 2 and 3 was built. The potsherds can all be assigned to the Recuay period, an indication that this old surface and the wall were exposed at the end of the Recuay period and the beginning of the Usú period.

10. *Cut 3.*
The areas defined by strings are 50 cm. square.

Depth measurements in Cut 3 were taken from the current ground surface. All levels were composed of fine-grained black alluvial soil with practically no rock (fig. 10).

Level 1: 0–98 centimeters. Light brown soil, small stones. Recuay period pottery types.

Level 2: 98–175 centimeters. Darker soil with carbonized areas, one cluster of stones. Recuay period pottery collected on old surface by washing down the hill.

Level 3: 175–200 centimeters. Light gray soil, small stones. Abundant Recuay period sherds washed down.

Level 4: 200–270 centimeters. Light gray soil. Recuay Yaiá phase pottery. The base of a stone wall ending about 1 meter from the great wall of El Caserón was found at the west margin of the cut. The wall was made of stone set in mud mortar.

Level 5: 270–370 centimeters. Dark gray soil. Recuay Quimít phase potsherds. An earlier wall curving eastward from the corner of El Caserón appeared in this level.

Table 2.
Summary of the Ceramics from Cut 2

	Level 1	Level 2	Total
Sherds	81	329	410
Rims	16	39	55
Pashash Orange & Vista Brown	67	251	318
Caserón Orange & Cabana Cream	14	78	92
Resist	0	4	4
Figurines	2	0	2

Table 3.
Summary of the Ceramics from Cut 3

	Level 1	Level 2	Level 3	Level 4	Level 5	Total
Sherds	1,016	2,136	3,386	1,747	332	8,617
Rims	127	154	402	415	22	1,120
Pashash Orange & Vista Brown	492	1,639	2,747	486	271	5,635
Caserón Orange & Cabana Cream	524	497	639	1,261	61	2,982
Resist	29	42	284	376	3	734
Painted	202	335	310	355	36	1,238

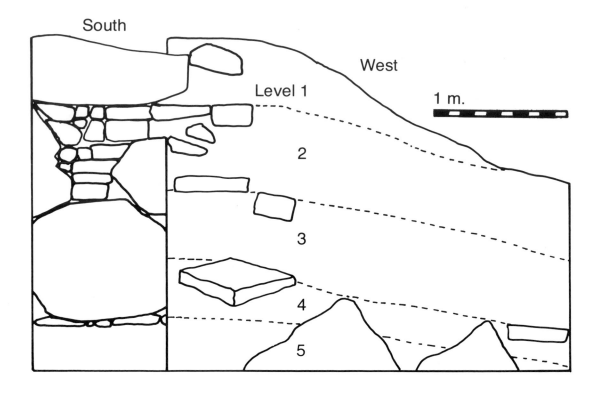

South

West

Level 1

1 m.

2

3

4

5

11. *Cut 7. South and west faces of the cut.*

Table 4.
Summary of the Ceramics from Cut 7

	Level 1	Level 2	Level 3	Level 4	Level 5	Total
Sherds	377	109	203	278	53	1,020
Rims	43	0	0	0	6	49
Pashash Orange & Vista Brown	249	77	162	207 / 36	45 / 0	776
Caserón Orange & Cabana Cream	128	326	41	34 / 1	2 / 6	538
Horno Buff	0	1	0	0	0	1
Resist	2	0	2	0	0	4
Painted	21	8	5	3	5	42

Note: Fragments of human jawbone were found in
Level 3 at a depth of 120 cm.; no other bones were
found. The bones presumably represent traces of a
burial eroded out at a higher level on the hill.

Cut 7

This was another unsuccessful attempt to determine the period of construction of a major wall. The wall faces north in the area of revetments between El Caserón and La Portada. The downhill side of the wall was selected for excavation in the hope that platform fill might be avoided and the foundation level more easily reached. Since all the deposit was alluvium, the strata are chronologically inconclusive. The foundation was reached and was proved to rest on sterile soil. A sample of carbonized wood was taken from the level of the base of the wall in an effort to determine the approximate period of construction. The period indicated by carbon testing was the sixteenth century, which shows that the wall was clear of debris at that time and that the accumulation of earth over the wall began with the introduction of colonial agriculture in the region. I was the supervisor of the work.

Measurements were taken from the top of the ancient wall. The area was 1 meter wide against the wall and 3 meters long perpendicular to the wall (fig. 11).

Level 1: 0–50 centimeters. Black alluvial soil collected on a stone floor. The 377 Recuay type sherds were washed down from areas higher on the hill.

Level 2: 50–115 centimeters. The natural levels decline as they move away from the wall, which indicates that they are natural accumulations. The base of this level is a large flat stone which seems to have been intentionally set against the wall. Above it are dry brown soil and rock supporting an irregular pattern of uncut flat stones, which certainly formed a narrow piece of floor set against the wall. The potsherds are all Recuay types, apparently in the alluvial soil which was leveled against the wall.

Level 3: 115–165 centimeters. Brown soil and rock, apparently laid by natural processes but leveled at some time at the edge of the wall.

Level 4: 165–205 centimeters. Hard gray brown clay with three large partly worked stones which may have fallen from the wall. This level rests on sterile soil. It contained 278 sherds of Recuay types.

Level 5: 205–250 centimeters. Sterile except for a small pocket of potsherds, all Recuay types, about 60 centimeters from the wall. The level is below the base of the wall. A radiocarbon sample (Tx-1330) from the top of this level gave an age of 420 B.P. ±80, which suggests that all these strata accumulated during the colonial period.

Cut 8

This excavation was also located against the wall of El Caserón, on the northeast side toward the upper end of the wall (fig. 12). It was intended to reveal the foundation of El Caserón, but the cut was terminated before the foundation was reached when it appeared that the wall of El Caserón was not sufficiently solid to endure without the support of the debris against it. The backdirt was then thrown against the wall.

A single stone wall of the small scale one might consider domestic runs perpendicular to the wall of El Caserón and was clearly built subsequent to the great wall. Also, a small sample of pottery fragments was recovered. The work was supervised by John W. Smith.

Measurements were taken from the top of the wall of El Caserón at the place where the excavation was made. The area of the cut was 2.5 meters against the wall by 4.5 meters perpendicular to the wall.

Level 1: 0–275 centimeters. From the top of the wall of El Caserón to the current earth surface.

Level 2: 275–360 centimeters. Sod and black soil which had collected against El Caserón.

Level 3: 360–440 centimeters. Cut stone fallen from the wall, with some soil sifted in.

Level 4: 440–500 centimeters. Among the cut stones and earth of this level was a low wall of small rocks running perpendicular to the wall of El Caserón. An earth floor may have existed but was not proved. Irregular stones and earth lay below this wall.

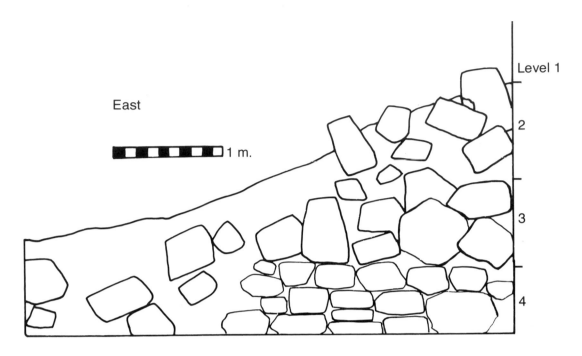

East

1 m.

12. Cut 8. Section.

Table 5.
Summary of the Ceramics from Cut 8

	Level 2	Level 3	Level 4	Total
Sherds	447	90	14	551
Pashash Orange & Vista Brown	337	68	14	419
Caserón Orange & Cabana Cream	98	20	0	118
Resist	1	1	0	2
Painted	28	11	0	39

Excavations on La Capilla Hill

The excavations on La Capilla Hill (fig. 13) have shown two kinds of building: (1) small chambers with sunken fireplaces, which I interpret as houses (Cuts 4–6 and 9), and (2) a two-room structure and its massive revetment, which enclosed a burial (Cuts 10–12). The offerings which accompanied the burial form the main body of material on which this study is based.

La Capilla Hill was originally a jagged stone outcrop on the western edge of the present hilltop. It dropped steeply on the west and more gradually on the east, only falling in precipices on that side some 30 meters or so east of the outcrop. The hilltop was inhabited, evidently being the most densely settled part of a village which clung to the highest part of the ridge throughout the site, in the Quinú period. At the beginning of the Recuay period, massive build-up of the hilltop began. Rock fill seems to be deepest on the north terrace, apparently as part of a general filling and leveling connected with the massive revetments of the South Wall and the great walls closing the north side of La Capilla Hill. Deep rock fill was also encountered on the south terrace, again evidently part of an

early Recuay filling and leveling project. At the end of the Yaiá phase—the second of the three Recuay phases—the eastern flank of the hill was filled and raised to its present form. The 5-meter-high east wall (fig. 14) was erected, with a projecting stringcourse at the middle, to enclose a small burial temple. The revetments and stairs (fig. 15) lower on the eastern flank were probably erected about the same time. The latest phase of the Recuay period, Huacohú, produced domestic construction evident in Cut 4. Some of the destruction of the Recuay buildings took place in the following Usú period, during which the upper parts of the walls of the burial temple were razed. But no Usú period constructions for which the stones might have been reutilized has been identified. Looting of the Recuay period walls for cut stone has continued into modern times. It resulted in a crudely built chapel in the early twentieth century, which gave its name to the hill and which was torn down by the local people in 1972. I supervised all the excavations in this sector except Cut 9, which was supervised by John W. Smith.

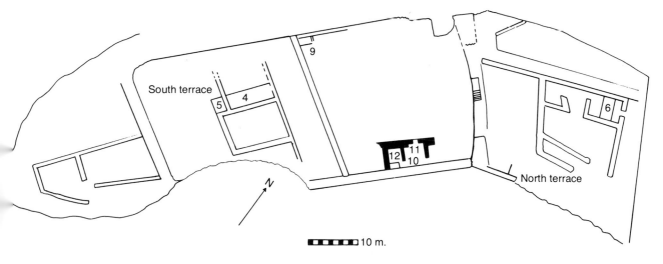

13. *The top of La Capilla Hill.*
Numbers are those of excavation cuts. The walls
of the burial temple are in black.

14. *East wall of La Capilla Hill.*
5 m. high. The stringcourse marks the middle.

15. *Stairway against a revetment on the east*
side of La Capilla Hill.

Cut 4

This excavation (fig. 16) was located on the south terrace of the hill within the walls of what I interpret as a house. Three walls remain—on the north, south, and east sides—the western wall and the floor in that area having eroded away. The interior of the chamber (fig. 17) measured at least 8.8 by 3 meters and surely had a width greater than 3 meters. The smooth cut stones which flank the doorway contrast with the crude walls. The roughness of the walls suggests that they were originally plastered, presumably with a mud plaster. The house, with its earth floor and its fireplace, can be placed at the end of the Recuay period. The latest floor (Floor 1) was set within the stone walls.

The other floors all pass beneath the stone wall on the east, and they were part of structures whose walls have not been located. The structure which accompanied Floor 2 presumably had wooden rafters which burnt and fell to the floor, where they remain as a heavy deposit of carbonized wood. Carbon from that deposit gave an age reading of 1490 B.P.±70 (Tx-941) in a radiocarbon test, suggesting a late fifth or early sixth century period for the burning.

A narrow (1 meter wide) trench was cut through the floor and taken to sterile soil through two more earth floors. Potsherds from beneath the earliest floor provide our only sample of Quinú sherds in isolation. Above that floor appeared a carbon sample which produced the oldest age reading from the site—1640 B.P.±80 (Tx-944)—suggesting a period of the late third

or early fourth century for the building of the earliest floor.

Measurements were taken from the highest point of the house wall, at the northeast corner.

Level 1: 0–140 centimeters. This level contains all the house construction above the latest floor, which is to say the remains of the stone walls and the doorway. The floor and hearth in Level 2 belonged to this house. The house was partially filled with alluvial soil containing a mixture of Usú and Recuay ceramic material.

Level 2: 140–170 centimeters. Floor 1 marks the top of this level, set on a foundation of small flat stones. A sunken rectangular fireplace was built with the floor, which was placed over a layer of burned logs, presumably rafters of an earlier building. The radiocarbon test Tx-941 suggests that they had burned during the late fifth or early sixth century.

Level 3: 170–200 centimeters. A brown earth floor resting on a foundation of flat stones, with earth fill below.

Level 4: 200–230 centimeters. A brown earth floor resting on a foundation of flat stones, with rock and earth fill below. There were just six potsherds in this level, but they span all three Recuay phases. Radiocarbon sample Tx-944 was found in this level, giving a late third or early fourth century date, which may apply to the floor in Level 5.

Level 5: 230–255 centimeters. An earth floor without a stone foundation. Brown earth fill. The potsherds are all Quinú period types. Sterile soil and rock were reached at 255 centimeters.

Table 6.
Summary of the Ceramics from Cut 4

	Levels 2–3	Level 4	Level 5	Total
Sherds	685	6	22	713
Rims	45	3	5	53
Pashash Orange & Vista Brown	664	4	22	690
Caserón Orange & Cabana Cream	21	2	0	23
Painted	2	2	0	4

Note: Sherds in aeolic and alluvial deposits are counted in Levels 2–3.

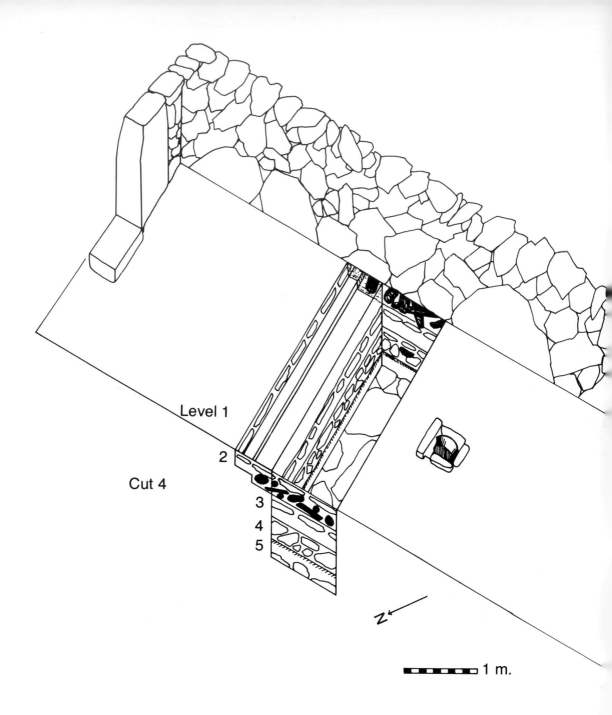

Level 1

2

Cut 4

3

4

5

1 m.

16. Cuts 4 and 5. Perspective plan.

17. *Cut 4. View from the fireplace eastward toward the doorway.*

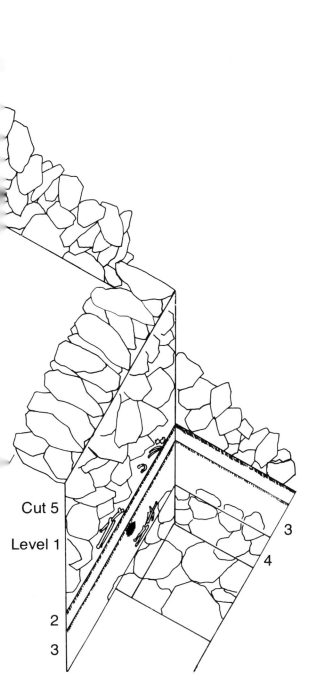

Cut 5

Level 1

3

4

2

3

Cut 5

Cut 5 (fig. 16) was located against the outside of the south wall of the same structure revealed in Cut 4 in the hope of learning more about the building and securing a larger sample of Quinú pottery.

An animal skeleton, probably a llama, in Level 3, looks as if it had been intentionally laid on the stone fill when the earth floor was about to be put down. Its position in the structure suggests human intervention, either placing it as a sacrificial offering, which seems most likely, or burying it beneath the floor, evidently as the floor was being built, since there is no indication of digging through the levels above. A human skeleton in Level 1 is a different case: if it was an intentional burial, it had been much disturbed (fig. 18). The vertebrae lay to the right of the jaw, which is all that remained of the head, and the bones of the arms lay to the left. The bones of the pelvis and lower extremities were missing. Little earth lay above the bones, and that may have sifted through the fallen rock which was the principal material of Level 1. This skeleton may be that of an abandoned victim of war or disaster, but two similar burials—one of them disturbed—appeared in Cuts 10 and 11, directly on or very close to the present ground surface. It is most likely that all three of these were really burials deposited in the Usú period (to judge by the ceramic offering in Cut 10, Level 1) on what was by then an abandoned hilltop. Erosion of the hilltop reduced the layers of earth covering the burials, which may not have been very deep to start with.

The two top floors in Cut 5 are assumed to be coeval with the upper floors in Cut 4, and the stone fill of Level 3 is assumed to be of the same period as Level 4 in Cut 4. The steep drop in the natural ground level implied by the depth of the fill in Cut 5 compared to that of Cut 4 is apparent on the site. The south terrace, like that on the north side of La Capilla Hill, was built up to a level with stone fill.

The excavation measured 3 by 2 meters down to 2.55 meters, where a layer of massive stone fill was encountered. The cut was narrowed to a sounding 1.2 meters wide and finally abandoned in the stone fill. Depth measurements were taken from the top of the remaining south wall of the surface structure in Cut 4.

Level 1: 0–170 centimeters. This level consisted of the collapsed stone rubble of the wall and the earth floor at the base of the level. A broken mortar and two pestles were mixed among the stones. A disarticulated human skeleton lay directly on the earth floor against the base of the wall.

Level 2: 170–190 centimeters. Brown earth fill supporting the earth floor.

Level 3: 190–255 centimeters. Brown earth floor resting on fill of earth and rock. An undated charcoal deposit appeared under the floor. The skeleton of an animal, probably a llama, was found in the lower part of the level.

Level 4: 255–310 centimeters. The cut was narrowed to 1.2 by 1.5 meters. Heavy rock fill. No potsherds or other cultural material. The excavation was abandoned at 310 centimeters.

Table 7.
Summary of the Ceramics from Cut 5

	Level 1	Level 2	Level 3	Total
Sherds	332	340	77	749
Rims	19	31	6	56
Pashash Orange & Vista Brown	264	265	53	582
Caserón Orange & Cabana Cream	68	75	24	167
Painted	6	5	0	11

18. *Cut 5, Level 1. Human skeleton.*

Cut 6

Cut 6 (fig. 19) was located on the opposite, or north, terrace of La Capilla Hill. The small stone chamber chosen for excavation was near the bedrock outcrop at the westerly edge of the hill. We hoped to reach sterile soil in that spot, but again the hole was abandoned in rock fill. The ceramics in Level 1 suggest an Usú period occupation on a floor built late in the Recuay period, since a mixture of the later types appears there. Below the floor the mixture is entirely of earlier types, obviously churned during the construction.

Depth measurements were taken from the top of the vertical stone set in the east wall of the house. The stone rose 80 centimeters above the earth surface, so the soil deposit in Level 1 was about 30 centimeters. The area of the cut was 2 by 4 meters, narrowed to 1 by 1 meters.

Level 1: 0–110 centimeters. Alluvial soil resting on Floor 1, with some fallen rock. The pot-

sherds are Recuay Huacohú phase and Usú period types.

Level 2: 110–160 centimeters. Loose earth fill supporting an earth floor, Floor 1. Sherds are Recuay period types.

Level 3: 160–260 centimeters. Rock fill with soil filtered through it. The top of this level consisted of large flat stones laid level as a foundation for the earth fill above. There is no discernible natural level at 260 centimeters, but below that level the potsherds seem to be all Recuay Quimít phase types.

Level 4: 260–310 centimeters. The cut was narrowed to 1 by 1 meters as a sounding into the heavy rock fill. No natural level appeared at the top or bottom of this level. The sherds are Recuay Quimít phase types. The cut was abandoned when we could no longer remove the massive rocks.

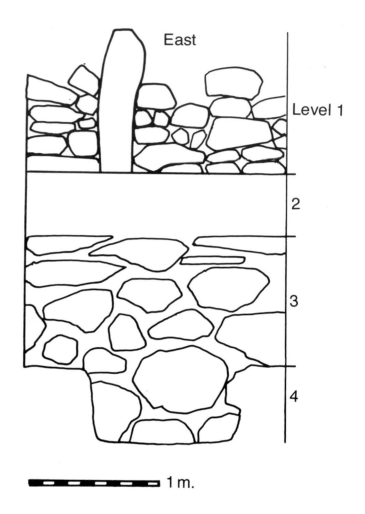

19. *Cut 6. Section of the east face.*

Table 8.
Summary of the Ceramics from Cut 6

	Level 1	Level 2	Level 3	Level 4	Total
Sherds	908	448	262	73	1,691
Rims	47	24	26	8	105
Pashash Orange & Vista Brown	703	376	168	65	1,312
Caserón Orange & Cabana Cream	205	72	94	8	379
Resist	0	1	0	0	1
Painted	12	17	12	1	42
Figurines	1	2	1	0	4

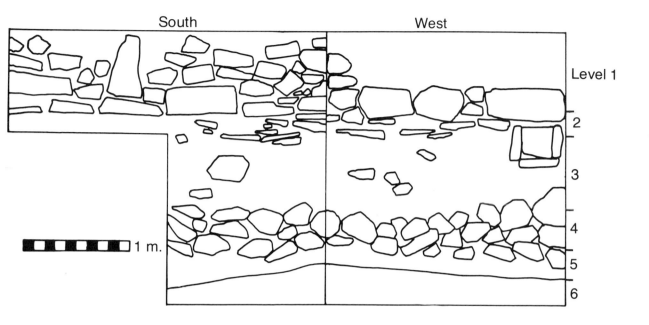

South   West

Level 1

2

3

4

5

6

1 m.

20. *Cut 9. South and west faces.*

Cut 9

This excavation (fig. 20) was set at the western edge of the top section of La Capilla Hill against a wall which was visible on the surface. Levels 1 and 2 contained the floor and hearth of a house and its outer (west) wall. The floor, easily discerned on its flagstone foundation, ended about 1.4 meters east of the outer wall, and it appeared that the earth had been disturbed beyond that point. To avoid the disturbed area, the cut was reduced and excavated to bedrock.

The levels span all the periods of Pashash occupation, with Quinú and Recuay Quimít phase types in the lower levels (Levels 4–6), Recuay Yaiá phase in the level of the house floor, and Recuay Huacohú phase and Usú period on the surface. Among the early sherds are nineteen which show areas of narrow lines of white paint on red slip, probably a late Quinú period decorative technique. On the surface are red-slipped sherds painted in broad bands and areas of white, sometimes with orange or black paint added. These belong to the Recuay Huacohú phase and represent the shift to positive polychrome painting at the end of the Recuay period. The mid-Recuay diagnostic resist decoration is extremely rare in this cut—just one sherd, in

Level 3. It may be that the house construction at the end of that period caused the removal of a surface level containing debris of that phase. The surface level was especially rich in Horno Black and Horno Buff types, which were assigned to the last phase of the Recuay period largely on the basis of this cut.

The house, to judge by the ceramics, was built late in the Recuay period. A radiocarbon determination (Tx-1332) gave an age of 1610 B.P. ± 170, centering in the early fourth century, for a sample from Level 4, earlier than the construction. A carbon sample from Level 3 (Tx-1331) gave a reading of 1110 B.P. ± 270 (or A.D. 570–1110), suggesting a date between the sixth and twelfth centuries. The earlier part of this long period seems most plausible even for the period of occupation of the structure and seems late for the period of construction.

Measurements were taken from the top of the superficial wall. The area in Levels 1 and 2 measured 3 by 2.3 meters. Because the ground had been disturbed in part of the cut, the cut was reduced to 1.5 by 2.3 meters in Levels 3 through 6.

Level 1: 0–80 centimeters. The superficial wall, of late Recuay period construction.

Level 2: 80–100 centimeters. Sod and some soil with many sherds lying on the earth floor of the structure whose wall appears in Level 1. The floor rests on a foundation of small flat stones. A rectangular fireplace was set into the floor. The floor had been destroyed about 1.4 meters east of the outer (west) wall. The sherds account for more than half of those found in this cut, with Recuay Huacohú phase and Usú period types dominating.

Level 3: 100–170 centimeters. Brown earth fill for the floor with some stones. At 120–140 centimeters a large stone had been laid flat; now it passes under the surface wall. The sherds were Recuay Yaiá and Huacohú phase types. The only resist-decorated sherd found in this cut was in this level.

Level 4: 170–210 centimeters. Stone fill with some soil filtered in. The sherds are Quinú and Recuay types.

Table 9.
Summary of the Ceramics from Cut 9

	Level 2	Level 3	Level 4	Level 5	Level 6	Total
Pashash Orange						
Plain	492	28	21	17	18	576
Painted	1	0	0	0	0	1
Brushed	8	1	0	0	0	9
Vista Brown						
Plain	743	49	79	84	96	1,051
Red slip	85	5	3	14	18	125
Stick-burnish	45	17	14	13	11	100
Caserón Orange						
Plain	93	0	3	1	0	97
Painted	19	5	0	0	0	24
Red slip	91	5	4	0	10	110
White/red	0	8	8	6	5	27
White/orange on red	52	0	0	0	0	52
Cabana Cream						
Plain	35	4	4	3	2	48
Painted	48	2	0	1	1	52
Resist	0	1	0	0	0	1
Horno Black						
Polished	62	16	1	0	0	79
Painted	14	14	0	0	0	28
Horno Buff						
Polished	97	4	0	0	0	101
Brushed	9	0	0	0	0	9
Total	1,894	159	137	139	161	2,490

Level 5: 210–235 centimeters. Brown soil of the original hillside before filling. The sherds are Quinú and Recuay Quimít phase types, including four sherds of creamware, one of them painted.

Cuts 10, 11, and 12

This series of excavations was done as separate cuts spread over a two-year period, but the cuts were all located within a small two-room structure on the eastern edge of the top of La Capilla Hill. This prolonged and piecemeal method had the important advantage that a relatively small amount of material could be analyzed before proceeding to open the next cut. Doubtful points could usually be rechecked in the subsequent excavations. Exceptions to this procedure were caused by vandalism, which was frequent and, in two cases, serious and which, despite our efforts, we were powerless to control.

The western edge of the stone floor in Cut 12, Level 3, was destroyed by vandals on July 29, 1973, and the altar platform in Cut 12, Level 2, was destroyed the next night. The stone floor of the outer chamber was restored after the excavations of 1971 but was found largely destroyed in 1973; it was relaid again when the floor was restored in Cut 12, Level 3, in 1973. Areas which remained unexcavated in September 1973 and which had not been vandalized were about a meter wide against the north wall of the outer chamber and against the east and west walls of Cut 12.

Cut 10 began as the exploration of a wall visible in the eroded northeast corner of the top of La Capilla Hill. The wall runs approximately parallel to and about 5 meters west of the large wall that encloses the east side of the top of the hill. When the doorway (fig. 21) was encountered, the cut was widened to lay bare the tops of the walls of Chamber 1, and the remaining levels were confined to the interior of that chamber. The pattern of the walls (fig. 22) suggested that another chamber may have been enclosed on the north side of Chamber 1, but erosion had completely destroyed any trace of the northern half of that supposed chamber. The pattern of the walls also suggested the existence of a chamber to the south of Chamber 1, which was later revealed by Cut 12. In Cuts 10 and 11, the southerly half of the interior of

Level 6: 235–260 centimeters. Shale which had been disturbed. Quinú and Recuay Quimít phase sherd types.

Chamber 1 was excavated to sterile soil (fig. 23).

Level 1 in Cuts 10 and 11 was measured from the top of the east revetment wall to a full definition of the walls of the chamber, ending at the level of the threshold stone. Since the temple walls were not visible on the surface, with the exception of the colossal east wall, the cut was redesigned with three sectors as the chamber came to light. Sector A was the area outside the north wall of the chamber, B was inside the chamber, and C was outside the west wall of the chamber. References to Cut 10, Level 1, in the text refer to Sector B unless otherwise specified, that having been the only sector to be further excavated.

Measurements in Cut 10 were taken from the top of the east wall (fig. 23).

Level 1: 0–175 centimeters. Except for the walls of the chamber, the level was entirely of earth, probably mostly laid as fill. A disturbed burial was found in Sector C, just west of the doorway of the structure.

Level 2: 175–210 centimeters. The level measured 2 by 4 meters across the eastern half of the interior of the temple chamber. The top of the level may have been an old surface but was probably not a constructed floor. The earth floor in this level was not discovered. The level ended at the stone foundation of the original floor.

Level 3: 210–255 centimeters. The area was reduced to 2 by 2.7 meters in the southeast quarter of the interior of the chamber. This level was composed of the stone foundation of the original temple floor and earth fill down to the large stones which lie over the main body of the offering.

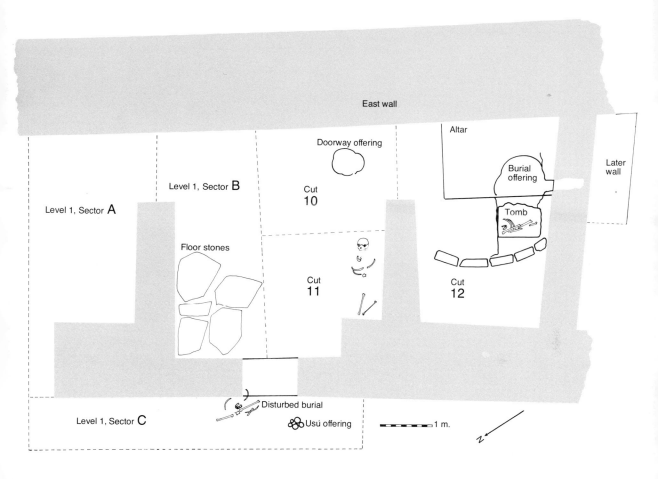

East wall

Doorway offering

Altar

Burial offering

Later wall

Level 1, Sector **B**

Level 1, Sector **A**

Cut
10

Tomb

Floor stones

Cut
11

Cut
12

Disturbed burial

Level 1, Sector **C**

Usú offering

1 m.

N

22. Plan of the burial temple.

Level 4: 255–300 centimeters. An area 2 by 2.7 meters. Its upper limit was defined by the heavy stones laid over the offering, one of which was built into the east wall. The lower limit was defined by the irregular brown stain which reveals the presence of a cloth on which most of the offering was laid. Earth containing some potsherds had been placed over the offering or had seeped into the open area of the offering. That the earth was not packed tightly around the offering is indicated by the subsidence of the stones, which crushed many of the vessels in the offering.

Level 5: 300–400 centimeters. An area 2 by 2.7 meters. The top of the level was defined by the brown stain indicating the cloth laid down to hold the major part of the offering. Offering material continued to a depth of 345 centimeters. Rock and shale fill and earth disturbed in construction, with scant cultural material, were found from 355 to 400 centimeters, where bedrock was reached.

The excavated material is listed in appendix 2.

21. Opposite: the doorway and outer chamber of the burial temple, looking southward. Level 1 has been cleared.

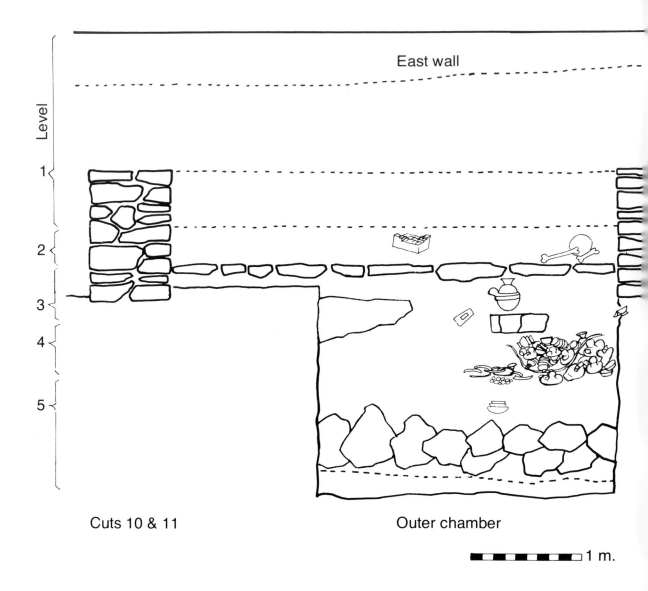

Cuts 10 & 11   **Outer chamber**

■━━━━━━━━━━▭1 m.

Cut 11 was located in the southwest corner of the outer chamber of the temple. It was excavated in 1973 in order to learn more about the context of the offering found in Cut 10 by taking the adjoining sector down to bedrock. The original intention was to excavate the entire interior of the chamber, but it was found that the central and northeast sectors of the chamber had been dug up by looters after the 1971 season. The southwestern sector had not been disturbed, so an area measuring 2 by 2.3 meters was completely excavated. Level 1 in this sector had

been removed in the 1971 excavations and is designated Cut 10, Level 1, Sector B; it includes material from the whole interior of the chamber. Cut 11 thus began 1.75 meters deep with Level 2. This sector of the temple was far poorer in cultural material than the back sector (Cut 10), as the count of ceramic material indicates. The most significant feature was the burial, which is distinguished from that in the inner chamber (Cut 12, Level 6) in almost every possible way. The body had been buried in an extended position aligned with the wall, with the head toward

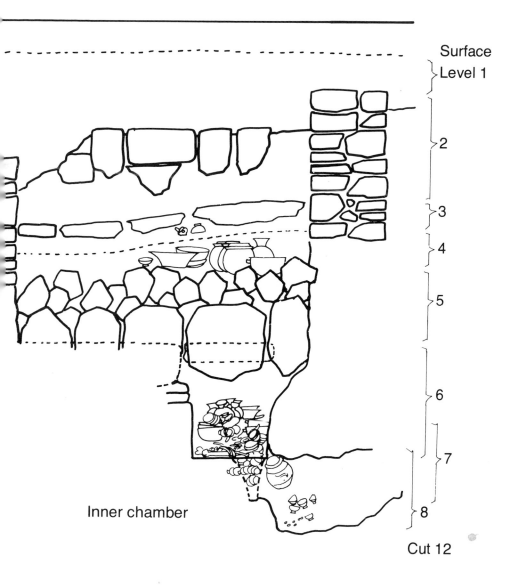

Surface

Level 1

2

3

4

5

6

7

8

Inner chamber

Cut 12

the east. Four snail shells were the only objects associated with the skeleton.

The levels were measured from the top of the east wall.

Level 2: 175–210 centimeters. Earth fill and floor. There was an extended burial oriented to the wall.

Level 3: 210–255 centimeters. Stone foundation of the floor and the earth fill beneath it. Pottery was the only cultural material.

Level 4: 255–300 centimeters. Earth fill. Pottery was the only cultural material.

23. *Section through the burial temple, showing Cuts 10, 11, and 12.*

Level 5: 300–400 centimeters. Bedrock was reached at 400 centimeters. Earth fill with some rock at lower levels. Pottery was the only cultural material, the most significant being fragments of large Pashash Orange Plain jars continuing the deposit found in Cut 10, Level 5.

The excavated material is listed in appendix 2.

Cut 12 (fig. 23) was excavated in 1973 to amplify the context of the offering in Cut 10. As the surface level was cleared an enclosed chamber was revealed, its only doorway opening into the chamber previously excavated. Measurements were taken from the top of the east wall, as in Cuts 10 and 11.

Level 1: 0–60 centimeters. An area 5.6 by 3.35 meters, which is the whole interior of the chamber plus the south and west walls, whose top surfaces mark the base of the level. The level was composed of sod and soil.

Level 2: 60–160 centimeters. An area 4.1 by 2.65 meters, the whole interior of the chamber. The soil in this level seems to be fill intentionally laid to level the ground for a later structure, now lost. The principal feature in this level was an earth and stone platform along the east wall, which stood 60 to 80 centimeters above the chamber floor and projected 150 centimeters into the room, running nearly the whole width of the chamber.

Level 3: 160–185 centimeters. An area 2.6 by 2.3 meters, the area of the platform along the east side of the chamber remaining unexcavated. The level began at the surface of the floor, which was made of gray clay with unworked flat stones, mostly shale, set in its upper surface. When the stones were raised, spots of red pigment were noted, as if powdered pigment had been scattered over the floor. The whole level was composed of the clay floor, in which offerings in the form of a whole vessel, miniature vessels, and whistles were deposited. The low percentage of Pashash Orange Plain sherds (38.8%) and the high percentage of Cabana Cream and decorated Caserón Orange sherds (45.9% together) suggest that many of the sherds were also considered offerings, that is, they were intentionally placed in the floor.

Level 4: 185–215 centimeters. An area 2.6 by 2.3 meters. Brown earth, contrasting sharply with the gray clay of Level 3. Spots of yellow

pigment, apparently added intentionally, were common in the earth. The level is composed of fill.

Level 5: 215–285 centimeters. An area 2.6 by 2.3 meters. Heavy rock fill with some mixture of brown earth. The principal feature was a curved wall formed by five upright stones crossing the level roughly north to south. The level ended at the stone cover of the tomb chamber inside the curve. The area outside the curved wall reached bedrock boulders and was not excavated further.

Level 6: 285–390 centimeters. This level consisted solely of the burial chamber, an area 60 by 55 centimeters. The top of the level was defined by a layer of flat stones. One large stone about 14 centimeters thick with a polished upper surface completely covered the chamber. Beneath that slab was grainy brown earth, apparently largely formed of decomposed textiles. Badly decomposed human bones lay on the smooth stone floor of the chamber. Two fragmentary lower jaws revealed the presence of at least part of a second skeleton in the chamber. The chamber was open on the east and the burial offering lay in the earth on that side.

Level 7: 360–430 centimeters. An area about 1 by 1 meters east of the burial chamber and extending below it. It contained the burial offering, which was partly laid on cloth whose presence was indicated by brown stains, and sherd material in the earth fill surrounding the offering. The level ended on sterile soil and bedrock boulders.

Level 8: Between the two large bedrock boulders which form the south side of Cut 12 is a natural crack about 20 centimeters wide. It was open and clear from about 400 to 460 centimeters deep, where it ended in bedrock shale. The only earth in this crack was a little at the bottom. Material from the offering in Level 7 seems to have fallen into this crack accidentally as the offering settled. The only cultural material in the level which was not part of the offering is the five potsherds (12/8.27), which were at the very bottom of the crack, separate from the other material. They represent types earlier than those in the offering. Three are rims of Form A and, probably, E-1 vessels.

The excavated material is listed in appendix 2.

3.
The Temple

At the time of the death of the important person in the burial, the east flank of La Capilla Hill was in its natural state, dropping steeply from the hillcrest, the slope broken by large boulders and outcrops. Fragments of pottery among the boulders, found in the lowest levels of the excavations, testify to the earlier presence of people on the hill, but no structures prior to the Recuay period have been found.

The tomb and its temple were constructed in one building campaign and express a single conception. The placement of offerings in the earth below, beside, and above the burial chamber, the absence of any easy access to the chamber, and the sheltering of the doorway offering beneath a stone tenoned into the east wall all indicate the unity of both the conception and its execution. The work must have been done after the death, since the construction could not have been completed until the body had been placed in the tomb chamber. The body must have been wrapped and put in some temporary place until the construction had reached the stage at which the body and the offerings could be put in place and sealed.

The first parts to be constructed were the small burial chamber (fig. 24) and the founda-tion of the east wall. The burial chamber was open on the east and enclosed by natural bedrock boulders on two of the other three sides. A stone floor measuring roughly 60 by 55 centimeters was cut from the living rock. A smooth stone wall was constructed on the north to a height of 90 centimeters, and a single large stone was shaped to form the west wall.

It is clear from the dimensions of the chamber, as it is from the position of the bones, that the body was interred in a sitting position, probably with the head facing toward the south. Abundant brown organic material in the burial chamber is presumably the decayed remains of layers of cloth in which the body was wrapped.

Among the bones of the buried person was the fragment of a second lower jaw, slightly smaller than the first but with worn teeth (fig. 25). This is the only indication we have that a second body was somehow buried in this narrow space. This may be compared with the "Warrior-Priest's Tomb" in the Virú Valley, which had three additional bodies, all presumably sacrificed to accompany the principal burial (Strong and Evans 1952: 198). The second body in this case must have been awkwardly placed at the east, or open, side of the burial chamber.

24. The burial chamber, Cut 12, Level 6, as the bones appeared.
The wall at the top is called the west wall.

At the time of the burial, the boulders surrounding the chamber were free of earth, for offerings were set in the crevices 40 and 70 centimeters lower than the floor of the chamber on the east, or downhill, side. As earth was added, a cloth was laid, evident now in brown stains in the soil, and more offerings were set upon it. Pottery vessels continued to be added to this first offering, designated 12/7–8 or the "burial offering," as earth fill was placed to seal the tomb chamber.

With the burial and its first offering in place, earth began to be added, presumably leveling to the partially completed east wall. The burial chamber was sealed with a large slab with a polished upper surface, and a curved wall of irregular upright stones was set along the western margin of the burial area. Once the burial was sealed, work may have shifted to other areas. No doubt the second offering, designated 10/4–5 or the "doorway offering," was set in place after the chamber was sealed, since it is mostly at a level

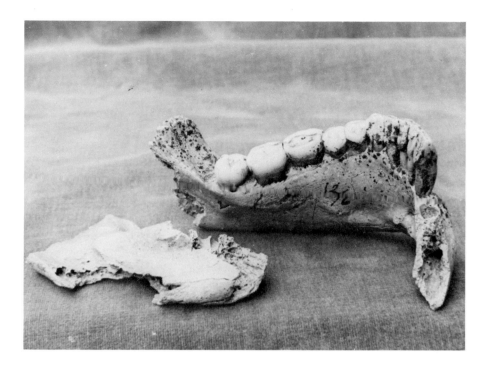

25. *The remains of the jaws in the tomb.*
The fragment on the left, which is the left side of
a lower jaw, suggests the presence of a second
body. Note wear on the molars on the larger
fragment. The teeth of the smaller fragment
were found, but are not shown.
12/6.

that would have been open when the burial chamber was closed. This second offering was sealed under heavy flat stones in the same way as the burial. One large stone was tenoned into the east wall, indicating that the wall was under construction when the offering was deposited. With the body and the two offerings sealed under stones, the upper levels of the construction were begun, the first step being a layer of heavy stones. Other offerings were included in the dirt thrown over the stones: copper-and-gold jewelry, broken ceremonial pottery and stone vessels, beads, whistles, spindle whorls, and figurines. Yellow pigment spots are common in the fill of Level 4 of Cut 12. The top layer, which formed the floor (Cut 12, Level 3), composed of 25 centimeters of clay, was especially rich in offerings but included only one whole vessel, except miniatures and whistles. The layer of clay was sprinkled with red pigment, and a layer

of flat stone slabs of irregular form was set into the clay. The temple walls were begun before the clay subfloor was laid, for they rest on the earth level (Level 4) and enclose the clay subfloor (Level 3). It appears that the plan of the two chambers was intended from the beginning, since the second offering lay beneath the doorway to the inner chamber.

The temple walls remain firm and smooth surfaced, but they are quite casual in construction (fig. 26). Stones of various sizes and shapes were laid in thin mud mortar with the smoothest face on the wall surface. Only a few stones appear to have been carefully shaped, then generally only on the face that was to be visible. The walls are all double-faced, the two surfaces being laid independently, with a mud and rubble core if the thickness permitted it. In spite of the irregularity of the stones, the walls have an even surface. It is likely that they were originally

26. *The burial temple.*
Foreground is the inner chamber, Cut 12, during the restoration of the stone floor. View northeastward.

faced with mud plaster, but no evidence of this remains anywhere in the site. Although the region gets considerable amounts of rainfall, adobe is the common building material now. The smooth stones of the doorway contrast so markedly with the walls that one is tempted to imagine a finished surface having been part of the original appearance of the walls. The much earlier buildings at Kotosh show a similar stone wall construction and a mud plaster finish coat of the sort the Pashash temple may have had. The Kotosh buildings were painted, which the Pashash artists must also surely have done if the wall surface permitted it. There is, however, no evidence to support this theory beyond the irregularity of the walls themselves.

The temple walls are now evenly cut off at about 1 meter above the original floor. My first impression was that the upper parts of the walls had served as quarries for later builders and had simply been carried away. Although the area around the temple is littered with building stones, there is no suggestion of collapsed walls

associated with the temple. Nor do the walls themselves appear to have fallen, all the remaining parts being perfectly sound. The best explanation for the absence of the upper parts of the walls rests on the several indications of later building over the temple, notably the wall along the outside of the south side of the inner chamber and, possibly, the uncertain upper floor level in the outer chamber. It is clear that the upper parts of the extant walls were removed down to an even height and the interiors of the chambers filled in order to permit new construction. What the later construction was may never be known, since the northern edge of the temple area is deeply eroded and the tops of the temple walls, half-destroyed as they are, were only just below the modern ground surface. The outer wall, just south of the south wall of the temple, may be a remnant of the later structure, which would thus appear to have been larger than the burial temple with its two small chambers (fig. 22).

The temple seems to have been centered between major boundary walls on the top of the hill. The distance from the south wall of the temple to the highest standing wall that divides the top from the south terrace is 7.25 meters. 7.4 meters is the distance from the exterior northwest corner of the temple to the wall that divided the north terrace from the top. The contemporaneity of these walls with the temple has not been proved, but they appear to rest on (for the south wall) and contain (for the north wall) fill contained by the east wall, which is part of the temple construction. Thus the north dividing wall would appear to be contemporary with the east wall of the temple, and the south dividing wall would appear to have been built after the east wall of the temple, although it may have been part of the same total design.

The area in front of the temple is irregular, with a slight depression leading toward the north dividing wall, where the path ascends onto the hilltop. The area may have been an open courtyard, but excavations have not been done. On the west edge of the hilltop at least one small house, and probably several, was present at the time the temple existed, although the exact historical relationship has not been determined. The excavated structure (Cut 9) was a stone-paved room 2.3 by 2.6 meters, enclosed on the north, west, and south but open on the east, toward the temple, with a small rectangular fireplace near the west edge of the floor.

The temple area, as reconstructed from our data, thus appears to have been an enclosed hilltop leveled with fill, especially along the east margin, reached by a stairway built parallel to the north dividing wall. The top of the hill appears to have had an open center, small domestic structure(s) along the west edge, and the temple centered at the east side, its doorway off-center to the north. Such errors as exist in this reconstruction are certainly on the side of oversimplification, for large areas, in the center and in the northwest section of the hilltop especially, contain evidence of constructions, which have not been excavated.

4.
The Burial
and the
Offerings

Although many burials have been excavated by archaeologists, and of course many more by looters, the published analyses of burials are still insufficient for very precise comparisons. By far the greater amount of evidence comes from the coastal region, very little from the highlands, reflecting both the larger amount of archaeological work done on the coast and the much better preservation of all materials, including cadavers, in the desert environment.

The feature which seems to have varied least from region to region and from Formative to Inca times is the deposition of offerings with the body. The burial which contains nothing but the remains of the body is the exception. By the offerings we can identify the social background of the person and, if the offerings are abundant or particularly revealing, read some of his or her history.

If the custom of leaving a burial offering was nearly universal, there was more variety in regard to the position of the body and its enclosure. The social status of the deceased person affected the enclosure of the body, the more elaborate and abundant offerings tending to appear in the more elaborate burial constructions. The sex of the deceased does not seem to have

been a factor in the complexity of the burial or its offerings; Duncan Strong and Clifford Evans remark on the "sex equality in the ritual of the dead" in Moche period burials in the Virú Valley (1952: 197).

The position of the body varies, at least on the coast, from period to period—flexed burials being characteristic of the Chavín period, extended burials dominating in Moche and early Gallinazo, and flexed burials reappearing in the Middle Horizon and later periods. In the Virú Valley, Strong and Evans find extended burial to be characteristic of the Puerto Moorín (roughly the time of the Recuay Quimít phase at Pashash), and it continued dominant in the succeeding Gallinazo period, although flexed burials also appear in Gallinazo (ibid., pp. 202–203). Rafael Larco Hoyle's (1945a: 1–2, 25–28) contention that both Gallinazo and Moche cultures preferred extended burial in their early phases and flexed in their late phases—those phases being partly simultaneous and perhaps blended—is supported by Strong and Evans. Wari traits appear at the close of those periods, bringing flexed burial "into almost universal vogue" in the later epochs, according to Strong and Evans (1952: 203). Flexed burial, wrote

Wendell Bennett, is "a position typical of the Highlands and the Late periods" (1939: 72). One may postulate that flexed burials found on the coast represent the dominance of highland traditions and, conversely, that extended burials in the highlands represent the dominance of coastal traditions.

According to the postulate, the flexed burials of the Chavín period in the Chicama Valley (Strong and Evans 1952: 202) and on the Paracas Peninsula (Engel 1966: 175) are evidence that the Chavín culture was highland in its burial traditions. The extended burials of Moche and early Gallinazo imply the independence of those cultures from the highland tradition during those periods.

The converse situation is found at Pashash in two of the burials in the La Capilla temple: a tightly flexed burial on sterile soil (12/6) and an extended burial associated with the level above the floor (11/2). The difference in period between the two burials, probably not more than two centuries, is just one of the many differences between them. The flexed burial shows signs of cloth wrappings not evident on the extended; a stone chamber and other structures enclose the flexed burial, but the extended is in simple earth; many objects accompany the flexed, but only very few accompany the ex-

tended. These differences suggest another: the flexed body was that of a person of much social power, while the extended was a person of little power. Social status may account for many of the differences, but the positions of the bodies accord with long-standing highland and coastal traditions and appear to reflect the dominance of those regional traditions at Pashash. The flexed burial is traditionally highland and is accompanied by predominantly highland style ceramics. The extended burial, taken with the Usú ceramic types found in the surface levels, becomes another element of coastal culture intruding at Pashash during its terminal phase.

Although the bones in all the Pashash burials are too poorly preserved to permit any conclusive identification of sex, in the case of the flexed burial some features of the burial offering and the fill offering suggest that the body was that of a woman. Spindle whorls (fig. 27), which form an important part of the burial and fill offerings, appear only in the graves of women of the Gallinazo and Moche cultures in the Virú Valley (Strong and Evans 1952: 75, 141–146). Moreover, in Burial 1 at Site V-163, which contained the body of a woman, there were two ceramic spindle whorls accompanied by a copper object which was interpreted as a spearthrower hook. In all other cases weapons were

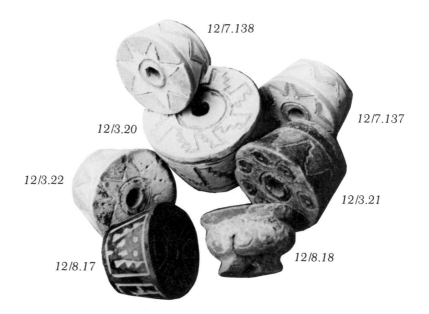

27. *Spindle whorls from Cut 12.*

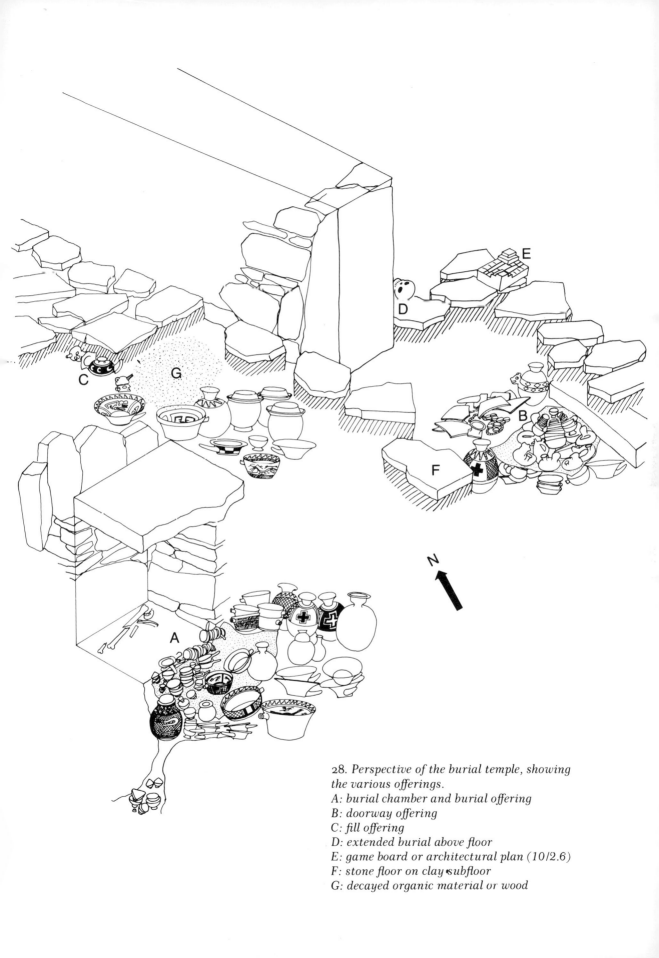

28. Perspective of the burial temple, showing
the various offerings.
A: burial chamber and burial offering
B: doorway offering
C: fill offering
D: extended burial above floor
E: game board or architectural plan (10/2.6)
F: stone floor on clay subfloor
G: decayed organic material or wood

29. *A selection of pottery from Cut 12, mostly from the burial offering.*

found only in men's graves, just as spinning and weaving tools were found only in women's graves. Although the "hook" is smaller than the curved pins (fig. 114) found at Pashash, its form and material are so similar that we can now identify the Virú object as a fragmentary piece of personal adornment.

In the Virú Valley graves, women were ordinarily accompanied by weavers' baskets containing yarn, spindles, and spindle whorls. Although there are traces of basketry in the Pashash burial, they are associated with jewelry, not weaving tools. The clustering of three spindle whorls in one case suggests that a completely decayed weaver's basket might once have held them.

On the other hand, the presence of earplugs suggests that the body was that of a man, since earplugs seem to have been worn only by high-

status men in Recuay and Moche art; during the Inca period, only men of the ruling caste were allowed to wear earplugs. Since the earplugs were not with the skeleton but in the offering, it appears that they might have been offered as treasures, which would seem to be less likely in the case of the spindle whorls. For that reason I am inclined to keep open the question of the deceased person's sex.

To judge by the remaining bones—the jaw (fig. 25) and the legs are the best preserved—the person in the burial was an adult. The teeth, nearly half of which are preserved, suggest that the person was not young, for they show heavy wear, similar to that of teeth found in the extended burial in Cut 11 and the disturbed burial in Cut 10, Level 1. In all these cases the molars were worn nearly smooth on the chewing sur-

30. *A selection of objects from Cut 12, mostly from the burial offering.*

faces. Thus, the evidence suggests that the flexed burial so elaborately entombed was that of a mature person, possibly a woman.

Three separate offerings (fig. 28) accompanied the flexed burial: the burial offering (Cut 12, Levels 7–8), which was immediately beside or in front of the body; the doorway offering (Cut 10, Levels 4–5), beneath the doorway to the burial chamber; and the variety of items, many of them just fragments, which were thrown into the fill before the floor was laid (Cut 10, Level 3; Cut 11, Level 3; and Cut 12, Levels 3–5). Each of these offerings has its own organization and distinctive contents, which implies that each offering has a particular significance.

The burial offering (figs. 29, 30) is composed of jewelry (pl. 7), pottery vessels and figurines, pottery and stone spindle whorls, and a few mis-cellaneous items such as bits of rock crystal. The central item is the large covered jar which was set against the base stone of the burial chamber. It was empty and clean. Next to it were placed pedestal cups containing iron red pigment, several sets of elaborate earplugs which may have been held in a small basket, and some copper-and-gold pins. Earth was arranged to hold the jar upright, and many more pottery vessels were put in around and above the large covered jar. Although the vessels are mostly fine ware, they are all at least potentially utilitarian (pl. 6). The figurines, on the other hand, are pure sculpture, not effigy vessels (figs. 140, 154). The burial offering was laid partly on a cloth in a rough semicircle around the burial chamber, the vessels being placed as close to the body as possible but not in any significant order.

Earth was being added as the offering was placed, so some vessels were at a higher level, but the main part of the offering was at the level of the burial chamber floor, at the level of the top of the large covered jar. This offering is distinguished from the second, or doorway, offering by the utilitarian forms of the vessels, the distinction between vessels and figurines, and the presence of jewelry and spindle whorls.

The second offering was begun with the laying of three simple bowls, nested, with red pigment thrown in, at about the same level as the burial (3.45 meters deep). The bowls were set about 75 centimeters above bedrock on a layer of rock and earth. The thick east wall was being built as the offering was laid, but the other walls of the temple were not yet evident. About 20 centimeters of earth was thrown on top of the three bowls, and a string of ten copper bells was laid on the earth, followed by four large empty storage jars. Just above and toward the east a cloth was laid, evident as a clear line of fibrous brown in the earth, covering an irregular area about 1 meter square (fig. 31). Nine effigy vessels were spread upon it in a rough circle, and various bowls and other forms, all richly painted in red and black resist on cream, were set around the periphery. Thirty-four pedestal cups of cream or black fine paste, all of them very thin-walled, were densely piled in nested groups at the center. With them were laid, at one side, ten plain polished stone pedestal cups of black or green. All these ceramic and stone pedestal cups show signs of having been made by rotary tools: lathes or potters' wheels. Opposite the stone cups were four nested vessels of unfired clay, one of dark red, one of chocolate brown, and two of golden yellow clay, each bearing relief figures of a rampant feline and a crowned god, with turquoise inlays (fig. 77). Two more effigy vessels, both representing spotted felines, were put in at this upper level (figs. 61, 62). Finally, at the top and center of the offering, was set a red stone pedestal cup bearing the same reliefs of a rampant feline and a crowned god, with green stone inlays and traces of iron red paint (fig. 156, pl. 4). Over it were laid massive stones, one of which was tenoned into the east wall. 45 centimeters of earth was deposited and a stone floor was laid.

The sixty-six stone, ceramic, and unfired clay vessels set on the cloth form an offering distinct in many ways from the burial offering. Many are of nonutilitarian forms and of obviously nonutilitarian material, in the case of the unfired clay. Effigy vessels comprise a seventh of the total number; they bridge the categories of sculpture and pottery, and this offering contains no figurines. Spindle whorls and jewelry are also absent.

The organization of the vessels on the cloth appears to be significant. A comparable plan was used for stone images in temples at San Agustín, in the Colombian highlands 1,100 kilometers to the north. At Mesita B, South Barrow, at San Agustín, the central image is a frontal human with a fanged feline mouth, holding a small human figure. The guardian figures are anthropomorphic serpents with feline faces. Four other stone sculptures, long ago removed from the same temple, represent feline-mouthed figures—one holding a snake, another a fish, a third with a tiny human figure, and one empty-handed (Reichel-Dolmatoff 1972: 45). The iconographic elements—feline mouths, serpents, human sacrificial victims, feline-serpent combinations—are similar to those found in the second offering, which encourages the belief that the offering was intentionally given a temple-like organization. The San Agustín sculptures are in the nature of tomb offerings, a further point of likeness to the Pashash offering. In both cases an anthropomorphic deity occupies the center—at San Agustín that figure has feline traits, while at Pashash the feline is a jaguar companion (fig. 156). In both cases feline and feline-serpent figures surround the central subject. The rich variety of designs on the surrounding vessels in the Pashash offering appear to be alternative and subsidiary images related to the central deity. The static frontal pose of the crowned figure at the center contrasts with the active profile pose of the jaguar companion, an expression of the enduring and the immediate, or Being and Becoming, of the eternal and the temporal aspects of divine power. Ideas in this general category could hardly have escaped the minds of the artists who designed the vessels and deposited the offering. It is evident that this second offering was organized as a set of temple images or as the expression of a theology. It was not simply a set of objects to accompany the person in death, as the first offering seems to have been.

The third offering consists of a variety of objects laid in the fill above the burial chamber.

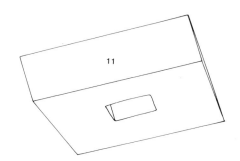

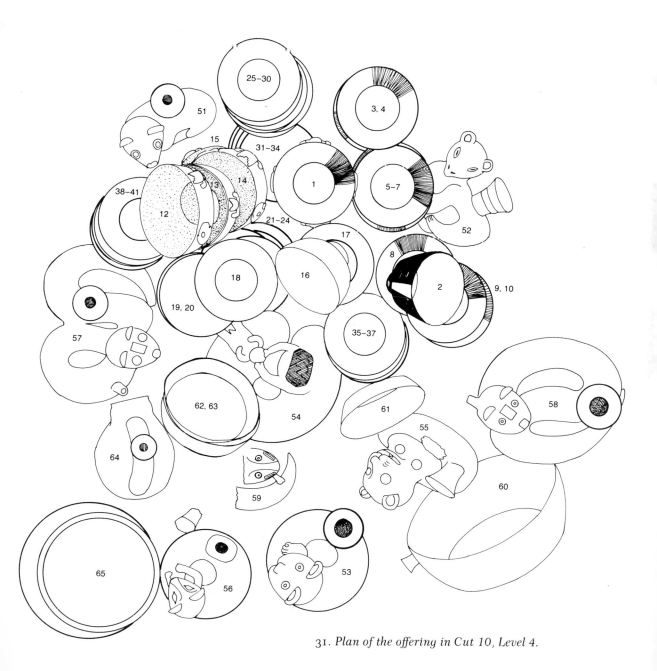

31. *Plan of the offering in Cut 10, Level 4.*

The fill contained a mixture of crude ware pot-sherds, which may be considered accidental inclusions in the fill dirt, and fine ware sherds, some of which are so decorative, so large, or so unusual that they seem to have been deposited intentionally. Except for whistles and miniature vessels, only one whole vessel (12/3.9) was found in Levels 3, 4, and 5 of Cut 12, but practically all the parts of several were found. It is clear from the way in which restorable vessels were found that breakage was part of the burial ritual. Three kinds of breaks appear: old breaks, in which just a fragment was deposited; breaks in which the pot was smashed and scattered in the fill; and breaks which occurred after the floor was laid, caused by settling. Level 3 of Cut 12, just below the floor, had the largest number of such offerings.

Pottery was not the only material deposited in the fill. A carved red stone cup, similar to that in the second offering, was scattered in Level 5, but parts are missing and it appears that it was broken before deposit. A rim fragment of a carved stone bowl (fig. 166) lay in Level 4, with some metal jewelry and what was probably a wooden object constructed with six copper nails. A granite ax head was found in Level 3.

This third offering is different from the other two in its casualness. It suggests something like family members gathered around the grave, smashing vessels and tossing them in or laying down treasured objects which had lost ritual usefulness by being broken. The burial and doorway offerings both have an official character absent from the material in the fill.

The three offerings are unique among the burial and ritual offerings previously recorded in the Andes, although so few have been described in print that a claim of uniqueness is hardly significant. The importance of the buried person is manifested by the number and quality of the offerings as well as by the architectural setting for the burial, and that immediately sets the offerings apart from the "average" burial offerings, just as the individual was distinguished in life. The discovery of the three offerings together, all related to a single burial, is valuable in providing a single gravelot of at least 277 items (Cut 10, Levels 3–5; Cut 11, Level 3; Cut 12, Levels 3–8; not counting potsherds). By contrast, Max Uhle excavated thirty-two Nasca burials in the Ica Valley, containing a total of 146 pots, or an average of 4 1/2 each, 15 being the largest number in a single grave (in Proulx 1970: 47 ff.). The Pashash offerings provide a very rich resource for the description of the Recuay period in Pashash art, technology, burial customs, and religious imagery. The value of a gravelot lies, of course, in the fact that all the items were available at one time to the people constructing the grave. (See Rowe 1962b for a critique of this principle.) Some items obviously were older than others, but they do not immediately declare themselves by style. One might assume that the previously broken objects in the offerings, particularly in the third offering, are the oldest. Yet the broken stone cup in Cut 12, Level 5, is similar to the complete one which is the centerpiece of the second offering. That, as well as the general unity of the style of the objects in the offerings, indicates that the three offerings in general represent a single phase in the middle of the Recuay period at Pashash. There is, moreover, good evidence that many of the vessels in the burial and doorway offerings were made especially for those offerings and were designed to carry out a prearranged plan (see chap. 5). Thus, the core of the offerings represents a single moment in the history of the site.

5.
Ceramic Types
and Their Periods

Pashash ceramics offer an opportunity for two kinds of studies which complement each other. The sherd collections from stratigraphic excavations provide evidence for a developmental sequence, and the funerary offerings broaden our knowledge of one phase of the sequence. This chapter will deal with the pottery from the first of these two points of view, emphasizing the sherd collections as evidence of the historical development of ceramic types and their decoration.

At this time, the definition of periods in the history of Pashash rests entirely on ceramics.

Ultimately more comprehensive criteria will have to be developed, incorporating architecture and stone sculpture especially, but the ceramics will probably remain the basic and most sensitive indicator of social changes and extramural relationships.

The features of the pottery most useful for defining periods are wares (the clay and the manner of its firing), vessel forms, and decorative techniques. Other aspects of the pottery, such as techniques of forming the vessels and decorative motifs, also show differences characteristic of particular periods.

Wares

The Pashash pottery wares have been divided into named types based on the color and texture of the clay body. The type is designated by the first two names, such as "Caserón Orange," in which the color name refers to the color of the clay body between the surface and the core, as visible in sherds. The varieties of surface treatment are designated by the third name: "Plain," "Painted," or "Resist." Thus, Pashash Orange is the name of a medium-fired orange clay body,

usually with a gray or black core (the result of incomplete oxidation) and heavy sand temper. This is distinguished from Caserón Orange, which is a hard-fired orange clay body, sometimes with a gray core, and very fine sand temper. Resist decoration is common on Caserón Orange but is very rare (seventeen sherds) on Pashash Orange. The positive-painted varieties of these two wares are also distinct. Pashash Orange Painted bears only casual red lines,

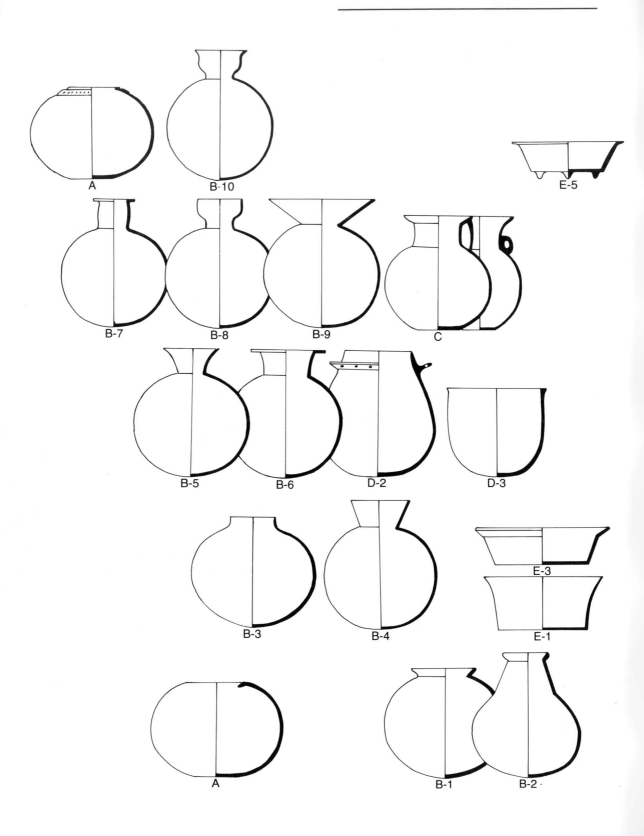

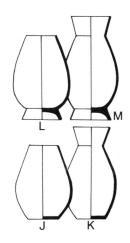

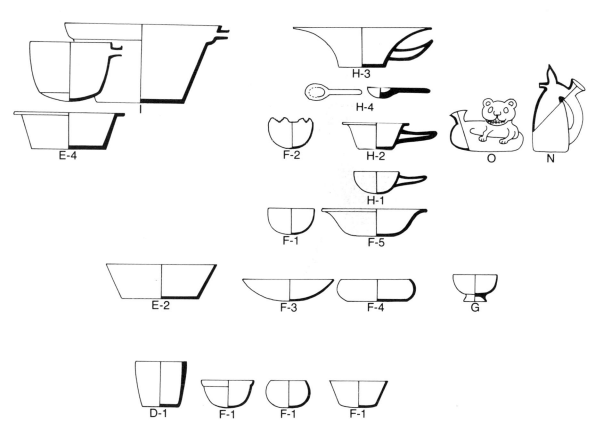

32. *Vessel forms.*
Forms characteristic of each period or phase are
shown together, earliest at the bottom, latest at
the top.

whereas Caserón Orange Painted may be elaborately decorated in five or six colors. These named wares are intended to reflect the categories in the minds of ancient Pashash potters.

Pashash ceramic wares give an impression of unity. The clay seems to come from a single source for most of the pottery, the type being the result of the addition of fine or heavy sand temper and the temperature of the firing. Thus Vista Brown is the lowest fired, heaviest tempered ware, a brown crumbly paste with a black core. Vista Brown can be distinguished from Pashash Orange, which is harder and lighter in color. Pashash Orange grades into Caserón Orange, which is thinner, harder, and a still paler orange. The finest temper and the highest firing temperature resulted in Cabana Cream ware, made of the same basic clay as the other wares. Cabana Cream ware was fired in an oxidizing atmosphere to produce the very pale orange, cream, or white pottery. The same clay fired in a reducing atmosphere, in which the vessel was buried in ashes or otherwise smothered, produced Horno Black. The rare Horno Buff seems to have been intentionally made by briefly oxidizing a vessel blackened by reduction. In summary, all the local pottery was made of clay from the same source, an indication that Pashash was self-sufficient in pottery at least. The rare fragments of pottery made from other clays stand out as imported pieces.

The potters of the earliest period, Quinú, produced Vista Brown, Pashash Orange, and Caserón Orange wares. A single Horno Black sherd is probably imported. The Recuay period opens with the introduction of Cabana Cream. The Yaiá phase added only Horno Black and Horno Buff. No new wares came into use during the Huacohú phase, and all the other wares remained in use. In the final Usú period the finest wares (Cabana Cream, Horno Black, and Horno Buff) seem to have disappeared, leaving the other wares still in use. Especially during the Recuay period, the potters were aware of the possibilities in tempering and in firing techniques and were proficient in controlling them.

Forms

The general development of vessel forms is presented in figure 32, in which the five horizontal rows represent periods and phases from the earliest at the bottom to the latest at the top. The particular forms are shown only in the row of which they are most characteristic, but most of the forms remained in use in later times. Neckless jars (Form A), for example, were used during all periods and phases with only minor changes in the form of the rim. Among the necked jars (Form B), on the other hand, later forms tended to supersede earlier ones, but Forms B-7 to 10 appeared at the end of the Yaiá phase and only gradually replaced the earlier forms.

The categories of vessel form are designated by letters and the varieties within each category by numbers. The categories are:

A. Neckless ollas ("jars"). This form continues throughout all periods and phases with only minor changes in the rim form.

B. Necked jars. Each period has its characteristic varieties, defined mainly by rim form.

C. Handled jars. Both circular and strap handles are found.

D. Wide-mouthed jars. D-2 has a pierced flange on the shoulder. This form is most common in Pashash Orange ware, but there are also decorated examples in Caserón Orange and Cabana Cream fine paste wares.

E. Bowls with out-slanted or flared walls and a flat floor. Tripod nubbin feet appear on this form in the terminal period.

F. Simple bowls in which the height does not exceed the rim diameter and the floor curves up into the wall. The rim form varies from slightly restricted to vertical, with rim tabs in one phase, to an outward flare or rim flange.

G. Cups or bowls with pedestal or ring feet. This form comes into use at the beginning of the Recuay period and remains the most common fine ware form until the site was abandoned. There are Pashash Orange ware examples in the terminal period.

H. Handled bowls, cups, and spoons. Hollow conical handles were used on the bowls and cups, solid handles being found only on the spoons. These forms were definitely present in the later phases of the Recuay period and may have been characteristic of the whole period.

I. Basins with pouring spouts. Despite their functional appearance, unpainted examples are rare, and the form is most common in Caserón Orange and Cabana Cream fine wares.

J. Plain goblets, defined by the height being greater than the rim diameter, with restricted openings.

K. Goblets with flared necks.

L. Goblets with pedestal or ring feet.

M. Goblets with flared necks and pedestal or ring feet. All the goblet forms are characteristic of the later periods.

N. Miscellaneous unusual forms.

O. Effigy vessels. The Pashash Recuay type is characterized by the whole form's being modeled into the subject. There is no Recuay example of a bowl or jar with a modeled figure attached to it, although there are figurines which may have been so attached (e.g., 12/7.136, fig. 185). Modeled additions are more characteristic of the Usú period, when they were probably both imported and made locally.

P. Figurines (not represented in fig. 32). Figurines appear in all periods except the first and show great variety in ware, subject, and decoration. There is no standard type.

Imported forms are not categorized by letter. The stirrup-spout bottle, for example (figs. 41–43), is represented only by three fragments defined by their paste as imported pieces.

Periods

Using the ceramics as a guide, we can establish three periods in the history of Pashash, with approximate dates based on radiocarbon tests. The periods are Quinú, of which the beginning has not been dated but which ended about A.D. 310; Recuay, A.D. 310–600; and Usú, A.D. 600–700. The Recuay period can be divided into three phases with dates intended to indicate the approximate time of developments in the style: Quimít, 310–400; Yaiá, 400–500; and Huacohú, 500–600.

The name of the earliest period, Quinú, means "father" in Kul'i (Rivet 1949), suggesting its ancestral position in relation to the later periods. The definition of the Quinú period rests on isolated deposits in Cut 4, Level 5, which had twenty-two sherds, five of them rims; Cut 12, Level 8, which had five sherds, three of them rims, isolated from the burial offering; and the deeper Levels 4, 5, and 6 of Cut 9, in which there was some mixing of early Recuay sherds. Vista Brown is the commonest ware, outnumbering the other common ware in this period, Pashash Orange, by about nine to one. Vessel forms are neckless ollas with various undecorated rims (fig. 33), necked ollas with low outward-curled rims or high necks slanting inward to an everted rim, and small bowls and basins, some with slightly elaborated rims of various

forms (fig. 34). Decorations include red slip, stick-burnishing, opaque white paint in simple patterns on red slip, postfire red paint, incised or grooved slashes or zigzag designs, and applied nubbins with a center pit.

Although the evidence is not sufficient to support the definition of phases, at least two phases appear to be represented in the Quinú material: an early phase using red slip, postfire red paint, and incised or grooved designs and a

33. *Rim sherds from Cut 12, Level 8.*
Quinú period neckless ollas with red slip. Upper left is interior, others exterior.

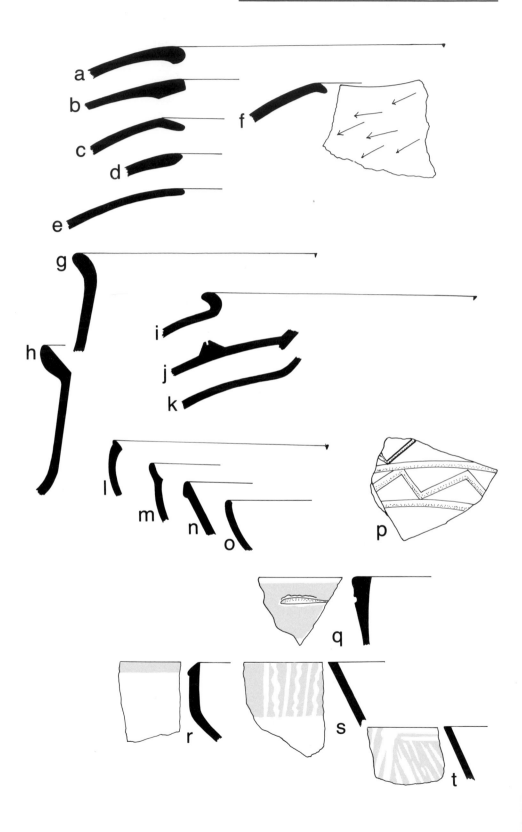

later phase in which white on red decoration was used. The white on red decoration was found only in Cut 9, where its stratigraphic relationships are ambiguous.

The deposit in Cut 4 lies below a level that held charcoal which gave a radiocarbon test date centering on A.D. 310 (Tx-944), serving as an arbitrary terminal date for the period, which must have spanned centuries. Perhaps the earliest single sherd is a polished blackware rim with a grooved slash and postfire red paint from Cut 9, Level 4, which looks like an early Chavín or Kotosh type and was probably imported to Pashash. But there are no decorative elements or other traits which definitely represent the Chavín style or any other identifiable tradition. Quinú period occupation of Pashash may not have been continuous, but its final phase was continuous with the initial Recuay period, for the ceramic wares extend from Quinú into Recuay.

The second period, Recuay, is named for the ceramic style of the Callejón de Huaylas. The name is intended to convey the presence of an oxidized creamware decorated with red and resist black, with effigy vessels appearing. The name does not imply that Pashash and the Callejón de Huaylas produced indistinguishable art, for there are unmistakable local differences, but it is clear that they participated in the same style.

The names of the three phases of the Recuay period are derived from Kul'i: Quimít means "brother," Yaiá "god," and Huacohú "fruit" (Rivet 1949).

34. Potsherds representative of the Quinú period.
Gray areas represent red paint in all illustrations of ceramics.
Material in parentheses refers to forms in fig. 32; cut/level numbers for specimens are given.
a–e (A): 12/8, 12/8, 4/4, 4/4, 4/4
f (with stick burnish): 1/2
g, h (B-2): 4/4
i (B-1): 9/6
j, k: 4/4
l–n (F-1): 9/5
o: 9/6
p: 9/4
q (D-1): 9/4
r: 9/5
s, t: 9/6

The Quimít phase represents the introduction of the Recuay style (fig. 35). The phase is typified by material in Cut 5, Level 3; Cut 6, Levels 2, 3, and 4; and Cut 9, Levels 4, 5, and 6. The Cut 9 levels have earlier material mixed in, and Level 2 of Cut 6 contains some later Recuay mixture; otherwise these appear to be purely Quimít phase deposits. The fine ware—Cabana Cream—makes its first appearance during this phase. It is indicative of the experimentation with firing techniques which characterized the Recuay period and led to the introduction of Horno Black and Buff in the next phase. Vessel forms show continued, but less common, use of neckless ollas and the introduction of a low vertical neck and an expanded neck, which was by far the most common. Large basins with flat floors and out-slanting walls become common, and a variety of bowls and cups, some with pedestal feet, are found. Modeled effigy vessels were made. Red or orange slip was applied on both coarse and fine wares, and cream slip was used on fine wares. Red is the most common paint color by far, but both black and opaque white are found. Incision and the other types of plastic ornament—modeled, punched, drag-and-jab, gouged, filleted, etc.—are absent or rare. Resist may have come into use in this phase, but it is characteristic of the succeeding phase, and individual pieces cannot be distinguished by phase. Typical decorations of this phase are red on cream conventional patterns, such as crosshatching and chains, rather than representational subjects.

The Yaiá phase represents the purest Recuay style (fig. 36), a restricted conventional style dominated by black on cream resist decoration. The phase is typified by the material in Cut 3, Levels 2, 3, and 4; Cut 7, especially Level 4; and by the funerary offerings in Cut 10, Levels 3 to 5; Cut 11, Levels 3 to 5; and Cut 12, Levels 3 to 8. The full range of Recuay wares is found, including Horno Black and the rare Horno Buff. The neckless olla is rare in this phase and shows elaboration of the rim, such as an incised line or an everted rim edge. More common are ollas with a flange near the rim (Form D), plain to support a lid or pierced for suspension. The most common olla form has a flared neck, often with a flat rim flange (Form B-6). Olla rims and necks vary, some forecasting the S-necks of the next phase. Large basins with plain or flattened rims are common. A variety of simple and pedestal

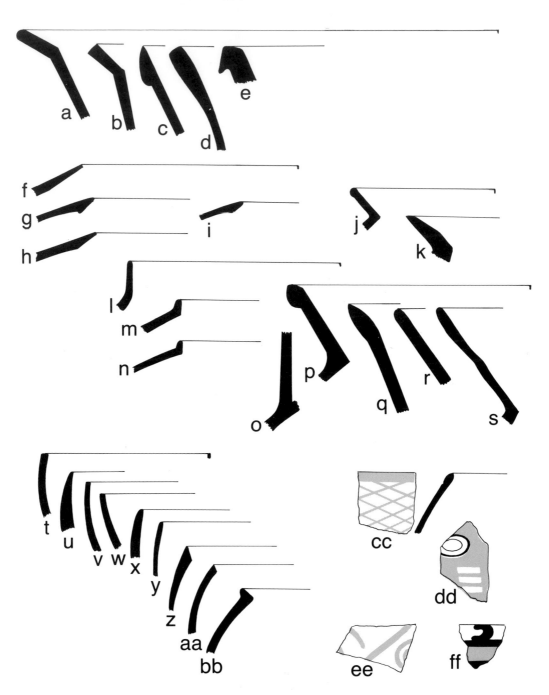

35. *Potsherds representative of the Recuay*
Quimít phase.
Material in parentheses refers to forms in fig.
32; cut/level numbers for specimens are given.

a, b (E-3): 6/3
c, e (E-2): 5/3, 9/4
d (E-1): 6/2
f (A): 6/2
g–i (A): 6/3
j, k (B-1): 5/3, 6/2
l–n (B-3): 6/3, 5/3, 5/3

o (B-2): 5/3
p–s (B-4): 6/3, 6/3, 6/2, 6/4
t–y (F-1): 6/3
z, aa (F-1): 6/4
bb (F-1): 6/3
cc: 6/4
dd, ee: 6/3
ff: 5/3

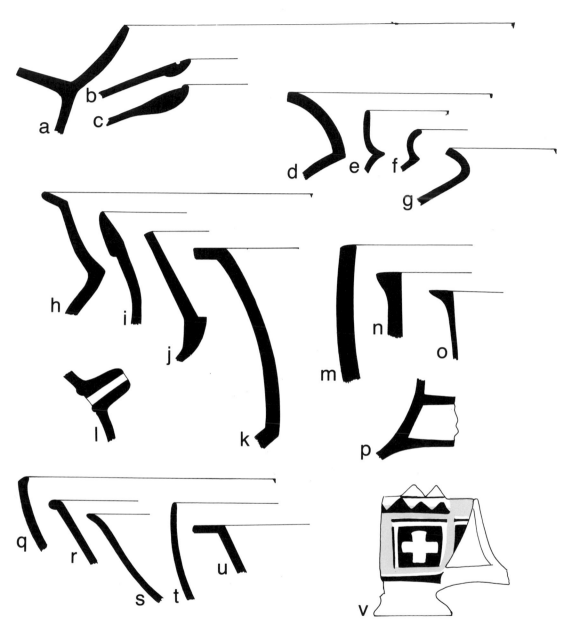

36. Potsherds representative of the Recuay Yaiá
phase.
Material in parentheses refers to forms in fig.
32; cut/level numbers for specimens are given.

a (D-2): 10/5
b, c (A): 10/4
d (B-5): 10/4
e, f (B-8): 3/2, 10/4
g (B-1): 3/2
h (B-10): 10/5
i–k (B-5): 7/4, 10/5, 10/5

l: 10/4
m–o (D-3): 10/5, 7/4, 3/2
p (H): 10/5
q, r, t (F-1): 10/4
s (F-5): 10/4
u (H-2): 10/4
v (double pedestal cup with rim tabs): 11/3

37. *Pedestal cup with cover of the Yaiá phase.*
Cabana Cream Plain ware.
11.8 cm. diameter. 12/7.77.

bowls and cups are found, some bowls with rim
flanges and others with rim tabs. Short spouts
are fairly common on basins and jars. Hollow
handles are common on bowls and basins. Broken handles were at first interpreted as tripod
feet, but no example of that use could be proved,
all the certain examples being handles. The ring
or pedestal is the only foot form. Modeled and
effigy vessels are common. Spoons and triangular and square vessels were made occasionally.
Matching covers were sometimes made for
cups, bowls, or jars (fig. 37).

Red is by far the most common positive paint
color, with others appearing in minor roles.
Black is found only as a smudged carbon color
used in resist decoration, distinguishable from
the heavy-bodied brown black pigment used in
the next phase. White, cream, and a range of
pale pinks and oranges appear mainly as slips,
which is to say as grounds for other decorations,
rather than as decorations in their own right.

Most of these features were carried on into the
final phase of the Recuay period, the Huacohú
phase, represented by the material in the upper

levels of all the excavations (fig. 38). Evidence
of this phase is found mixed in all levels of Cut
1; Cut 3, Level 1; Levels 1 and 2 of Cuts 4 and 5;
Cut 6, Level 1; and Levels 1 and 2 of Cuts 7, 9,
10, and 12. The name Huacohú, meaning
"fruit" in Kul'i, is intended to imply the final
fruition of the decorative tendency of the
Recuay style in colorful unconventional decorations. A wide range of paint colors is found: positive mineral black, brown, tan, gray, red, orange,
and yellow. A bright orange background was
especially popular. Although black and cream
resist remained common, painting with positive
white slip paint is diagnostic of the phase. Olla
forms include neckless examples with elaboration of the rim area, flanged examples, and the
most common type with a flared neck. The
S-neck, curving out and in, is typical of the
phase. Basins are common, usually with a reinforced or flanged rim. Bowls and cups, both
simple and pedestal-footed, are common, with
simple or flanged rims. Vessels with the body
(not the neck) modeled as a head are known in
other Recuay pottery (Larco Hoyle 1965? shows
three examples); the noses found in deposits of
this phase, and rarely in the Yaiá phase, probably represent that form. Spoons and square and
triangular cups are found, and the only spindle
whorl from a subsurface level outside the burial
offerings belongs in this phase.

Huacohú phase ceramic decoration represents a reassertion of traditional local decorative

38. *Potsherds representative of the Recuay*
Huacohú phase.
Material in parentheses refers to forms in fig.
32; cut/level numbers for specimens are given.
a–c (A): 5/2, 9/1, 5/2
d (D-2): 10/1
e (B-6): 10/2
f, g, l (B-5): 10/1, 10/1, 5/2
h (B-4): 10/1
i (C): 6/1
j, k (B-8): 5/2
m–q (E): 10/1, 5/2, 5/2, 4/1, 4/1
r–v (F-1): 9/1, 9/1, 5/2, 9/1, 6/1
w: 4/1
x: 4/1
y: 10/1
z (H-2): 10/1
aa (F-5): 12/3
bb–hh (F): 9/1, 9/1, 10/1, 3/2, 10/1, 10/1, 4/1

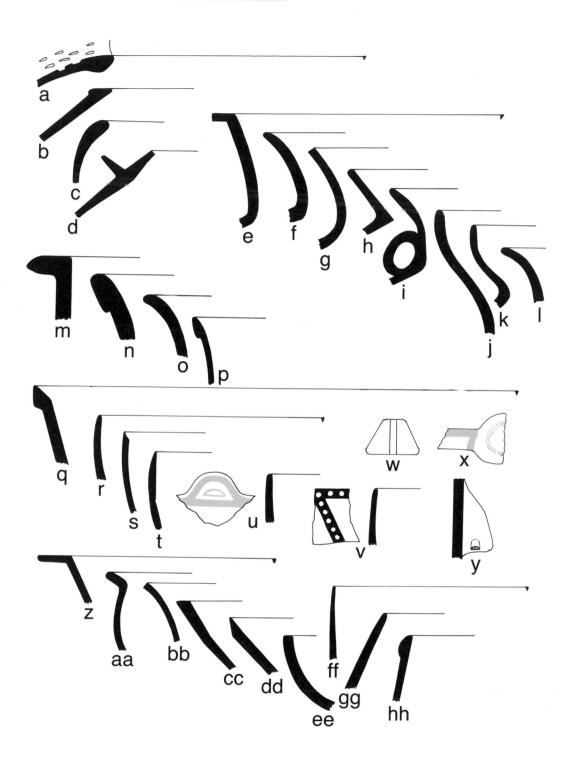

preferences against the more disciplined intrusive style of the Yaiá phase. The high Recuay style of the Yaiá phase shows connections with the southern coast and the southern highlands in motifs and decorative techniques (see chap. 10), and it remained an elite style which had only slight influence on pottery style in the smaller centers in this district. By the Huacohú phase, we find the independence of that courtly style waning as local tradition revived. The local tradition shared the use of step and fret designs and the mixture of positive and resist with the Lima style. It shared vessel forms, wares, and decorative designs with the beginnings of the Cajamarca cursive style. The positive white dots on dark bands found in Huacohú decoration are shared with the Wari style, whose expansion was just beginning, and they may manifest a continued connection with the southern highlands.

Usú, the final period in the ancient occupation, is represented throughout the site, especially in Cut 2, Level 1, and Cut 10, Level 1. The name Usú, which means "man" in Kul'i (Rivet 1949), is given to suggest the mundane simplicity of its style, lacking the ritual forms and iconic decorations typical of the Recuay style. In most cases Usú potsherds are mixed with Huacohú phase debris on the surface, but an isolated set of vessels in Usú style was found in Cut 10, Level 1C. This set of at least twenty-three ves-

sels was evidently an offering with a burial, the disturbed traces of which were found on the surface (fig. 39).

Usú period ceramics (fig. 40) are unlike those of any earlier period at Pashash: they are typically unslipped coarse wares with plastic ornament. The only paint color is red, applied in casual lines on unslipped or orange-slipped surfaces. Usú period pottery is a local product, to judge from the clays and the vessel forms, but there are also more sherds of clays which do not appear to be local than are found in deeper levels.

The presence of the traditional Vista Brown and Pashash Orange coarse wares—the finest creamwares and blackwares disappear—and the retention of most of the traditional vessel forms show that the Usú occupation was continuous with the Recuay period and that the basic population remained intact. Neckless ollas are found with punched or slashed ornament or reinforced rims. Necked jars continued in use; the typical form has a recurved neck, adding an outward curve to the Huacohú S-neck. Simple bowls and pedestal cups are found, but only in the coarse Pashash Orange ware.

Although the periods at Pashash are defined by ceramics, they are also useful for the description of stone and metal artifacts and architecture. Descriptions of the development of those arts will be presented in separate chapters.

39. *Whole vessels from the Usú period offering in Cut 10, Level 1C.*

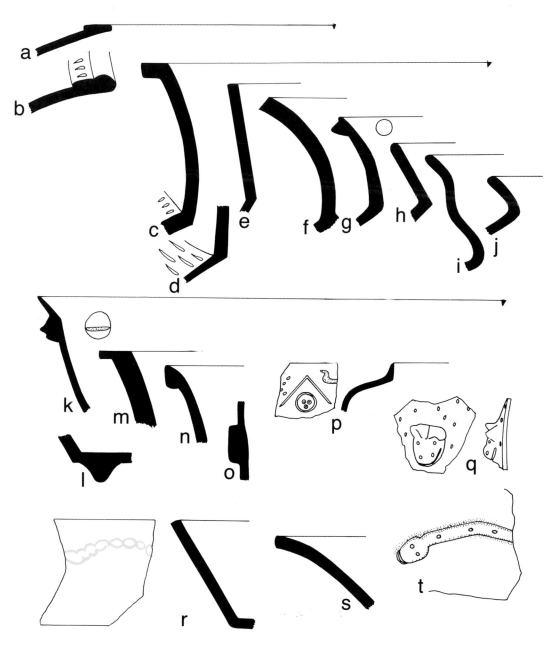

40. *Potsherds representative of the Usú period.*
Material in parentheses refers to forms in fig.
32; cut/level numbers for specimens are given.
a, b (A): 7/1, 9/1
c, d (B-6, 7): 2/1, 10/2
e, h (B-4): 10/1
f, g (B-5): 10/1, 7/3
i (B-10): 7/2
j (B-1): 10/1
k, m, n (E): 5/1, 7/2, 6/1

l: 10/1
o: 6/1
p: 6/1
q: 2/1
r (E-2): 1/2
s (F-5): 10/1
t: 10/1

Imported Pottery

The number of potsherds which can be distinguished as imported is statistically negligible, but the sherds are nonetheless interesting for what they tell us about contacts with other cultures.

A sherd which is the earliest in style of any on the site—a Kotosh or early Chavín style polished blackware with a broad groove and postfire red paint—was found in Cut 9, Level 4. The flattened rim was thickened to 7.5 millimeters from a wall thickness of 2 millimeters. This single sherd implies some Quinú period contacts, probably southward with Chavín or Kotosh related styles (fig. 34, q).

In the burial offering, Cut 12, Level 7, was a fragment of a small (8 centimeter high) moldmade stirrup-spout bottle representing a human figure wrapped in a blanket (figs. 41, 42). This

bottle was already broken before deposit, and only this fragment was found. The dark orange paste was slipped in orange, and stripes of black and white were painted on the blanket. Black and red lines were painted on the face, running from the eyes. The person had something, probably a hand, touching its mouth. Two small holes through the back show where the spout was attached. Except for the paint, the vessel looks like Moche style. Moldmade pottery is so typical of the north coast that an origin in that region is a first presumption. The paint might even have been added at Pashash.

The Moche style is also represented in two sherds from stirrup-spout bottles, one being part of the stirrup with the base of the spout, the other just a long section of the stirrup (fig. 43). Both are of orange paste not assignable to

41. *Fragment of an effigy stirrup-spout bottle in the Moche style.*
12/7.130.

42. *Side view of fig. 41.*

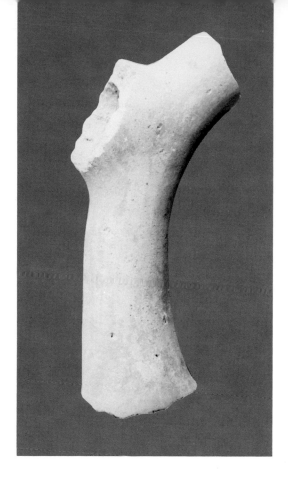

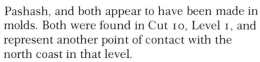

Pashash, and both appear to have been made in molds. Both were found in Cut 10, Level 1, and represent another point of contact with the north coast in that level.

In Cut 10, Level 1, there were also two ceramic effigy heads attached to the exterior of vessels. The larger and hollow one is made from clay which falls in the Pashash Orange category, and it may be a local product (fig. 44). The other (fig. 45), which is smaller and solid, is of a gray clay not found in other Pashash pottery. This fragment may be assigned on the basis of style to the Castillo Modeled type found in the Virú Valley (cf. Strong and Evans 1952: 309–310).

There are a few other sherds whose category is doubtful and which may be imported, but none of them can be assigned a provenience. The abundant ceramic material at Pashash gives the impression that there was little importation of pottery made at other centers even when foreign styles were influential.

We have long been accustomed to tracing highland traits on the coast, but coastal influence on highland cultures has not been much in evidence. That people, women as well as men, of coastal culture were actually present

43. *Above: fragment of a stirrup from a Moche style bottle. Orange ware.*
9 cm. long. 10/1.

44. *Below left: hollow head of an animal, probably a guinea pig, from the shoulder of a Pashash Orange Plain vessel.*
8 cm. high. 10/1B.20.

45. *Below right: solid head from the shoulder of a jar in Virú Valley style.*
10/1B.19.

at Pashash is implied by the finding on the surface of La Capilla Hill of a single spindle whorl
in a style associated with the Moche culture (fig.
46). It is a perfect example of the type found by
Christopher Donnan on Moche sites in the
Santa Valley (1973: 100, pl. 8, L–T), with a
rounded top and bottom. Nine other spindle
whorls have been found at Pashash (Cut 4,
Level 1, and Cut 12, Levels 3, 7, and 8), all of
the same form: trapezoidal in section, with
slanted walls and a flat top and bottom (fig. 27).

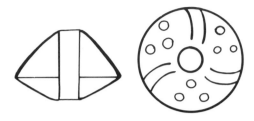

46. *Coastal style spindle whorl found at
Pashash on the surface.*

Contemporary Related Styles

Of the various cultural features surviving at
Pashash, comparable material is most abundantly available for ceramic vessel forms and
decorations. Comparisons offer evidence of cultural regions and their boundaries and of the
relative chronologies and cultural contacts between regions.

The local styles of the Early Intermediate
period in the Callejón de Huaylas to the south,
the Huamachuco district to the north, and the
coastal valleys to the west show a complex pattern of similarities and differences when compared with Pashash (see table 10).

Wendell Bennett's description of the Recuay
style in the Callejón de Huaylas shows it to be
very similar to the style found at Pashash (1944:
99–103). In decoration, he notes the presence of
both positive and resist painting in all the color
combinations common at Pashash (red on white
being most common, followed by white on
orange, black on orange, and red on orange;
black-white-red in both positive and resist; and
black-white resist). The white on red style was
absent in Bennett's Recuay excavations.

In vessel form the similarities are so great that
it is easier to point out the differences. What
Bennett calls "measuring bowls"—restricted-
orifice handled bowls—are absent at Pashash,
as are hollow tripod supports, bridge spouts, stirrup spouts, and trumpets. Vessels with small
modeled figures of humans and animals attached are rare. Among Bennett's modeled vessels are "castles" in which the vessel has been
designed as a building, but at Pashash effigy
vessels are modeled as a single being, the idea of
the container being entirely dominated by the
representation. Pashash also shows a greater va-

riety of round-based and flat-based bowls,
utilitarian jar forms, and large bowls and basins.

The Recuay style of the Callejón de Huaylas
was more closely related to the Gallinazo style
than was Pashash Recuay, a relationship especially evident in the globular bridge-spout double vessels found in both styles (Bennett 1944:
100, fig. 32, I; Proulx 1973: pl. 2), a form not
found at Pashash. The two styles are nevertheless distinguishable even in the coastal valleys,
with some evidence suggesting that Recuay is
the older. In an excavation at Gallinazo in the
Virú Valley, Bennett found five sherds of three-
color "negative" (resist), about which he wrote:
"Four of these, found at almost 2.00 meters
depth in Pit G4 [80 to 90 centimeters below
Gallinazo period graves], are pure Recuay style,
with the white clay base, the black-on-white
negative, and the additional red line" (1939: 73).

The ceramics of the Virú Valley epitomize the
relationship between Pashash and the coast.
The Guañape and Huacapongo jar types of the
early periods are similar to the early utilitarian
forms at Pashash, and in the Virú Gallinazo
period there are wide-necked jars comparable to
the B-9 form at Pashash. Resist decoration is
characteristic of the Virú Gallinazo period, although the designs are distinguishable from
those in contemporary Recuay pottery. The
greatest similarities to Virú pottery are found in
the surface levels at Pashash, where plastic or-
namentation, especially filleting and modeled
heads, like that in the Castillo Modeled type in
the Virú Gallinazo period appears. Before the
terminal period at Pashash, the similarities between the ceramics of the two regions occur in
very widespread traits, which suggests that

Table 10.
Pashash Periods in Relation to the Virú Valley and the Huamachuco District

Date	Pashash		Virú	Huamachuco
600	Usú		Tomaval	
				Amaru
			Huancaco	
500		Huacohú		
				Huamachuco
400	Recuay	Yaiá	Gallinazo	
				Purpucala
				Blanco
300		Quimít		
			Puerto Moorín	Campana
	Quinú	late phase		
		early phase	Guañape	Mamorco

there were few direct contacts between the coastal valleys and Pashash.

The ceramics of the Huamachuco district, north across the canyon of the Chuquicara River from Pashash, have been studied by Theodore McCown (1945) and John Thatcher (1972). Although the similarities are considerable, it is evident that the Chuquicara Canyon was a cultural frontier in all periods. The scanty material representing the Quinú period at Pashash makes comparison with Thatcher's early phases difficult, but the two regions shared the basic olla forms (A and B-1). With Thatcher's third phase (Blanco), which shows white paste wares, white paint, and two-color resist with incision, there are some parallels in early Recuay ceramics at Pashash, although no example of resist with incision has been found there. The fourth phase (Purpucala) has white paste wares and two- and three-color resist, which correlates with the Pashash Recuay Yaiá phase. The latter half of the Pashash Recuay period (late Yaiá and Huacohú phases) may be equated with Thatcher's fifth phase (Huamachuco), which shows the long-popular white paste wares, pedestal bowls, and positive painting in the Cajamarca cursive style. Resist decoration had disappeared from Huamachuco phase pottery but remained in use in the Pashash Huacohú phase. Thatcher comments on the heavy fortifications constructed during the Huamachuco phase and notes that the unrest was not emanat-

ing from the Cajamarca region, to which Huamachuco was allied in style. He attributes the unrest to Wari expansion, evident in the pottery of the following period (1972: 84–85). Pashash shows similar fortifications, but relatively few Wari traits are found in Pashash pottery compared with the strong Wari influence evident in Huamachuco pottery. Thatcher's sixth phase (Amaru) represents a mixture of Wari and Cajamarca traits, and Wari style architecture is represented by the Viracochapampa storage center. Pashash may have been abandoned by this time.

The comparison here is between the single site of Pashash and many sites in the Huamachuco region, yet it is clear that there was a shared trend of development. Many of the differences can be attributed to the fact that Pashash had an especially high production of decorated fine ware which had much more in common with the Recuay pottery of the Callejón de Huaylas than it did with the northern regions. The analysis of Huamachuco area vessel forms given by McCown (1945) confirms that Pashash shares utilitarian bowl, basin, and jar forms with those at Cerro Campana East and perhaps overlaps with the earlier phases at Marca Huamachuco. This implies southern, rather than northern, connections for the symbolic forms and decorations imposed upon a widespread northern tradition of functional pottery wares and forms.

Decorative Techniques

The only decorations definitely assignable to the Quinú period (fig. 34) are red slip, some patterns of straight white lines on red, and a small nubbin or lug on the shoulder of a jar. Some sherds in the deeper levels (1/4, 9/3–5) show incision and gouge marks, both techniques of plastic ornament which should also belong in this period. With the advent of the Recuay style, we begin to find more painted pottery. A white paste or slip is a common feature of Recuay fine wares, and it served as the background for painted designs. Red on white or cream was the first color combination to appear, and it remained common throughout the period.

Black first appeared as the background for white or cream resist designs, to complete the red, black, and white (or cream) color scheme typical of the Recuay style (fig. 47). Experiments by Robert Sonin suggest that, on the three-color vessels, the red on cream was fired first in an oxidizing atmosphere. After firing, a very liquid slip was painted on the vessel in areas to be reserved cream and over all the red. A liquid organic substance—almost any organic material will serve—was painted over the vessel, or the vessel was dipped into it. The vessel was then subjected to low heat sufficient to scorch the organic material, leaving a carbon residue in the clay, but insufficient to fire the slip, which was finally rubbed off to reveal the red and cream areas.

Resist decoration had a long history in the Andean region, beginning before 1000 B.C. in the Chorrera and Early Cerro Narrio styles of Ecuador and in the earliest pottery of the Peruvian south coast (Lathrap, Collier, and Chandra

47. *Pedestal cup showing Recuay red-black-cream resist decoration.*
10/4.39.

1975: 34), and it continued to appear in Paracas pottery from at least 600 B.C. (Menzel, Rowe, and Dawson 1964: 4, 21). Pashash resist decoration is a relatively late manifestation of an old technique, but one which had been thoroughly mastered.

The last phase of the Recuay style turned toward positive painting with a great variety of colors in many combinations (fig. 48). Ground colors tended to white or orange, with positive paint in several reds, orange, brown and black, gray, and opaque white. During this phase both black and white appear as positive paint, as well as in resist designs. The white is a very white slip paint, applied thickly. The black gives a different appearance from the carbon black used for resist. The positive black, which is probably an iron oxide or manganese, coated the surface without much penetration and did not fade. It tends to grade into brown. The gray blues and purples of contemporary Nasca pottery are not found at Pashash.

During the Huacohú phase, decoration was often applied to the coarse wares. Opaque white, red, orange, and black are found, often in combination in simple geometric designs (fig. 49).

48. *Above: Huacohú phase painted sherds from Cut 9, Level 1.*
Left: opaque white on brown;
right: tan, black, and wine red on white.

49. *Below: white and red on orange sherds of the Huacohú phase. 9/1 and 10/1.*
The sherd from 10/3 (upper right center) is late Yaiá phase, anticipating these later decorations on coarse wares.

50. *Plastically ornamented sherds of the Usú
period.*
9/1, 10/1.

Usú period pottery seems to have nearly
eliminated painting in favor of plastic ornament.
Incision, filleting, and modeled additions show
up in Huacohú phase pottery, but in the Usú
period these plastic techniques are the principal
decorations (fig. 50). Incision and gouging,
brushing, punching, fingernail marking,
applied nubbins and fillets, and modeled heads
all appear. Painting appears definitely only in
the form of casual red lines on an orange-slipped
or unslipped body (fig. 51), although the mixing

of sherds in the surface level makes it uncertain
whether some earlier techniques may have remained in use.

That the Usú period directly followed the
Recuay period without a break in the occupation
of the site is indicated by the continuity of the
ceramics. Coarse wares and Caserón Orange
remained in use, and vessel forms and decorative techniques show many similarities. The
radiocarbon tests tend to confirm the continuity
of the occupation and suggest that the site was
abandoned after the Usú period.

51. *Usú period jar with two red lines.*
10/1C.27.

52. *Opposite: potters' marks on the bases of
pedestal cups. Base diameter has been standardized.*
a–g: incised marks
h: black paint
i–r: red paint
b, c, g, h, j, m, o: 3/3
d, f: 3/2
e, k, l, n, r: 12/7
p: 12/2
q: 10/2

The Identification of Artists and Studios

A unique glimpse of the working conditions of pre-Inca artists and their relations with their patrons is provided by the fine ware vessels in the offerings, a large number of which can be grouped as the work of single individuals. That this might be possible was first suggested by the incised or painted marks which Pashash potters sometimes placed on pedestal cups. Potters' marks have been recorded in the Santa Valley in both ancient Moche and modern cultures by Donnan (1971; 1973: 93–95), but they differ from the Pashash examples in being exclusively on coarse vessels and in appearing on the necks of the vessels. At Pashash all the marks are on fine wares (Caserón Orange and Cabana Cream), and they appear only on the underside of pedestal feet. The marks are about evenly divided between incised and painted examples; all but one of the painted marks are red, and the remaining one is black. The full range of marks is shown in figure 52, but several of the marks appear repeatedly.

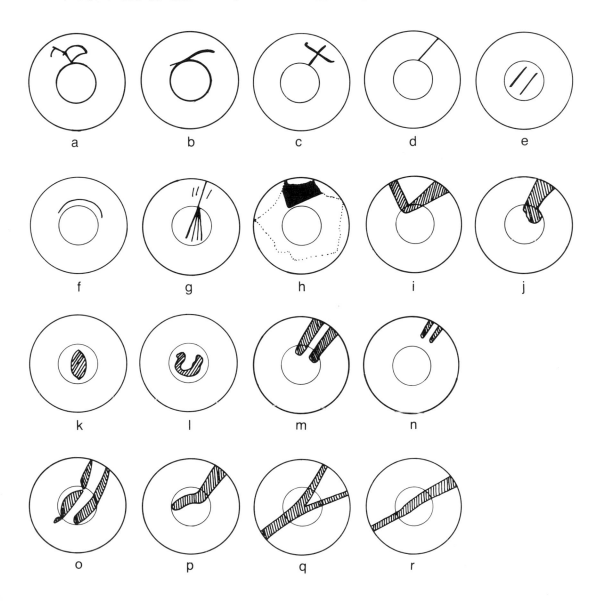

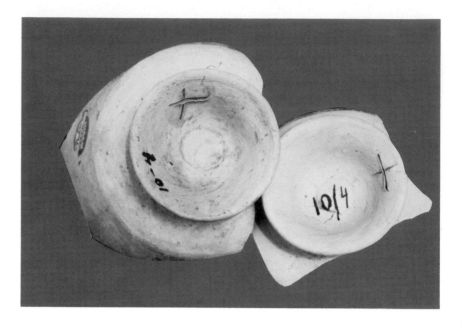

53. *Bases of two cups from the doorway offering, showing incised crosses.*

The modern potters mark their vessels only when they are being fired in common with other potters' work, a measure which economizes on fuel. The modern pots are made for sale, and for that reason it is important that potters be able to identify their own work. It is hard to believe that a commercial motive accounts for the marked vessels at Pashash. The marks were applied before the bisque, or first, firing, the incised ones while the clay was still moist (fig. 53) and the red painted ones with the first coat of slip paint.

Analysis of vessel characteristics (size, thickness, proportions, and ware) in combination with the decorations (motifs, colors, lines, and shapes) shows that individual artists can be identified by their styles even when no mark is present. The ceramic effigy vessels in the doorway offering, none of which is marked, provide a good example. They divide into pairs with definite individual or studio styles in both modeling and decoration. A single individual was surely responsible for two feline serpents, probably both originally holding victims (figs. 54, 55), both originally about 14 centimeters high, with similar zigzag and triangle designs in the stripes on their bodies. The two serpents with feline heads (figs. 56, 57) can also be assigned to one artist, and there are traces of mates for two

other feline serpents: figure 58 for figure 59 (also pl. 5) and effigy fragments listed as sherds for figure 60. The two pure felines on pedestal bases (figs. 61–63) look like the work of master and assistant, very closely related but one (figs. 62, 63) superior. These pairs of effigies are so different from each other that they must represent unrelated studios. They appear to be contributions from independent elite studios, the subject having been specified by the patron of the offering.

That the style of an individual artist cannot be traced from one form to another, with some rare exceptions, suggests that artists specialized in the creation and decoration of a certain form or that each form had a decorative tradition of its own to which the artist had to conform. For example, in the burial offering there are two rim-flanged jars, one large, the other small (figs. 64, 65), identical in form and decoration and surely made by the same artist. As usual, the distinctiveness of the pottery vessel is matched by the individuality of the decoration, which shows that the whole process was carried out by one artist, without specialization in any one part of the process. This implies that the vessels were considered "works of art" in the same way we would use that term today, both the form and

54. *Feline serpent with human victim.*
10 cm. high. 10/4.54.

the painting expressing the individuality of the artist.

One large group of vessels, mostly pedestal cups but also a small spouted basin and simple bowls, can be set apart as the production of a single studio. Since these vessels were produced by artists most closely in touch with the intentions of the patron or the representatives directing the fabrication and deposition of the offerings, this group of artists may be designated as the "Palace Studio." The work of the Palace Studio is characterized by the use of Cabana Cream paste, the spin marking of pedestal feet, the exceptional thinness of the pottery walls, and the exceptional fineness of the painted decoration in most cases. When the interiors are painted, they show motifs in open-topped frames. Forty-one vessels can be grouped in pairs or larger units and assigned to this studio,

but it appears likely that all the pedestal cups in both the doorway and the burial offerings, as well as some other forms, were produced in this studio. There were at least twelve artists associated with the studio, each making and decorating his own vessels. (Though we cannot be certain of the sex of the artists, the pronouns "he" and "his" are used for the sake of convenience.)

The two outstanding personalities in the Palace Studio were artists we can identify as Red Football, from his mark (fig. 52, k), and the Vulture Painter, who may have marked his work with a single small incision (fig. 68) but is more easily identifiable by his specialization in fancy vulture designs. Both these artists placed work in the burial and the doorway offerings, and the Vulture Painter is represented just below and probably also above the floor in the

55. *Feline serpent, probably originally holding a victim.*
14 cm. high. 10/4.55.

56. *Serpent effigy with feline head.*
10.7 cm. high. 10/4.57.

burial chamber (12/4 and 1). The Vulture Painter, an exceptionally fine craftsman, did not change his style at all between the two offerings. His work includes the finest pedestal cup in the burial offering (fig. 66), a cup showing vultures and felines (fig. 67), and a thin-walled wheel-made cup with red and black bands showing vultures and felines (fig. 68). Fragments of a large flared handled bowl in Cut 12, Level 1, have an unusual black and cream resist design on the interior with a rim border of birds which look like his work (fig. 69).

If the Vulture Painter is the classical master of the style, Red Football is the expressionist, the most original and imaginative painter in the Palace Studio. Seven vessels can be attributed to him—three bearing his mark, an elongated red spot, in the burial offering and four others identified on the basis of motif and style. His work is distinguishable by its relatively larger size and

thicker walls, but it is his use of chained loop borders and crests and of original versions of the standard motifs which identifies his work. Two of the marked cups (12/7.67 and 74) (fig. 70) have chained loops as their borders, and the same border appears on a small cup (12/7.86) with a unique version of the feline mouth. Chained loops reappear in the crests of the felines on a cup in the doorway offering (10/4.37, fig. 70), and the idea of chaining is found on another cup (fig. 71), in which the felines are chained by their tongues. A simple bowl attributable to Red Football has profile felines whose tongues swing below and back to end in feline heads (12/7.121, fig. 165). The third cup which bears his red mark (12/8.21, fig. 70) has the standardized exterior required in the burial offering, but the three profile feline serpents on the interior are a unique treatment of the theme.

57. *Serpent effigy with feline head.*
10.5 cm. high. 10/4.58.

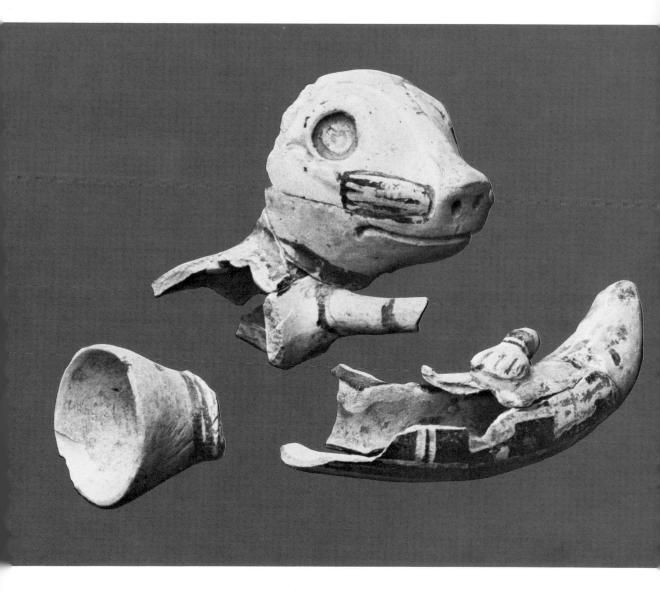

58. *Feline-serpent effigy, fragments.*
10/4.59.

59. Feline-serpent effigy.
9.5 cm. high. 10/4.56.

60. *Feline-serpent effigy.*
13.5 cm. diameter. 10/4.53.

61. *Feline effigy.*
13 cm. high. 10/4.51.

62. *Opposite: feline effigy.*
13 cm. high. 10/4.52.

63. *Opposite: front and back views of the feline effigy in fig. 62.*

64. *Opposite: large jar with cover from the*
burial offering.
28 cm. high without the cover. 12/7.55.

65. *Rim-flanged jar, attributable to the artist*
who made the jar in fig. 64.
14 cm. high. 12/7.128.

66. *Opposite above: pedestal cup attributed to
the Vulture Painter.
Red and resist black on cream.
8 cm. high. 12/7.57.*

67. *Opposite below: pedestal cup attributed to
the Vulture Painter.
Black resist on cream.
7 cm. high. 10/4.36.*

68. *Above: pedestal cup attributed to the
Vulture Painter.
Felines in positive white on red, birds in cream
and resist black.
7.5 cm. high. 12/4.7.*

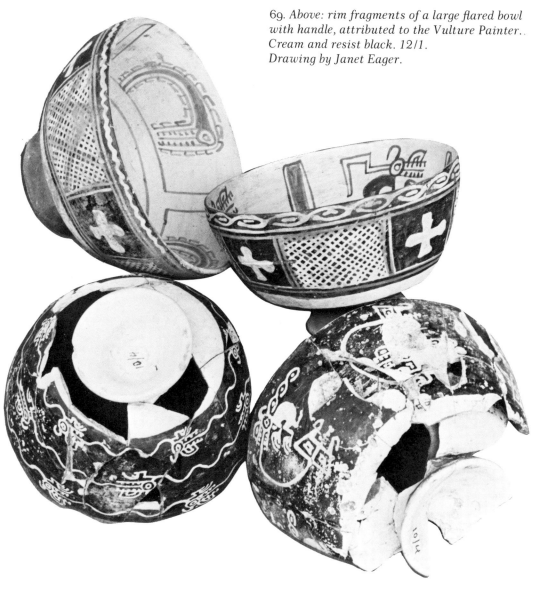

69. *Above: rim fragments of a large flared bowl with handle, attributed to the Vulture Painter. Cream and resist black. 12/1. Drawing by Janet Eager.*

70 *Opposite: vessels attributed to Red Football.*
Upper left: 12/8.21;
upper right: 12/7.67;
lower left: 10/4.38;
lower right: 10/4.37.

71. *Pedestal cup attributed to Red Football.*
Approximately 7.8 cm. high with base, not restored. 10/4.38.

It has usually been imagined that ancient American burial offerings contained merely whatever treasures were available, but that was clearly not true in this case. The differences in the cups made by Red Football conform to patterns obviously required by the patron, the burial offering containing cups with interior designs in red with cross and crosshatch on the exteriors, the doorway offering usually containing cups with plain interiors and subjects related to an anthropomorphic deity (faces, felines, birds) on the exteriors. Thus the vessels which follow these patterns were produced on commission for the particular offering and were decorated according to a prearranged plan.

That helps explain the use of potters' marks.

The Palace Studio was evidently firing its pottery in common, but, since the potters wanted to decorate their own vessels, the artists marked their work to avoid confusion among vessels all bearing the same red paint patterns, as required by the patron. Red Football was apparently uncertain that his red felines could be told from those painted by his colleagues. None of the vessels in the doorway offering is marked, which implies that the artists firing together were confident that they could distinguish their own work. Red Football's paintings appear, as usual, on the largest and thickest cups, so we may assume that he did recover his own pots from the fire, perhaps recognizing them by those traits.

Wheel-Thrown Cups

The great majority of Pashash pottery was formed by hand. If a spinning device was used at all, it was probably of the type of the palala (Tschopik 1951: 209), simply a round shallow ceramic plate which would hold the clay and turn easily as the pot was built. Other Pre-Columbian ceramic traditions have similar devices; the Mayan *k'abal* (Morley and Brainerd 1956: 373) and the Oaxacan *molde* (Foster 1955: 22–23, 31–32; Sayles 1955: 953) are examples. All these devices lack a center shaft and thus give the potter only a relatively friction-free turntable; they do not cause the clay to move against the potter's hand as on a potter's wheel. On the palala the clay is rotated by the potter's hand; on the potter's wheel the shaft, with its own source of power, turns the clay, while the hand only forms it.

Since no examples of wheel-thrown pottery have been discovered before in Pre-Columbian contexts, it has been assumed that the shaft-centered potter's wheel was not known in Pre-Columbian America (Willey 1966: 87). But among the fine ware pedestal cups at Pashash are seventy-one examples partially or completely formed by spinning the clay on a shaft-centered potter's wheel. At the present time, these vessels

are unique in Pre-Columbian ceramics and represent the adaptation of technology to ritual requirements rather than to economic ends, since the majority of the wheel-thrown vessels were probably made only for deposition in the offerings.

The best evidence of the use of a potter's wheel would be to find the tool with a partly formed pot sitting on it. That has not been found; whatever parts were wooden would probably not have survived in the highland climate. A second-best piece of evidence consists of marks on the completed vessels which can be reasonably attributed only to the use of the wheel. This evidence is found on pedestal cups but on no other vessel form. The clearest marks are concentric shallow grooves on the underside of the foot, which was not smoothed or painted since it would not ordinarily be seen (figs. 72–74). Experiments by potter Steven Howell at the University of Texas at Austin have shown that this appearance can be duplicated by an electric potter's wheel turning at moderate speed, using a cloth or a tool to smooth the surface. Examination of the drag marks of the tool in the clay shows that in all of the few cases examined the wheel was spinning counterclockwise.

72. *Opposite: spin-marked base from the door-*
way offering.
10/4.16.

73. *Above: spin-marked base from the door-*
way offering.
10/4.

74. *Below: spin-marked base from the doorway*
offering.
10/4.

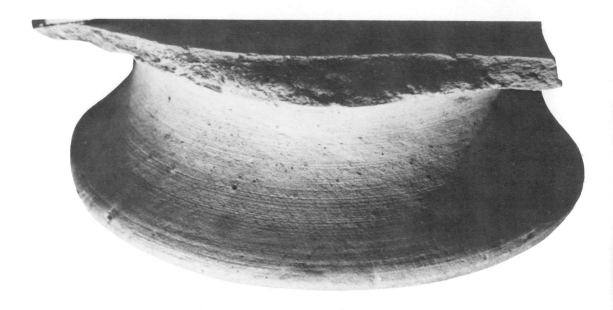

75. *Above: spin marks on the exterior of a pedestal base from the doorway offering.*
10/4.

76. *Below: spin-marked base separating from cup at joint.*
10/4.23.

77. *Opposite: fragments of pedestal cups of unfired clay. The fragments were preserved during excavation by covering them with plaster.*
10/4.14 and 15.

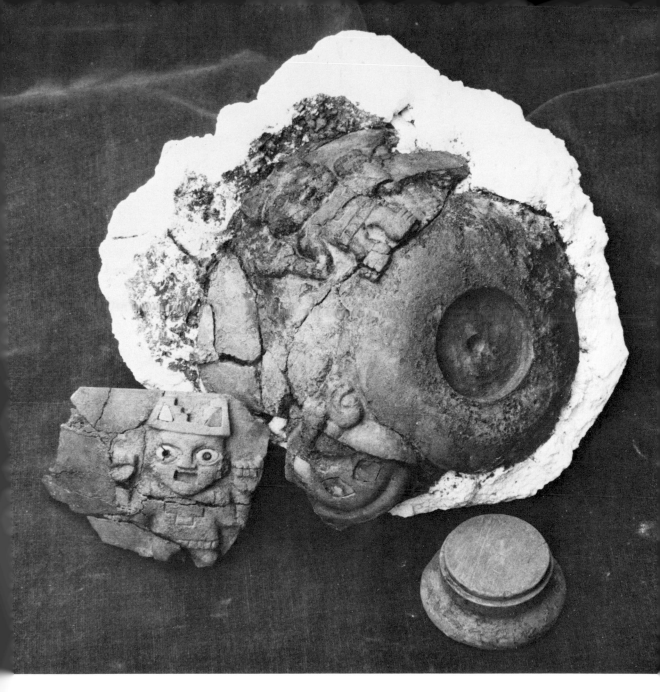

The outer side of the foot and the exterior walls of the body of the cups sometimes show marks of tools used while the vessels rotated, but usually these parts were more carefully finished and painted (fig. 75). Measurements of the circularity of the rim of the cup and of the base confirm the general circularity of the vessels, but the nature of pottery, which has to be handled before firing and which shrinks in the fire, makes these measurements inherently too remote from the forming process to be meaningfully precise. The walls of the cups are very even in thickness, but it is the thinness of the walls, as narrow as 2 millimeters in the wall and 1

millimeter at the rim, which distinguishes the wheel-thrown cups from the others.

An odd feature of the ceramic cups is the separate formation of the cup and the foot (fig. 76). A flat circular depression was cut into the base of the cup, and the foot was made with a circular projection which exactly fitted into that socket. This feature is seen in one of the four unfired clay cups in the offering in Cut 10, Level 4 (fig. 77). As the offering settled, one of these vessels fell over and the foot fell from its socket (fig. 78), revealing the circular depression about 3 millimeters deep in the base of the cup. A small pit in the socket is off-center, and its func-

78. *The foot of the unfired clay cup.*
10/4.15.

tion is unknown (fig. 79). Among the fired cups are several on which the foot has cracked away from the base. The tight fitting of the foot on the fired cups was accomplished with slip, and the joint was covered with slip. One stone cup (10/4.10) also had the foot made separately, but no socket was made to hold it. The mark where the foot was placed, evidently with some sort of glue, can still be seen on the smooth base of the cup. In the making of the foot separately, the ceramic cups differ from most of the stone cups.

In other respects the stone and the ceramic cups are closely related. They are similar in size and form, and they appear in the same funerary context, as well as showing comparable tool marks. The stone cups could not have been cut without a shaft-centered lathe, which strengthens the argument that a similar tool was used for the ceramic cups. The source of power

for the shaft can only be imagined, taking into account what archaeological and ethnological evidence we have. There are no rotary tools or parts of rotary tools certainly identifiable at Pashash except spindle whorls (but see chap. 6 on stone artifacts). Although cord-operated tools have never been described in native American contexts (Easby 1968: 19–20), the cultural background of ancient Andean artisans might easily have accommodated that principle, and the tools used for spinning thread might have inspired it. Besides clothing, the Andean people produced an astonishing variety of cordage and textile products, from bridges and architectural elements to boats, quipus, and slings, which were preferred over bows as weapons. The feet of the ceramic cups show a single direction of spin like the sling, rather than the reversal of motion which the use of a bow-driven shaft

79. *Base of the unfired clay cup, showing the*
socket which held the foot.
The pit is off-center.
10/4.15.

would produce. This suggests the use of a continuous cord wrapped around the shaft, which
gives a rapid even rotation when the cord is pul-
led, especially if the shaft has a flywheel. But the
use of rotary tools was never part of utilitarian
technics but, rather, a symbolic activity which
dramatized the relationship between human activities and the cosmic order evident in the rotating circle of the heavens (see also chap. 10 on
symbolism).

6.
Art
and Artifacts
of Stone

Pashash stone artifacts are easily divided into two period styles, one associated with Recuay ceramics and the other with Usú. Both sets are noteworthy for the rarity of utilitarian objects. Among the few purely utilitarian objects are mortars (fig. 80) and round stone pestles (fig. 81). A granite ax head was found among the offerings under the temple floor, but it shows no signs of wear (fig. 82). Natural minerals were also kept by the ancient inhabitants, especially, it appears, during the Usú period, for two pieces of coral (fig. 83) and a piece of stalagmite (fig.

82. *Granite ax head abraded for hafting. 12/3.1.*

80. *Opposite above: stone objects from the La Capilla excavations.*
From left: mortar, 10/1B.5;
rectangular pierced stone, 10/4.11;
mortar, 10/1A.2;
half a mortar, 5/1.

81. *Opposite below: stone artifacts from 7/1.*
Counterclockwise from upper left:
a fragment of a stone vessel, a waterworn pebble, a round pestle, a ground stone, two worked stones of unknown use.

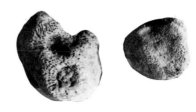

83. *Two pieces of coral.*
6 and 4.5 cm. long. 10/2.8 and 9.

84. *Calcite, part of a stalagmite.*
11/2.4.

85. *Gray slate palette.*
6.6 by 5 by 1.2 cm. 11/2.5.

84) were found above the temple floor. Some other pieces of worked stone appear to have been containers and tools (fig. 81).

Recuay period stone objects will be described together, there being no good evidence of phases. The distinctive feature of Recuay stonework is geometric form, either rectangular or circular. Every worked piece shows some effort to attain one of these simple geometric forms, the circles by drilling and the rectangles—more accurately described as quadrangles—by percussion and abrasion. Circles were the more accurately achieved, an indication that a tool was available, but there can be no doubt that the quadrangular stones with quadrangular holes (10/3.1 and 10/4.11) (fig. 80) and the small palettes stones (figs. 85, 86) were conceived as rectangular or subrectangular. Clearly, there was no method available for measuring the right angle. A right angle is most easily judged by eye in small scale, and it is in the small pieces that Pashash artisans came closest to achieving right angles.

Among the best examples of the Recuay desire for geometric form are the stone pedestal cups (figs. 87, 88, pl. 4) and the lapis lazuli whorl (fig. 93, pl. 1) placed in the funerary offerings. Measurements of diameter can be taken with precision only on unrestored pieces or parts, which leaves only the whorl and two of the cups for measurements around the whole rim. One of the cups is black (fig. 89), the other green (fig. 90). The black cup has an exterior

86. *Sandstone rectangle.*
5.5 by 3.7 by 1 cm. 12/7.47.

rim diameter varying from 10.2 to 10.26 centimeters and an exterior base diameter varying from 4.5 to 4.55 centimeters. The green cup has an exterior rim diameter which varies from 11.1 to 11.15 centimeters and a base which does not vary from 4.33 centimeters in exterior diameter. The lapis whorl has a perfect hole 1.8 centimeters wide through it, but there are variations in all the other measurements: wall thickness from 1.46 to 1.58 centimeters and a total diameter from 4.83 to 4.95 centimeters.

In the case of the cups, the maximum wobble was .06 centimeters in a 10.2 centimeter rim, with a .05 centimeter wobble in a 4.5 centimeter base (figs. 91, 92). A variation of 1 part in 90 is the maximum in these two vessels. That degree of wobble makes the use of a tool certain. That the tool was a lathe, rather than some type of hollow drill, for example, is shown by the varying radius of the wall of the cup as it tapers toward the base.

87. *Seven stone cups from the doorway offering.*
Clockwise from left front: 10/4.1, 2, 3, 4, 8, 9,
and 10.

88. *Stone cup from the burial offering.*
6.6 cm. high. 12/7.49.

89. *Black stone cup.*
7.9 cm. high. 10/4.2.

91. *Base of stone pedestal cup.*
10/4.2.

90. *Green stone cup.*
7.3 cm. high. 10/4.3.

92. *Base of stone pedestal cup.*
10/4.3.

93. *Lapis lazuli whorl.*
4.9 cm. diameter, hole 1.8 cm. wide. 12/7.46.

The lapis whorl (fig. 93, pl. 1) was perforated with a very steady drill, but the irregularities in the external dimensions can be detected with the naked eye. The variation reaches 1.2 millimeters in about 49 millimeters, a variation of 1 part in 40.8, a 2.45% error. That is a considerable wobble, but it is still a very small error if one imagines the piece carved freehand. The exterior shows no faceting, which one would expect in hand cutting. The outer wall has a luster which distinguishes it even from the ends, which are smooth but not highly polished. The luster was certainly produced by polishing the stone as it was spun on a shaft-centered tool, probably with the shaft through the center hole, and it seems most likely that the outer wall was given its final form with a handheld bit while the whorl spun on a shaft. The wobble is easily accounted for by imagining the artisan smoothing the roughed-out form as it rotated. To reach a more perfect circularity, the bit would have had to be pressed hard against the stone; thus more of the rare and beautiful stone would have been sacrificed. The artisan chose to leave a larger error in order to retain more of the precious material and to keep larger, more impressive dimensions. Circularity was very valuable since the center of the stone and an indeterminable amount of exterior stone were destroyed to obtain it, but once a reasonable appearance of circularity had been achieved the value of the material had to be considered.

The use of shaft-centered tools distinguishes the technology of Pashash from other ancient American centers. That they were used in the making of pottery vessels as well as stone artifacts is indicated by vessel forms and tool marks in the clay (see chap. 5). The rotary tools used for work in stone appear to have included a solid drill; a hollow drill, presumably made of reed or bamboo or perhaps bone; and a lathe, in which the stone was attached to the shaft. No evidence of such tools remains, and it may be assumed that they were mainly of wood.

The stone cups are good evidence of the use of a shaft-centered lathe, since the stones of which they are made are too hard to be cut on a loose rotating platform without a shaft, the sort of turntable known in modern indigenous potterymaking. The green stone of one of the cups, for example, measures 6.5 to 7 on the Mohs scale; quartz measures 7. This technology has been examined earlier in the discussion of wheel-made pottery, which was formed by techniques copied from stoneworking (see chap. 5).

There are a number of other stone artifacts which show the marks of rotary tools. Perhaps some of them even served as parts of the tools, although all have other, more conventional identifications. The numerous small pieces of slate with small drilled holes which were found in several of the excavations are similar to pieces found in post-Chavín levels at Chavín de Huantar and considered by Tello (1960: 305–306) to have been loom weights (fig. 94). Since the loom was used in the region throughout a period of some three millennia, it is strange to find "loom weights" only in deposits identified with Recuay occupations. That suggests that they may have served in connection with rotary tools, which are also associated particularly with the Recuay culture. They might, for example, have served as supports for the butts of rotating shafts, in which case the holes are the unintentional results of wear. A hollowed stone, which we have called a mortar (fig. 80, left), has an even circular hole which also might have served to support a shaft. Three stone rings (10/1.8, 8/2, and 4/3) (fig. 95) of the sort identified as club heads might have served as flywheels on

95. *Half of a stone ring.*
12.7 cm. diameter. 8/2.

shafts. The spindle whorls, one made of a veined green and white stone (12/7.48), were flywheels, and it is reasonable to call the lapis lazuli whorl a flywheel. Its size would make it useful for weighting a shaft for some heavier duty than spinning thread. The beauty and rarity of the material suggest that it may have been part of a tool used in ritual.

Among the other stone artifacts assignable to the Recuay period is the block, found in Cut 10, Level 2, bearing twenty-one shallow rectangular depressions on one side (fig. 96). The diagonal symmetry of the pattern of depressions is typical of this well-known type, which has been called a game board or an architectural plan (Kubler 1962: 315–316, pl. 163, B). The context in which it was found offers no clues to its use, but the double-headed feline incised on the sides places it conclusively in the Recuay period.

94. *Slate circle with drilled hole.*
3.8 cm. maximum diameter. 1/1.

96. *Carved stone, perhaps a game board or architectural plan.*
23.5 by 20 by 9.8 cm. 10/2.6.

A stone ax head, found in the surface level no more than 10 centimeters deep in erosion deposits on the stairway leading onto the north side of the top of La Capilla Hill, relates Pashash to various sites to the southeast (fig. 97). Similar T-shaped axes have been found at Chavín de Huantar (Tello 1960: 308–309), Kotosh (Izumi and Sono 1963: 147–148), and Shillacoto (Kano 1972: 142). The type is found throughout the Formative period at Shillacoto and in late Formative (Sajara-patac and San Blas) levels at

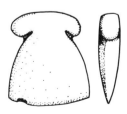

97. *Stone ax head from the surface of La Capilla Hill.*

Kotosh. The examples from Chavín de Huantar cannot be assigned to a level or period but may be assumed to be no later than the superficial Recuay levels at that site. The surface level at Pashash in which this example was found was formed in the Usú period, probably at least a century later than the period when the ax was made. It was very likely imported from some site to the southeast, where it might have been made centuries earlier.

Usú period stone artifacts are distinguished by their production by hand carving and their rejection of both geometric forms and the use of rotary tools. A fragment of a green stone cup (fig. 98) depicting a hooded human head represents the transition from Recuay to Usú tech-niques. The use of a rotary tool survives in this piece in the pit which represents the mouth. The measurements of 6.8 centimeters for both the height and the breadth (the back is broken off) suggest that the block from which the cup was carved was a measured cube. Nevertheless, the geometry plays a secondary role to the free carving, and the result is very different from the stonework in the offerings. Perhaps this cup was made by an artist trained in the Pashash Recuay tradition working for a foreign patron, a patron accustomed to the use of the three-dimensional human head as an ornamental motif, such as we find in Usu pottery. A fragment of another green stone cup shows a carved handle, another form not produced by the use of a rotary tool (fig. 99).

98. *Green stone cup fragment with a carved face.*
6.8 cm. high and wide. 10/1B.1.

99. *Fragment of a green stone cup with a carved handle.*
6.7 by 5.1 cm. 10/1B.2.

100. Polished stone animal, probably a guinea pig.
9 cm. high. 10/1B.6.

101. Right: polished stone animal, probably a guinea pig.
3.4 cm. high. 10/2.7.

A typical stone work of the Usú period is a polished stone animal which probably represents a guinea pig (fig. 100). It retains the amorphous massiveness of the original stone, which was abraded into a barely recognizable but still natural form. A similar but much smaller carving was found in the next deeper level (fig. 101).

102. *Carved red stone, suggesting a grass-hopper.*
5 cm. long. 10/3.3.

103. *Carved white stone, suggesting a butterfly.*
4.8 cm. high. 10/3.4.

Two other small stone carvings were found in Level 3 of Cut 10 and may have been associated with the extended burial in Level 2 of Cut 11, the head of which was within about half a meter of each of these pieces. One is a reddish pebble cut into a form which suggests a grasshopper (fig. 102), the other a white stone cut into a nearly symmetrical butterfly form (fig. 103). Both were made by sawing the stone with a fine-bladed tool, which might have been of metal or of stone.

At Pashash the great period of art in stone was the Recuay, which saw the construction of cyclopean walls as well as the creation of a considerable body of relief sculpture and the finely crafted objects in the burial offerings. Recuay stonework in all its forms emphasized shape, pattern, line, and geometry, reflecting a graphic tradition. The few small pieces of Usú period stone carving give evidence not only of less interest in stone as a material but also of an entirely different aesthetic in its use, one in which mass was the primary expression, emphasized by softly abraded forms and by saw cuts which gave relief to the forms they defined.

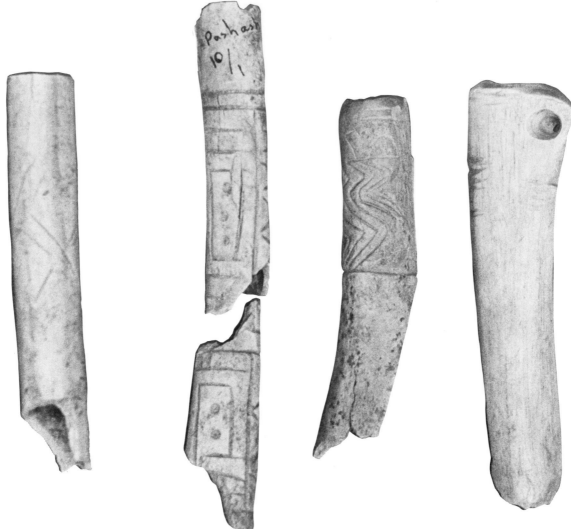

104. *Four carved bones.*
From left: 10/1B.13, 14, 12, and 17.
No. 17 is 10 cm. long. The first three are hollow
tubes with traces of red paint.

7.
Art
and Artifacts
of Bone

All the bone artifacts—distinguished from un-worked bone by evidence of incision, drilling, carving, or painting—were found in Cut 10, Levels 1 and 2, inside the temple chamber. Of the nine bone artifacts (figs. 104–109), six are hollow tubes between 8.2 and 11.2 centimeters long. The seventh is an elaborately carved bone closed on one end. The eighth is the simplest, a 10-centimeter-long sliver of bone with a biconi-cal hole at one end and several lateral incisions, and the ninth is two parts of a carved bone.

All these bones were found scattered in a small area in the center of the outer chamber, but there was no evidence of associations. It was as if they had been tossed into the fill, but the nature of the levels near the surface is not clear. It is possible that they were offerings placed in the fill above the extended burial in Cut 11, Level 2, but they were not directly above that burial. In short, their appearance together in a small area suggests that they were deposited in-tentionally, although casually, since they were not closely associated among themselves or with other things. Their use is likewise uncertain. They show no evidence of wear, burning, or adaptation as flutes or whistles. Only the simplest is pierced for suspension.

105. *Hollow mammal bone with traces of red paint.*
8.2 cm. long. 10/1B.15.

106. *Left: hollow mammal bone with traces of red paint.*
9 cm. long. 10/1B.16.

107. *Right: hollow bird bone with incised rings, two painted red, the other black.*
9.1 cm. long. 10/2.3.

108. *Fragments of carved mammal bone with traces of red paint.*
10/2.1.

The source of six of the bones has been identified by Dr. Ernest Lundelius. The bones cataloged as 10/1B.15 and 16 and 10/2.1 are bones of some large mammal, possibly a llama, deer, jaguar, or human. 10/1B.13 and 10/2.3 are the bones of large birds, and 10/2.2 is the ulna of a condor. The presence of a condor bone is interesting since the condor and other vulture species were represented in art. Condors and the other vultures are absent from the earlier Chavín art, in which hawks and eagles were present (Rowe 1962a: 18).

Three of these bones (10/1B.12, 14, and 15) show the use of small pits in their decoration, and on at least two of them (10/1B.14 and 15) the pits were probably made by drilling. Three (10/2.2, 10/1B.15 and 16) have excised areas.

All show incisions. By their style the bone artifacts appear to belong to the later part of the Recuay period, when diamond-shaped and triangular conventional patterns were common. The levels in which they were found were laid down in the Usú period. The absence of bone tubes in earlier levels suggests that this type of artifact may be characteristic of that period; at the earliest the bone tubes might be placed in the Recuay Huacohú phase, an assignment more consistent with their style.

The best of the bone artifacts (10/1B.12, 10/2.1 and 2) are very delicate carvings and rank as works of art. The small triangular excisions on the condor bone, still colored with a bright red pigment, suggest what Pashash textile patterns might have looked like.

109. *Carved condor ulna with red paint in the excisions, closed on one end. About 11 cm. long. 10/2.2.*

8.
Art
and
Artifacts
of Metal

Sixty-four objects or sets of objects made of metal have been discovered at Pashash, all of them in Cuts 10 and 12. The inference one draws from that location is that all the recovered pieces had been deposited in a ritual context. The concentration of metal objects around the burial is a good indication that metal was valuable and was applied to ornamental uses.

The metal objects appeared in two groups separated by the floor of the building, but all the objects appear to be the work of Recuay artisans. The few items above the floor may be later than those in the offerings, but that is not certain. The pieces below the floor can be sub-

divided into three sets: objects in the burial offering (12/7–8), objects in the doorway offering (10/4–5), and those in the fill above the burial (12/3–5). All the items in the burial offering were partly made of gold, and most of them were made by lost-wax casting. Some of these pieces had inlays of stone or metal. A string of ten copper bells (fig. 110) is the only set of metal in the doorway offering. The bells were made by hammering out sheet metal. In the fill above the burial were found broken gold-and-copper pins and copper nails, two of which had heads cast in the form of conventional felines (fig. 111).

The items found farthest from the body were those least intimately connected with the dead person in life. The most distant were the copper bells, which may not have been the personal property of the dead person but were more likely used in the funeral ceremony, or perhaps they were sanctified by some other ritual use.

In the fill above the burial were found six copper nails (fig. 112). They were lying in an area of grainy brown decayed organic material totaling about half a cubic meter. No form could be discerned, and the original material might have been textile, matting, or wood. The nails are best accounted for by assuming that the decayed ob-

110. *Opposite above: copper items from Cut 10. Left: curls of wire about 1 mm. thick, 10/2.5; center: strip with diamond perforations, 5 cm. long, 10/2.4; right: one of the ten copper bells on a string, each 5.5 cm. wide, 10/5.1.*

111. *Opposite: feline-headed pins, cast copper. The heads are about 1 cm. long. 12/4.1 and 2.*

112. *Opposite below: two copper nails. 12/4.3.*

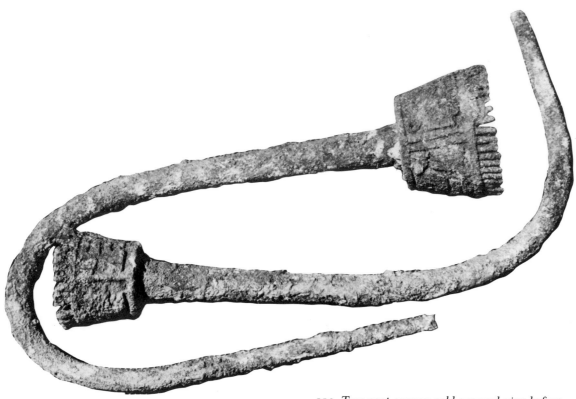

113. *Two cast copper gold-covered pins before cleaning.*
Both about 11 cm. long.
Left: 12/7.2;
right: 12/7.1.

ject was of wood. The two small pins with cast feline heads, like miniature tenoned heads, are from the same level, but they were not associated with the organic debris. They are both pierced about a centimeter from the pinhead, like the larger pins in the burial offering, and they probably functioned as ornamental clothing fasteners rather than as nails.

The most spectacular metal objects are the nineteen gold-plated pins in the burial offering (figs. 113, 114). They are important not only as examples of metalworking technique but also for the rich assortment of symbolic images they provide. The imagery, which includes frontal male heads (fig. 115), felines (figs. 116, 117), and owls (fig. 118), will be discussed in a separate chapter; only the techniques will be described here.

Technically, the pins are divided between those with solid heads (nine examples) (fig.

119) and those with hollow heads (ten examples). The solid heads, which appear to have been cast in single pieces, are found on the smaller pins. The heads of the larger pins were probably cast hollow to reduce their weight. The shafts appear to have been forged of pure copper and the heads of copper that was perhaps alloyed to facilitate casting. About 1 centimeter from the upper end of all the shafts is a small hole, which in one case still held bits of thread. That suggests that the pins were sewn or tied onto some support, probably clothing. Presumably the pins were used to fasten clothing; yarn might have been wrapped around the point of the curved shafts to secure them.

The hollow heads were made by modeling the intended design in wax over a core material. To judge by the unpolished interior surfaces of the castings, the core material was fine-textured and easily worked. The decoration of the top,

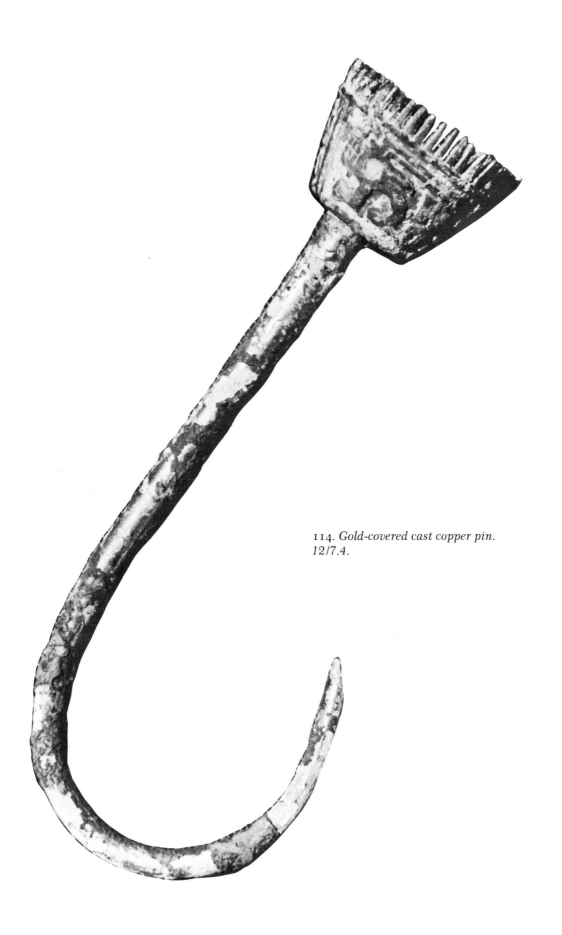

114. *Gold-covered cast copper pin.*
12/7.4.

115. *Top of the head of a pin showing a warrior head in turban and earrings.*
Top is 3.2 cm. in diameter. 12/7.3.

116. *Left: gold-covered cast copper pin showing four spiraling feline serpents on the shaft. Head of pin is 2.8 cm. in diameter. 12/7.9.*

117. *Below: top of pin with a frontal feline head in the center. 12/7.13.*

118. *Top of pin depicting an owl.*
2.8 cm. diameter. 12/7.9.

including the fringed border, was done entirely in wax, but the walls were left smooth. Even the wire hoop earrings of the frontal heads were made in wax and cast (fig. 115). When the wax model was complete, wax rods were attached as gates and vents; a gate still in place on the interior of one piece is visible through a break. The wax model was then covered with the mold material, probably of the same material as the core. Next, the wax was burned out of the mold and the molten copper poured in. Finally, the molds were broken open and the castings removed and cleaned, and the gates and vents were removed from the exterior. The shafts to be connected to the hollow heads were hollow at the top to ac-

commodate the pin which attached the head.

A white plasterlike material on the inside of some of the broken pieces may be a corrosion product, or it may be the remains of the core material, which otherwise was entirely removed. That is an indication that the interior space was accessible, which had to be the case in order to fasten the head to the shaft. Where the opening was located is not entirely clear. At ten-power magnification, a joint between the wall and the base plate is visible on one broken pinhead, and it may be that the base plate was pinned to the shaft separately and that the head was then soldered onto the base plate.

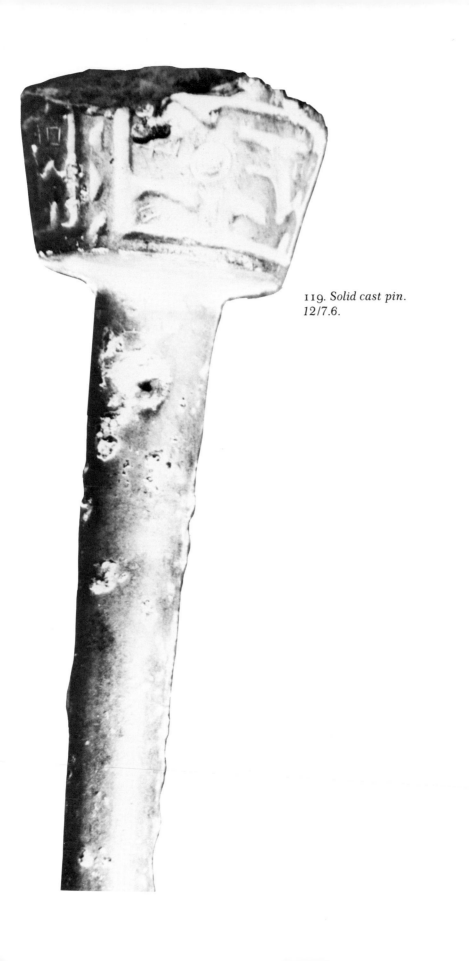

119. *Solid cast pin.*
12/7.6.

120. *Fragment of the head of a pin, showing the joining of the feline and the frame onto the wall and the gold surface on the cast metal of the core.*
Head is 1.4 cm. high. 12/7.41.

121. *Opposite above: head of a pin with panels of felines with eyes inlaid with green stone.*
Head is 3.5 cm. in diameter. 12/7.10.

122. *Opposite below: hollow gold head (center) made by joining two repoussé halves.*
1.7 cm. high. 12/7.32.
Two hollow gold fragments, 12/7.34 and, on right, 12/7.33, with traces of copper inlays.

The three plano-relief felines in frames which ornament the walls of all the hollow pinheads were made separately and soldered in place. On broken pieces the joint is visible even to the naked eye (fig. 120). These plaques might have been cast flat in open molds and curved to fit the surface by annealing and bending. The feline and the frame, which are separate pieces, were soldered into place (fig. 121).

The final step was the application of gold leaf to the whole surface. The purity of the copper core and the tendency of the gold to flake off show that depletion gilding was not used.

Several other techniques are found among the metal objects in the burial offering. A small gold bead (fig. 122) 1.7 centimeters high, representing a human head, was made by soldering together two sheets formed by repoussé. Stone inlays were set on many of the pins, most commonly as the eyes of the felines on the walls.

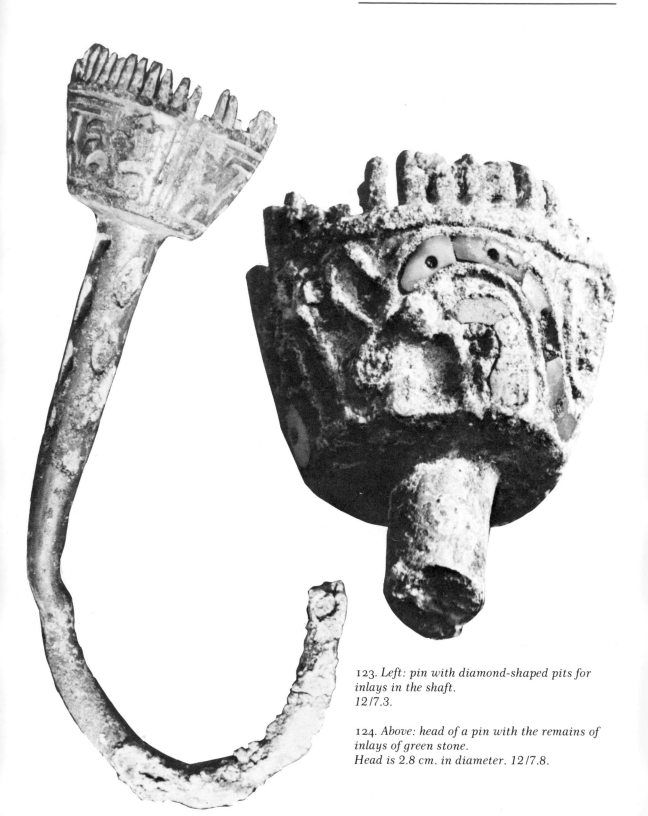

123. Left: *pin with diamond-shaped pits for inlays in the shaft.*
12/7.3.

124. Above: *head of a pin with the remains of inlays of green stone.*
Head is 2.8 cm. in diameter. 12/7.8.

One pin had sixteen diamond-shaped pits in the shaft which must have held inlays, probably of turquoise (fig. 123). Another pin (fig. 124) had stones set in cloisonlike frames both on the walls, where ten pieces of green stone remain in place, and on the top, where a frontal male head seems to have been represented. No inlays remain on the top, but the subject must have required a variety of colors. Besides stone, there is evidence of the inlay of metal into metal: thin diamond-shaped pieces of copper were set in shallow indentations on a hollow gold form (fig. 122, right), which must have been done by using a gold solder. The objects in the burial offering give the impression that Pashash metalworkers had their craft under absolute control.

Other items of personal adornment found in the burial offering are earplugs and four tiny (1.9 centimeter in diameter) double disks. The double disks (12/8.5) are of very thin sheet copper, and the disks are jointed at one edge and folded over. They were found in a triangular pedestal cup but may have been intended to be sewn on cloth as an enrichment. The earplugs are represented by parts of at least nine pairs of ear ornaments of three different types: metal flares (fig. 125), of which there are eight identical pieces, or four pairs; two pure gold rings (fig. 126) which formed the frames of wooden disks; and nine fragments of inlaid mineral disks which may have been the ornamental faces of ear ornaments, making at least four pairs (figs. 127, 128). Two pieces of wood (12/8.20) may have served as parts of ear ornaments. The metal items in this group stand out for their fine technique. The metal flares, although they were made of unequal mixtures of gold and copper (some being much more corroded than others), are identical in size and shape. Although their form suggests use as ear spools, their number might suggest some other ornamental use. The gold framing rings, which retain fragments of wood in the channel of the frames, are precisely circular, and both measure exactly 3.4 centimeters in diameter.

125. *Gold ear spools with copper alloys. 2.5 cm. diameter. 12/8.2.*

126. *Two gold flanged edges of earplug disks*
with traces of wood in the flange.
3.4 cm. diameter. 12/8.3 and 4.

127. *Mineral disk with yellow adhesive and*
traces of inlay.
Probably part of an ear ornament.
4.1 cm. diameter. 12/8.10.

128. *Mineral disk with green stone star inlays.*
Probably part of an ear ornament.
2.3 cm. diameter. 12/8.12.

129. *Copper cover for the end of a wooden shaft*
or staff.
4 cm. long, 2.5 cm. diameter. 10/1B.18.

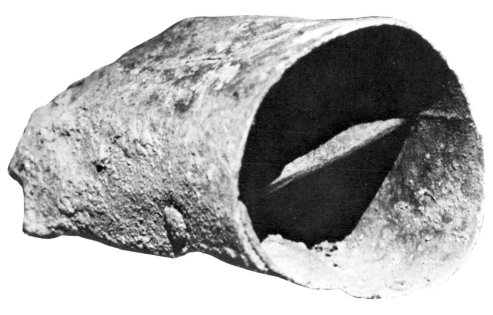

The three metal objects found above the floor were all in the outer chamber in Levels 1 and 2 of Cut 10. In the deeper level were a cluster of copper wire curls and a copper strip 5 by 1.8 centimeters (fig. 110). The strip, broken at both ends, has five diamond-shaped holes through the thin metal. The wire is about 1 millimeter thick, in curls about 5 centimeters in diameter. Both probably served a decorative purpose.

In the surface level of the outer chamber was found the head of a wooden staff or shaft encased in a copper cover 4 centimeters long by 2.5 centimeters in diameter (fig. 129). The sheet metal had been wrapped around the staff and held in place by a copper nail. Fragments of the wooden staff were still in place. A sample of the wood has been examined by R. C. Koeppen of the Forest Products Laboratory, but it was too degraded to identify beyond assignment to the Dicotyledoneae, or hardwood group.

It is tempting to assign these cruder pieces to the Usú period, which would accord with their discovery in levels above the floor and with the simpler techniques found in Usú period pottery and stone carving.

However, the similarity of the nail in the staff head to those in the burial fill as well as the diamond shape of the perforations in the metal strip—diamonds being common in Recuay borders—suggest that these pieces represent Recuay technology.

9.
Imagery

The imagery used by Pashash artists is rich but restricted to a few themes. The frontal figure or head of a man, members of the cat family, birds with large beaks or ringed eyes, and snakes practically complete the catalog of subjects found in Pashash art, along with an alphabet of abstract designs which appear to have been conventional symbols. It is apparent that we are presented with an art devoted to the expression of a very limited part of human experience, one far-removed from mundane activities. Agricultural work never appears, no women or children are represented, construction of houses and walls (obviously a time-consuming activity at Pashash) is not shown, nor is the practice of any art or craft depicted. The animals shown are almost certainly not those used for food, with the probable exception of the small stone sculptures of guinea pigs from the Usú period. In short, there is no representation of daily life.

What other life is there but "daily life"? To the inhabitants of Pashash, a superior reality evidently existed in an invisible realm accessible to the mind—a spiritual life. Apprehension of this invisible realm was possible through art and, it appears from the art, through ceremonies and warfare. Art formed part of a complex glorifying the military ideals in its imagery, manifesting the spirits, and providing the material accessories for ceremonies dedicated to them. The unity of this conception of a supernatural order is evident in the restricted range of themes and motifs.

The themes express concepts which unify several motifs, or particular designs. Our understanding of the concepts is entirely dependent on the shared elements in the motifs. To us, accustomed to literary documents, the reading of pictorial and design motifs for conceptual expressions seems imprecise and subjective, but to the ancient people of Pashash, who did not use a literary form, these motifs must have been quite definite and objective in meaning. The narrow range of subjects and the repetition of motifs reinforce the argument for their objectivity as expressions of shared concepts.

In this analysis we will consider the themes and the motifs which express them, disregarding whether they appear in ceramics, stone sculpture, or metal. Themes will be designated by numbers, motifs by letters. Granting that naming is speculative, analysis of the themes and motifs requires their naming.

1. The crowned figure
   A. Frontal, raising both hands
   B. Capturing an armed warrior
2. The head with emanations
   A. Four feline emanations from ears
   B. Four feline-headed serpent emanations from ears
   C. Cactuslike emanations
3. The circular head
   A. Forehead band
   Ḃ. No forehead band
4. The turbaned figure or head
5. The helmeted head
   A. Isolated frontal head, crested helmet
   B. Frontal, large earplugs, diagonal rays, crested helmet
6. The trophy head
   A. Frontal, no headdress, no attributes, eyes open, slash mouth
   B. Frontal, no headdress, grasped or pecked by three birds
   C. Frontal, no headdress, held by profile feline
   D. Frontal, no headdress, held by large-beaked bird
7. The splayed figure with a double crest
8. The frontal warrior armed with a club
   A. Club across body diagonally, helmet, trophy head in hand
   B. Club vertical away from body, crested helmet
   C. Club across body diagonally, profile birds flanking head
   D. Head grasped by crowned man, no helmet
9. The figure in a tall hat
10. The naked prisoner
    A. Frontal male figure held by feline serpent
    B. Frontal male figure alone
11. Feline animals
    A. Rampant, without crest or metaphorical attachments, with diamond spots
    B. On four feet, no crest or metaphorical attachments
    C. Rampant, crested or metaphorically augmented
    D. On four feet, crested or metaphorically augmented
    E. On four feet, turbaned, with diamond spots
    F. Double, with frontal heads on each end, crested or metaphorically augmented
    G. Double, with profile heads on each end, crested or metaphorically augmented
    H. Double, splayed into geometric patterns, with cross on body
    I. Double, reversed heads
    J. Serpent body and tail, no headdress
    K. Serpent body and tail, turbaned head
    L. Frontal head, no body
    M. Serpent body, feline heads on both ends
12. Snakes
    A. Natural snake, extended, with wavy body
    B. Coiled or curled snake with feline head or ears
13. Birds
    A. Profile bird with large beak, simple (condor or vulture)
    B. Profile bird with large beak, metaphorically augmented (condor or vulture)
    C. Frontal head with large round eyes (owl)
    D. Profile body, frontal head (owl)

14. Conventional designs
    A. Serpent-related designs
    B. Feline-related designs
    C. Space-defining designs

The conventional designs which accompany the representational motifs act as frames and backgrounds, as decoration on the bodies of represented subjects, and sometimes take over the pictorial field. At least some of these designs have symbolic meaning in their own right, as their use makes clear. Their symbolism will be examined later. Geometric precision is a primary feature of the conventional designs. The principal ones are the circle, square, checkerboard, equal-arm cross, step design alone or with a curl or fret attached, S-curve, zigzag, triangle, and a whirling design. This design vocabulary is subject to endless permutations.

The Crowned Figure

The crowned figure is represented a total of nine times, eight of which are a single motif—that of the frontal figure with raised hands (Theme 1, Motif A) (fig. 77, pl. 4). The other expression of the theme shows the crowned figure grasping the hair of an armed warrior as a sign of capture (1B) (fig. 130). The former examples all have a profile rampant jaguar at the left of the figure, facing toward him (fig. 156). George Kubler has postulated that "frontal figures have more rank than profile figures," and "frontal representations probably describe cult images" (1967: 7). Motif A certainly gives the impression of a cult image. The formality of the erect symmetrical pose, the strange gesture, and the emphasis on the inlaid eyes draw our attention to the figure's ceremonial and spiritual nature. The large eyes focus on the observer, and their inlaid pupils sharpen the gaze, which is clearly intended to make a psychological contact with the observer. A cult image is, of course, the image of a god. The Pashash god departs from northern Peruvian tradition in his purely human form, which distinguishes him from the half-feline gods of Chavín and from the contemporary fanged god of the Moche culture. This god has a purely human face, with the mouth open but no teeth shown in one motif (1A). He wears small earplugs, the stepped crown, a tunic with the step design, and a kilt. His fingers and toes are abbreviated, each hand having only four fingers and each foot just three toes, a trait perhaps surviving from late Chavín art. The appearance of a raised little finger probably represents the thumb, true space relationships being neglected. The meaning of the gesture is unknown, but it is found in Andean art of all periods in representations of both male (Sawyer 1968: 23) and female (Kauffmann Doig 1973: 436) ritual figures. It is probably related to the jaguar with extended paws found in some headdresses (Sawyer 1966: 34). Rather than a human gesture of adoration, it appears to signify the manifestation of divinity—a "here I am" pose—which may conveniently be called a gesture of apparition.

The open mouth is not usual in Pashash heads unless the teeth are shown, so the impression that the god is speaking or singing is probably intended. This suggests that the god manifested himself in speech or song, perhaps through a human medium. His attributes emphasize his human nature: the tunic, kilt, and crown could all be worn by men, and the pose, gesture, and facial expression are within human capabilities. His jaguar associate shows his superhuman status and makes clear his supreme rank, for the jaguar is likewise superior to men, as other motifs show.

The depiction of the god capturing an armed warrior (fig. 130) also shows him in a human role. The painting is in thick glossy black slip on a dull black ground on a large sherd from the rim of a basin which measured about 47 centimeters in rim diameter. The rim is bordered by a running step design which appears to refer to the insignia of the god. The sherd lay just beneath the floor of the burial chamber and was evidently a keepsake tossed in to represent the crowned god once more in the burial. Only enough remains of the painted design to identify the deity: the stepped crown on his head. His

130. *Painting of a crowned god taking a captive, in shiny black on dull black on the interior of a large basin fragment.*
13 cm. high. 12/4.9.

131. *Top of the head of a pin showing a feline with a trophy head.*
3.5 cm. diameter. 12/7.10.

body was not painted solid, as was that of his prisoner, but a single line begins to cross it from the shoulder, almost certainly an indication of a step design on his tunic. In his right hand he holds the hair of a warrior, who is still armed with a club. Perhaps the god also held a club in his other hand, now lost. The face of the god has the round eyes, large earplugs, and toothy mouth found in many depictions of human faces, such as that of his captive. Even though the design of the face is different from that of Motif A, both motifs agree in representing the god's face as human.

It is difficult to find comparative material, for the god is unusual in his humanity. A small ceramic figure of a nude male in a tall crenelated headdress is shown by Luis Lumbreras (1959: pl. 10, B), attributed to Wari. A similar ceramic figure in an openwork helmet with square bosses is presented by a giant feline on a vessel from Virú approximately contemporary with the Pashash examples (Bennett 1954: fig. 39), but in this example the roles of the god (if it is him) and the feline are reversed. The Pashash examples lead one to the art of classic Tiahuanaco, where the images are similar in form but are more covered with symbolic attributes, or to the much later images of gods or chiefs in Chimu and Lambayeque art of the north coast.

Despite his human appearance, it is evident that the crowned god exacts tribute from men. His capture of a warrior suggests the taking of human life, if only symbolically. That the tribute was a blood tribute may be the implication of the jaguar attendant's appearing with a captive (fig. 54) and a trophy head (fig. 131). The tunic bearing the step design worn by the god himself also appears on apparently human figures at Pashash, in Moche art, and in a variety of examples from later cultures. The widespread use of the costume gives us some clues for interpreting the significance of the crowned god. The numerous appearances of the step-patterned tunic in Moche art occur on the fanged god, on an anthropomorphic owl, and on phallic and copulating male figures (e.g., Benson 1972: figs. 2:17, 19, 5:24, 6:17; Emmerich 1969: no. 12). In sum, roles associated with the step-patterned tunic are killing, hunting, fertilizing, and ruling nature. The idea of a supreme god as creator and destroyer is widely held throughout the world, and ancient American examples are well known, so that in general the interpretation has the appearance of validity. The utility of the interpretation lies mainly in its ruling out the association of the god exclusively with water or sky or any other particular aspect of nature. His realm seems to have been nature in general. His human representatives seem to have been distinguished by their roles as chiefs, as warriors, and, at least among the Moche, as patriarchs, with emphasis on their fertilizing powers.

The Head with Emanations

The head with emanations is a striking design much favored by Pashash artists in both painting and relief sculpture. The basic feature of the motifs which express this theme is a frontal human face with four snakelike strips attached to the head: two at each of the ears or the sides of the head, one curving up, the other down. The principal differences in the several motifs are in the use of top-view and profile heads on the ends of the emanating strips or bands. The profile heads, which are more common, are standard conventional feline heads. The top-view heads are also a standardized motif of the feline head, but they have sometimes been considered to represent a snake (fig. 180). The combination of feline and serpent is common in Pashash art and seems to have been the idea

behind this motif as well, the serpent being represented only by the body, never by the head.

Two examples in stone relief show the head in a circular band which seems to be a helmet or turban, with a wide band across the brow. Both have felines emanating from the ears, one showing both the front and back legs and the tail (fig. 132), the other just the front legs and a snakelike body (fig. 203). The curls below the eyes on this example are not found on any other.

There are several painted versions of this motif. The most complete example is on the spout-handled vessel, 10/4.64 (pl. 2). It has an unusual face with a toothy mouth and a block nose set high on the forehead. The cross-marked and spotted earplugs have lost the character of attachments and have become large

132. *Stone relief of a circular frontal head surrounded by four felines.*
Collection of the church, Cabana.

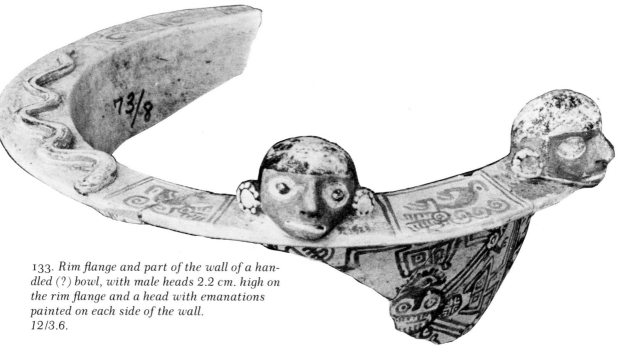

133. *Rim flange and part of the wall of a handled (?) bowl, with male heads 2.2 cm. high on the rim flange and a head with emanations painted on each side of the wall. 12/3.6.*

134. *Below: head with emanations. Sherd from 12/7. Drawing by Janet Eager.*

flaps on the head. From the earplugs emanate angular snakelike ribbons, ornamented with a fringe element. The snakes meet at top and bottom in top-view feline heads. From the mouth of each head emanate two more snake bodies which end in top-view feline heads. The divisions are emphasized by the contrast of cream on black resist for one side and positive red paint for the other. On the right margin appears a profile feline with a crest, its body marked with a cross. This is a particularly valuable design for the study of Pashash imagery.

More orthodox versions are found on the exterior walls of a wide-rimmed bowl (fig. 133). The two sides give different versions but agree on the main points of the face and the felines with front legs. One side has a top view of the feline heads with their tongues joined. Fragments of a bowl from the burial offering show a similar version in red and black (fig. 134).

Red
Black

135. *Head with emanations and large-beaked birds on the interior wall of a large basin fragment.*
12/7.

136. *Head with emanations and a crested feline in red line and wash on orange on the interior of a large basin.*
Diameter was about 68 cm., height of wall about 27 cm. 10/3.5.

Fragments of a large basin in the burial offering show the design on the interior wall (fig. 135). The motif was presumably repeated around the walls. The face has emanations from above and below the earplugs, terminating in feline heads. Long-beaked birds surround the head. The birds are standard subjects, but this is the only case in which they appear in the head-with-emanations motif.

The simplest version of this theme is painted in red line and red wash on the interior walls of a large basin which was smashed in Level 3 of Cut 10. The framed panel shows a smiling circular face with strange cactuslike emanations surrounding it (fig. 136).

The head with emanations is the first of a series of five themes to which the human head is fundamental, appearing in each with different attributes. There are two principal ways to represent the frontal head: one which we may call the painterly motif, another the sculptural motif, although there are paintings which use the sculptural motif (fig. 137) and vice versa. The painterly motif (figs. 138, 148) has a circular head and round eyes with concentric brows joining to form the sides of the nose, plus a mouth

137. *Paintings from a handled bowl.*
The interior shows a warrior head surrounded by crested double feline serpents.
The exterior has large-beaked birds.
12 cm. diameter. 10/1C.28.
Drawing by Janet Eager.

made of a horizontal line in a rectangular frame from which short lines extend to suggest teeth. The sculptural head (figs. 140, 144, left center and right center) has larger round eyes, a rectangular nose in relief, and a slash mouth. These two head motifs were interchangeable, for both appear in heads with emanations, not always confined to their normal mediums. In that theme they may both be taken as images of the same god, but both head motifs could also be used as trophy heads. There may be some deeper significance to this fact, but perhaps they are just alternative ways to represent any head.

The head with emanations may be the most complete expression of the concept of a celestial deity surrounded by the symbols of the four directions, an idea we shall return to in chapter 10. The circular head may be merely an abbreviated expression of the same theme.

The Circular Head

There are numerous examples—three stone tenoned heads and fourteen painted ceramic cups in the offerings—of a turbaned head without any projecting elements. In the painted versions the head is a perfect circle (fig. 138), like that on the finest relief of a head with emanations (fig. 203), the circle evidently representing a band of cloth which encloses the head vertically. The ears are portrayed by a downward curl or by a circle, as on the tenoned head in the collection of the Artisans' Center, Cabana (fig. 139). The eyes are open circles and the teeth are shown in the painted versions. This motif is associated in the paintings with crested felines, birds, crosses, and feline serpents, which suggests that this head is a manifestation of the divine power in some way, rather than a trophy. The turban is the only attribute shown on the stone tenoned heads, but in their original settings the other motifs, such as feline serpents

and birds, were probably associated by being represented on other tenoned heads or on reliefs attached to the same structure.

The circular head seems to have been just one element of a complex idea more fully expressed by the head-with-emanations theme. Its frontality and circularity emphasize its iconic nature and recall the circularity of the revolving heavens, to which the design probably referred.

139. Stone tenoned head.
Collection of the Artisans' Center, Cabana.

140, Below: male figure in "winged" headdress and step-patterned tunic, red on cream. 7.8 cm. high. 12/7.129.

The Turbaned Figure or Head

A turban with winglike flaps or appendages is the identifying feature of this theme, represented both in a full figure and by heads. A pottery figurine of Cabana Cream Painted ware 7.8 centimeters high (fig. 140) depicts a standing figure wearing a turban with winglike appendages and cross-marked earplugs. Like one set of warriors, the figure wears a step-patterned tunic which allies him with the crowned god. Since the figure is broken on the right side, we cannot be sure of all his attributes, but the turban suggests that he plays a role different from that of the helmeted warriors.

Two heads broken from larger vessels, which were found in the fill offerings (12/3–4) (pl. 3), share the winged turban and the cross-marked earplugs with the figurine. Two of these items have faces with large round eyes and a slash mouth, a design more typical of stone sculpture than of ceramic decoration.

Among the examples in which only the head was shown, the simplest is a modeled sherd found by children on the south flank of La Capilla Hill and preserved in the Artisans' Center in Cabana. Wearing a cream turban with a black crown, the strongly modeled head was bodiless, framed by a double border of step frets.

138. Opposite: pedestal cup with frontal faces, probably a celestial deity, in red and cream on black resist.
10/4.16.

A small patch of cream ground was left in the black background to signify appendages like those on a stone tenoned head, probably from Pashash, which appeared for sale in New York in 1968 (Emmerich 1968: no 56).

This theme appears only in three dimensions, in stone and ceramic versions.

It is helpful to examine comparable works from other places. A notable example in the Recuay style, of unknown provenience, shows a seated full figure with hand- or winglike appendages having five "fingers" (Larco Hoyle 1966: pl. 110). A small rectangular projection at the front of the turban bears a design of a toothy mouth, suggesting that the turban represents a feline and that the appendages are its paws. The figure wears disks marked with a cross in his ears, which is unusual, piercing for a pendant being the common element in this theme. He holds a small square shield and a stubby spear, both of which are unusual for the theme and seem discordant with his seated pose. The face is a standard sculptural motif.

Moche pottery has two ways of representing turbaned figures—one way showing somber men full-figure, seated crosslegged with their hands on their knees (Larco Hoyle 1966: 32–33; Emmerich 1969: no. 1), the other way showing only the head, set on a tapering pedestal base narrower and higher than usual in Moche head vessels (Benson 1972: 3–24, pl. 4; Larco Hoyle 1966: 53, pl. 31), which may indicate highland influence.

We may assume that the role indicated by the turban was shared by Callejón de Huaylas Recuay, Pashash, and Moche societies. Rafael Larco Hoyle calls the figures high dignitaries, and it would appear that sitting was part of their role. Although the Moche fanged god could play the role, it appears that it could also be played by men. Weapons were not foreign to the role, but perhaps their active use was not required. One might imagine a priest of a militaristic cult being so represented, probably acting as a surrogate for the god.

The Helmeted Head

Helmets bearing a transverse crest define the theme and presumably define the subject as a warrior. The theme is represented by the remarkable tenoned head in the National Museum in Lima (fig. 1), attributed to Pashash by Tello (1929: fig. 46). The head, about life-size, has earplugs in addition to the helmet. In 1973 a comparable stone tenoned head, slightly smaller than life-size and battered, was found in building excavations flanking the church in Cabana (now in custody of the church fathers in Cabana). The crest of the helmet had been almost entirely broken away, and the nobility of the Lima example is missing, but the theme is the same.

In addition to the painted design in the sculptural motif mentioned earlier, there are several cups or bowls painted with heads in the painterly motif, all of them wearing crested helmets with diagonal rays emanating from their heads (figs. 141, 142). The rays remind one of the heads with feline and serpent emanations, but the crested helmet is taken to identify the warrior theme. The significance of the plain rays is unknown. Other kinds of helmets were also shown, but we can only guess at the different meanings their designs conveyed. One warrior wears a helmet with two lobes instead of a crest (fig. 143). The lobes are similar to the design for jaguar ears. Other sherds show a variety of helmet and emanation designs whose significance is unknown (fig. 144).

141. *Opposite above: helmeted head, red on cream.*
Interior of 12/7.61.

142. *Opposite below: helmeted head, red on cream.*
Sherd from 12/5.

143. Above: head in lobed helmet, red on cream.
Interior of 12/7.82.

Black and red on cream, 2/2

Gray and black on red-washed white slip, 2/2

*Opaque white
and black on red, 3/2*

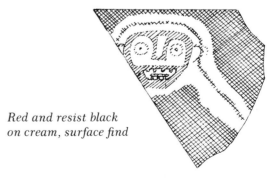

*Red and resist black
on cream, surface find*

144. *Head motifs from sherds of Huacohú
phase.*

The Trophy Head

The human trophy head is unquestionably represented in just three cases: one in which it is threatened by a feline on the top of a gold-plated pin (fig. 131); one in which it is in the talons of a bird in a stone relief (fig. 145); and in Relief 1, where a human warrior holds it (fig. 150). (See Schaedel 1952: 204–206 for the catalog of the Pashash stone sculptures. Reliefs are numbered according to that catalog.) The style of the heads held by the bird and the feline is similar to that of four heads framed on another relief (fig. 146). Their lack of headdresses or any other indication of a social role suggests that they are imagined in the role of "basic man," conceived as a sacrificial role.

There is a relief sculpture showing another head in the same motif, but in this case three birds touch the head with their beaks (fig. 147). It is impossible to determine whether the birds are intended to be seen as feeding on the head or as relating the head to that of warriors or priests, whose heads are flanked by similar birds. Two other isolated heads appear at the top of Relief 3 (fig. 148), adapting the painterly face motif to the relief medium. Repetition of the motif suggests trophy heads rather than a god, whom we would expect to be unique.

Although trophy heads were definitely represented, the propensity of Pashash artists for isolated heads intended to convey various meanings makes identification of some of the heads uncertain. The more attributes attached, the less likely it is that the head is a trophy or the full figure a victim. Death was evidently not glorious to the inhabitants of Pashash but represented total sacrifice. The placement of offerings in a burial, like the addition of attributes to the figure, must have brought distinction to that which was common.

145. *Stone Relief 4, showing a large-beaked bird with a trophy head.*
Location unknown.
Photo by Abraham Guillén.

146. *Stone relief, showing four frontal heads.*
44 cm. high, 46 cm. wide.
Collection of the church, Cabana.

147. *Stone Relief 8, showing a head with three birds.*
45 cm. high, 55 cm. wide.
Collection of the church, Cabana.

148. *Stone Relief 3.*
Formerly in a private collection in Cabana, re-
ported lost 1969.
Photo by Abraham Guillén.

The Splayed Figure with a Double Crest

Although the crested feline is a common motif, the human figure with a symbolic crest is represented in Relief 3 (fig. 148) and at least twice on painted basins, one smashed and scattered in 12/3 and 7 and another in 12/8 (fig. 149). Perhaps the theme is related to the head with emanations, but in this case the "emanations" emerge from the top of the head, rather than from the ears, and on Relief 3 end in ambiguous rectangles, rather than in feline heads. The diamond-shaped body with its central cross recalls the splayed motif of the feline (11 H),

and there is little doubt that the cross symbolizes the jaguar's spots. In this sense, the motif represents another crested feline. But the face is clearly that used for humans, as the trophy heads at the top of the relief show. The theme reminds one of Peter Furst's assertion that "shamans and jaguars are not merely equivalent, but each is at the same time the other" (1968: 148). This image is a notable example of the languagelike permutation of a series of pictorial symbols, which is a major characteristic of Pashash art.

149. *Fragment of the floor of a large basin with parts of a splayed figure in brown on cream. 6.3 cm. between the feet. Sherds from 12/7 and 8.*

The Frontal Warrior Armed with a Club

Theme 8 appears in various motifs and in both painting and relief carving. The basic conception seems to be expressed by the stone relief which shows a frontal warrior bearing a long club and a trophy head (fig. 150). His helmet has a central knifelike crest and three projections on each side, somewhat reminiscent of the stepped crown. The stone reliefs—there are three bearing this theme—always show the club held across the body, and two (17 and 18) (fig. 151) have birds attached to the warrior's head as if pecking it and lack both the crown and the trophy head. The painted examples, which appear on three pedestal cups—one from the burial offering and two others from the doorway offering—show the club held like a tall lance, away from the body (figs. 152, 153). The club is shown in a double view, its handle from the side and its pierced circular head from the top. In

150. *The helmeted warrior with a trophy head represented on Relief 1.*

151. *Stone Relief 18.*
48 cm. square.
Collection of the church, Cabana.

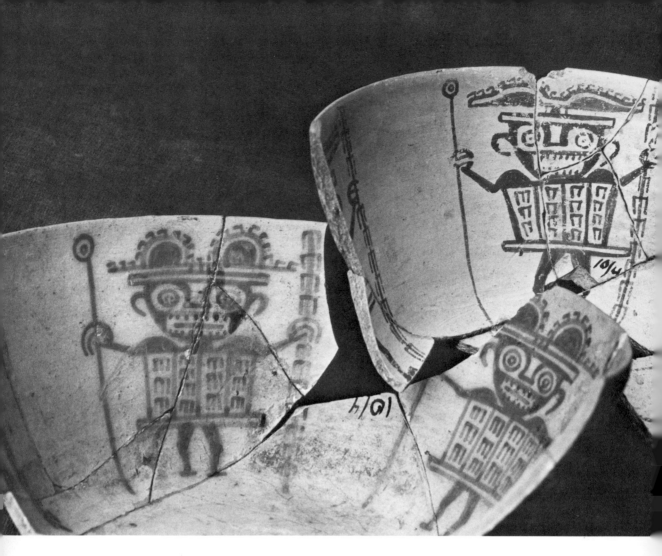

152. *Warriors painted in red on the interiors of cups.*
About 4 cm. high. 10/4.20 and 25.

these examples the helmet has a wide low crest or lobes marked with a fringe element. The warrior depicted in the burial offering has the step design on his tunic; the design on the tunics of the others is found on the banner borne by the warrior in the burial offering. The warrior's face has the standardized circular eyes, toothy grimace, and a three-fingered hand. The ex-

terior of the cup from the burial offering has resist checkerboard step designs which remind us again, as the tunic does, of the crowned god. We see another armed warrior on the black basin (fig. 130) as the captive of the crowned god, and on Relief 1 the warrior is imitating the divine action by taking a trophy head (fig. 150).

153. *Warrior with a club in red on cream from*
the interior of a cup.
Sherds from 12/7.

The Figure in a Tall Hat

This figure is depicted in a ceramic figurine of Cabana Cream Painted ware 6.3 centimeters high (figs. 154, 155). The figure is complete except for the hands, which were raised in front of the chest, perhaps holding something. The figure, presumably a man, seems to wear a long gown with vertical stripes of red and brownish black on a cream slip. His tall crownlike hat has a pattern of spots in those colors, forming vertical bands. His face is of the "sculptural mode": eyes left blank in the red face color, blocky nose, and slash mouth. His earplugs bear a pattern of brown triangles radiating from a red spot, forming a cross. The side view (fig. 155) suggests that the figure is seated on a throne, surely a prerogative of spiritual or secular authority. If costume distinguishes role and status, this figure is uniquely specified. The spots may pertain to the jaguar and be another example of the use of spotted designs with that sacred reference. But the absence of other figures in this costume makes it impossible to reach any conclusions beyond the general idea that the figure fulfilled some authoritative ceremonial role.

154. *Male figure in a tall hat, painted red and brownish black on cream.*
6.3 cm. high. 12/7.131.

155. *Side view of fig. 154.*

156. *Opposite: rampant jaguar on a red stone cup. The feline is repeated on the other side, where more of its green stone inlays are intact. 10/4.1.*

The Naked Prisoner

Another theme definitely represented by only a single example is that of the naked human prisoner (10/4.54, fig. 54). The little figure, about 10 centimeters high, lies over the body of a feline serpent, the monster grasping him by the hair. He is entirely naked, lacking even earplugs. The round eyes with their dotted pupils give an impression of fear, but his hands are free at his sides.

Relief 21 has a similar naked figure with no attribute to indicate his role. His pose with curled arms is the same as that on figure 54, with nothing, such as bound hands, to indicate that he represents a prisoner.

A comparable subject is the trophy head threatened by a feline represented on the top of a gold-plated pin (fig. 131). The idea of humans devoured by mythical feline monsters must have been common, but full-figure representations of the victim were rare, in contrast to Moche art, in which naked bound prisoners are a frequent theme.

The proportions in figure 54 are those common in Andean art: the prisoner is about four heads tall, his legs being even more abbreviated than usual. In other respects the figure is generally natural, with the fingers and toes indicated and a flesh-colored slip painted over the basic cream body, leaving only the eyes and the penis in cream. The role of prisoner did not require an attribute, such as bound hands; it was available to basic man.

Feline Animals

There is a rich variety of feline motifs ranging from fairly naturalistic to extremely conventional. Among the more naturalistic is the rampant feline represented in low relief on a red stone cup (fig. 156, see pl. 4 for another side). It has no metaphorical attachments. The three turquoise inlays on the body show that a spotted cat is meant, and it appears that all the feline images were to be understood as spotted. They may be taken as jaguars, that being the largest spotted feline found in South America, one abundantly represented in Pre-Columbian art

and in the ethnology of the surviving peoples.

The spotted feline appears again without metaphor, although conventionalized, in two effigy libation vessels (10/4.51 and 52, figs. 61–63). The pelage spots are conventionalized as black diamonds filled with dots in resist.

The sculptors of the stone reliefs ordinarily evaded the problem of representing the spots, but we may assume that such examples as the four-legged beasts emanating from a frontal face are also jaguars (fig. 132). Those are among the most natural, having the tail as well as the front and back legs shown. Another stone relief shows just the feline in left profile with emphasis on the male genitals, a feature not represented in any other example (fig. 157). A tiny circular relief in the top of a cast pinhead (12/7.10 and 31) (fig. 131) shows a feline without spots attacking a masklike face, presumably a trophy head, with

its front and back paws. An inlay in the eye, now lost but very likely of turquoise, was the only addition.

There are, however, numerous examples of felines with pelage markings represented in ceramics, and there is one example in metal (fig. 158). The markings are never casual but are always set within a restricted range of conventional designs: cross, diamond, checkerboard, square, or crosshatch. All these designs could be used independently and will be described in the section below on conventional designs.

The feline head was the subject of several motifs which were the bases of various feline and feline-serpent designs. The feline head appears as a full round sculpture, as a high relief, and as a low plano-relief of the frontal head. The most common is a profile view used in plano-relief and painting. A top view, for which two

157. *Stone relief of a feline.*
49 cm. high, 36 cm. wide.
Collection of the church, Cabana.

basic motifs were invented, was used mostly for secondary heads on the ends of crests or tongues (fig. 180).

The ceramic effigies show several examples of full round modeled heads (10/4.53, fig. 60). The emphasis is on the gigantic mouth with a double row of straight teeth, angled fangs being relatively uncommon in Pashash felines. Round eyes and large rounded ears are the other important traits. Stone tenoned heads from the Huamachuco region show this full round feline head, but there is no example in stone at Pashash.

That the idea of the tenoned head depicting a feline was known at Pashash is suggested by two kinds of feline representations in metal. The tops of metal pins from the burial offering include frontal jaguar faces in full relief as a common decorative subject. The emphasis is on the large ears and the large mouth full of straight teeth (12/7.2, 6, 12, 13, and 14) (fig. 117). The same motif appears in a simpler version in copper pins (12/4.1 and 2, fig. 111),

which follows very closely the form of a stone tenoned head, looking somewhat like a miniature version of the stone tenoned head from Huamachuco described by Theodore McCown (1945: pl. 17, d–e).

At Pashash the frontal feline head was represented more commonly in a flatter design, evidence of the graphic propensities of Pashash artists of the Recuay period. That motif is found, for example, on the top of a small solid pinhead (fig. 158). The jaguar's body has four diamond-

158. *Right: turbaned feline on the top of a gold-and-copper pin.*
2 cm. diameter. 12/7.5.

159. *Below: crested feline, red on cream.*
12/7.

shaped spots and a striped tail, but its frontal face could be mistaken for a human face if it were not for the semicircular feline ears projecting from its turban.

By far the commonest version of the feline head is the profile, used for painted and low plano-relief representations. A circular eye and a toothy mouth, sometimes with fangs, are the essential features (fig. 159). A tongue, a projecting nostril, a pointed ear, and a long crest emanating from the head are frequent additions to the basic motif. All these elements are variable, as is the body which accompanies the head. The tongue, for example, may be a single straight line; it may divide into curls (figs. 160, 161) or end in a top-view (figs. 162, 163) or side-view (figs. 164, 165) feline head. The nostril and the crest

often carry a step design (fig. 166), and the crest may be a plain strip (fig. 167) or may end in a feline head (fig. 168). The body of the feline is ordinarily rampant, with both a front and a hind leg represented (figs. 169, 170), but the hind leg is often replaced by a snake body (figs. 171, 172) and, in a few cases, the front leg is likewise eliminated (figs. 173–175). The fine pedestal cups in Cut 10, Level 4, ring all the changes on this subject.

Another common alternative in feline compositions is to double the heads. Double-headed felines employ all the alternatives among the elements (fig. 176). The simplest version appears on a large covered jar (12/7.55, fig. 64) from the burial offering, which has an S-curve suggesting a serpent body, ending in feline

160. *Pedestal cup with frontal faces and crested felines.*
The felines are positive white on a red band.
10/4.26.

heads composed of just the circular eye and the mouth with teeth and tongue. A stone relief (fig. 177) has frontal faces on a double-headed feline and has crests with steps and profile feline heads on the ends. Another stone relief (fig. 178) has the principal heads in profile and top-view heads on the tongues, crests, and even on the raised border.

One small fragmentary bowl has an amusing combination of feline motifs around the inner wall, painted in red and orange on cream (fig. 179). One half of the wall has a double-headed feline. The other half has two very abstract and elemental profile felines in series. The spiritual potency of the theme did not keep the artists from playing visual games with the motifs. This kind of inventive play with the elements was the aesthetic motive of the style.

161. *Pedestal cup with two registers of felines, upper in resist, lower in positive white.* 10/4.23.

162. *Above: stone relief of a feline with head and tongue crests.*
The circles for the eyes were cut with hollow drill bits measuring 7, 10, and 12 cm. in diameter.
41 cm. high, 38 cm. wide.
Collection of the church, Cabana.

163. *Below: pedestal cup with felines with tongues ending in top-view feline heads. 10/4.21.*

164. *Stone relief, showing feline with crested head and tongue.*
38.5 cm. high, 41 cm. wide.
Collection of the church, Cabana.

165. *Bowl with felines with tongues ending in double profile feline heads.*
Attributed to Red Football.
12/7.121.

166. *Crested felines on fragment of black stone bowl.*
Traces of red paint in the excised areas.
4.8 cm. high. 12/4.6.

167. *Stone Reliefs 2 (top) and 16, attributed to Pashash, showing a crested feline and a step fret.*
Location unknown.
Photo by Abraham Guillén.

168. *Feline with head crest ending in a top-view feline head.*
Red on cream. About 2 cm. high. 12/7.96.

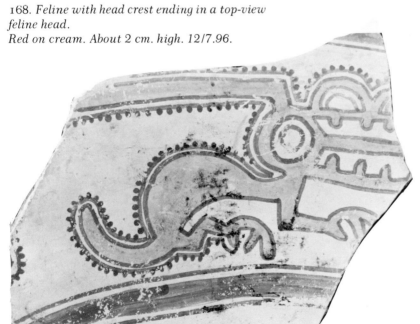

169. *Crested feline in red on cream on the interior of a large flared bowl broken and scattered in 12/2.*

170. *Feline monsters with profile and frontal heads.*
Both panels are in resist; alternate panels have a red wash.
Panels are 5.5 cm. high. 12/2.2.

171. *Spotted feline serpents in panels.*
The cup is 7.1 cm. high. 12/3.9.

172. Above: feline serpents in red on cream on the interior of a double pedestal cup fragment. 11/3.2.

173. Below: pedestal cup with decorations including feline serpents as the middle register. 10/4.30.

174. *Above: feline serpents in frames and linked feline heads suggestive of tenoned heads, on a square-rimmed pedestal cup found in the ruins of Pashash by children.*
Collection of the Artisans' Center, Cabana.

175. *Feline serpents in black and cream resist. Sherd from 12/7.*

176. *Below: double feline designs on Recuay Yaiá phase sherds from Cut 12.*

177. *Stone Relief 9, showing a double-headed feline.*
Collection of the church, Cabana.

178. *Stone Relief 22, showing double feline designs.*
Location unknown.
Photo by Abraham Guillén.

179. *Felines in series and doubled in red and orange on cream.*
12/7.

Snakes and Felines

Some feline subjects are easily mistaken for snakes, but when all the motifs are examined there is no standard motif in Pashash art for a snake's head. The two snake effigy vessels (10/4.57 and 58, figs. 56, 57), which at first glance seem to represent pure reptiles, have feline ears and noses. The heads were evidently intended to be purely feline. There are some snakes represented on the wide rims of handled bowls (e.g., 12/7.109), but the heads are featureless except for two small punches for the eyes.

There are two basic motifs for the top view of a feline head (fig. 180). These are really conventional, elemental versions of the plano-relief front view as found on Relief 9, but "top view" distinguishes them for descriptive purposes. There is no case in which either of these motifs can be shown to represent a snake. The places in which they appear (ends of tongues, crests, etc.) can be filled with profile feline heads. The stone reliefs (figs. 177, 178) mentioned above are good examples.

The triangular head motif has often been con-

sidered a snake, as in Paracas art (Bennett 1954: 37, fig. 35), but Paracas artists were careful to define the snake's head as feline whenever the design permitted (Sawyer 1966: 81–82, 118–119), just as we find in the art of Pashash.

It is the snake body, not the head, which plays an important role in the art. The serpent body with a feline head is the only really composite creature, as opposed to those which have metaphoric attachments to a single creature, in Pashash art, and it is one of the dominant themes. The effigy vessels in the doorway offering provide examples of two versions: the serpent body with a feline head, the head distinguishable as feline mainly by its ears (fig. 56, 57), and the serpent body with the forelegs, shoulders, and head of a feline (figs. 55, 59, 60). The serpent bodies always end in a simple point, not in rattles. The feline-serpent theme is not unique to Pashash, for effigy vessels on the same theme are found in Paracas art (Sawyer 1966: 80–81, 86, 118, nos. 107, 108, 115, 194, 195). The theme must have carried an impor-

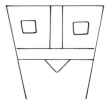
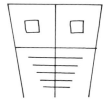

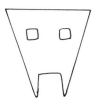

tant and widely shared meaning. Probably the feline serpents stood at the four cardinal directions of the cosmic plan.

This brief review scarcely suggests the importance of the feline as a theme in Pashash art. Even for the conventional designs felines, along with serpents, provided the basic ideas, as we shall see.

180. *Four versions of the two basic motifs for the top view of the feline head.*

Birds

Bird motifs were never so highly organized as feline motifs, a good indication that their importance as symbols was inferior to that of felines. There are just two categories of birds: those in which the large beak is the most important element, and those in which the large eyes are most important. The large-eyed bird can safely be called an owl, but the large-beaked birds

probably include at least two kinds: the Andean condor and the *alliguanga* (figs. 181–183), a vulture native to the northern highlands of Peru.

181. *Stone relief of a large-beaked bird. 41 cm. high, 56 cm. wide. Collection of the church, Cabana.*

182. Above: large-beaked bird in a framed panel on a spouted basin.
Red and black on cream.
10/4.60.

183. Below: effigy and figurine fragments from various locations in the ruins.
Top row: birds, all Recuay types;
middle row: mammals, left and center Usú types, right Recuay;
bottom row: human eyes from hollow effigy vessels, Recuay.

A stone relief (fig. 184) which shows a bird with a large cere may represent a condor, and there is also evidence of the condor in the period subsequent to the burial in a carved and painted tube made from the ulna of a condor (10/2.2, fig. 109). A small ceramic bird (fig. 185), probably broken from the rim of a vessel, has been identified by Alberto Bueno as an *alliguanga*. That seems to be the bird most commonly represented at Pashash.

184. *Stone relief of a large-beaked bird, the most natural depiction.*
42 cm. high, 51 cm. wide.
Collection of the church, Cabana.

185. *Large-beaked bird painted black and white.*
3.8 cm. high, broken at feet. 12/7.136.

It is difficult to interpret the roles of the condors or vultures shown flanking human heads, for there are two contrasting subjects represented by similar motifs. A headdress ornamented with two birds, of a type shown in full round in Moche pottery (e.g., Benson 1972: fig. 3-24), seems to be the subject of such works as Reliefs 17 and 18 (fig. 151). Reliefs 4 (fig. 145) and 8 (fig. 147) show condors or vultures grasping or pecking trophy heads. The feline images present a similar situation, in which the feline may serve as a headdress or may ornament a head crest (fig. 148) but may also grasp a naked man (10/4.54, fig. 54) or a trophy head (12/7.10, fig. 131). These motifs were no doubt easily distinguished by the people of Pashash, who understood that one group of people was under the protection of jaguars and condors or vultures while another group was threatened by them.

Two views of the condor or vulture are presented on a fine resist-decorated cup (12/7.57, fig. 66) from the burial offering, one in profile,

the other in top view. This cup probably gives an accurate impression of the mosaic compositions formed by tenoned heads and reliefs set in stone walls, compositions in which the condor or vulture played a supporting role in the mystico-military drama dominated by the frontal face and the jaguar.

Owls must have been part of such compositions, since there are stone sculptures representing large-eyed birds both as a profile body with a frontal head (one example: fig. 186) and as tenoned heads (two examples) (fig. 187). The owl motif is very consistent. The whole motif is composed of a profile body and a frontal face, large round eyes, a small beak, and earlike tufts, probably meant to show the owl as similar to a jaguar. A fragmentary cup (fig. 188) has the motif complete in a freely rendered red line, and we find it also on the tops of two gold pins (12/7.9 and 12/7.15 [fig. 189], in which the body is very abbreviated). Relief 31 (fig. 186) shows the same design, but the ears are lacking. Two stone

186. *Stone Relief 31, showing an owl above the door of a house in Cabana.*

187. Top: *stone tenoned head of an owl, the beak broken.*
The eyes were made with a hollow drill.
The head is 15 cm. high, 24 cm. wide.
Collection of the Artisans' Center, Cabana.

188. Middle: *owls in red on cream on the interior of a cup.*
12/2.2.

189. Left: *an owl on the top of a copper-and-gold pin. Green stone inlays in the eyes and black inlaid centers in the eyes and "ears."*
2.9 cm. diameter. 12/7.15.

tenoned heads show only the eyes; there are broken places on both where the beak must have been (fig. 187). As usual, the motif may be represented fully or in any abbreviation which leaves the basic identifying traits.

The owl always appears alone in Pashash art, without any attribute which would suggest the role it played in myth or symbolism. A Recuay style figurine of unknown provenience shows a "standing warrior with elaborate owl mask headdress, llama at his side" (Sawyer 1968: 38–39, no. 216). The warrior's head is capped with a spoutlike flared headdress on which the

large owl eyes rest. A tiny figure in a helmet with a transverse crest emerges at the top. Red-spotted black ears, presumably jaguar ears, are largely broken off. Small white-ruffed black condors or vultures crouch at the sides. A double-headed feline in resist ornaments the warrior's tunic. As this piece shows, under some circumstances the owl could take precedence over all other symbolic beasts. Although the owl is important in Pashash imagery, we have to look to the art of different sites for evidence of its relationship to other subjects.

Conventional Designs

During the Recuay period, Pashash artists began to use a new set of conventional designs. Only two of the sixteen most common designs at Pashash—the S-curve and the equal-arm cross—have clear Chavín antecedents. Of the other fourteen, six—stripe, concentric painted circles, step, fret, diamond, and zigzag—appear in Paracas style, which must be assumed to have served as a source of Pashash designs. The remaining eight—concentric squares, checker-board, diagonal crosshatch, football spot, triangle, curling frame, chain, and whirl—are new in the Recuay style. The uses to which all these designs were put in the decoration of

Pashash pottery produce such distinctive results that one accepts the originality of the artists, for they employed their design vocabulary with a confidence and a consistency not characteristic of provincial followers of a borrowed style.

There are three major categories of designs: (1) those related to the feline theme (equal-arm cross, concentric circles, concentric squares, diamond, checkerboard, crosshatch [fig. 190],

190. *Spouted basin with crosshatch design containing crosses and a three-dot design, perhaps representing a jaguar spot or a bean. 15.5 cm. high. 12/7.115.*

and whirl); (2) those related to the serpent theme (step, fret, zigzag, triangle, S-curve, curling frame, and chain); and (3) those used to define space (stripe), which may also figure in symbolic designs. It may be that many of these designs became mere spacefillers in this style, which preferred a lively well-filled space, but one of the distinguishing features of the Recuay style is the symbolic foundation of every mark. Among all the world's styles, it would be difficult to find one more unified in philosophy and design concept than the Recuay style at Pashash. Thus the conventional designs emerge from the representational designs as ways of filling areas

and borders, still symbolic but formally adapted to the secondary role.

A flat rim of a bowl (12/3.6, fig. 133) has both a realistic snake in relief and small panels of profile felines with unusual spiral crests. These rim ornaments may be taken as the naturalistic end of a continuum, for both the snake and the conventional feline were more commonly represented by an abbreviation when they appeared on rims and in bordering areas. The jaguar was ordinarily reduced to nothing but its spots, which might be represented by any one of a variety of designs (figs. 191–194).

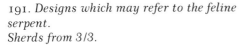

191. *Designs which may refer to the feline serpent.*
Sherds from 3/3.

192. *Pedestal cup with red dots on cream.*
4 cm. high. 12/7.64.

193. *A selection of conventional designs referring to the jaguar.*

194. *Left: spotted designs which refer to the jaguar.*

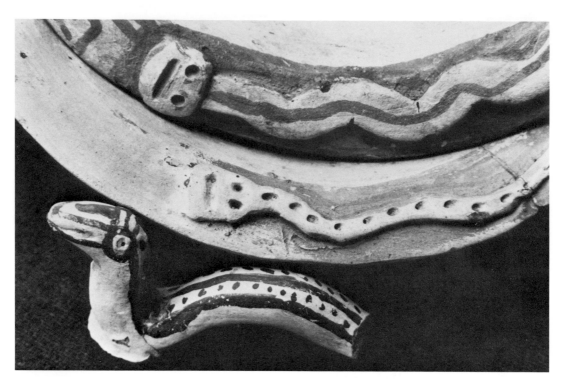

195. *Above: snake designs on the rims of handled bowls from Cut 12.*
The lower fragment is broken at the base, probably from a rim.
All are painted red on cream.

196. *Below: designs referring to the snake on the rim flanges of handled bowls from Cut 12. All are painted red on cream.*

The serpent was commonly represented by a wavy line or zigzag or some development of that shape such as a step, a spiral or rectangular fret, or a chain (figs. 195–197). The symbolism of the S-curve (fig. 198) and the curling frame (fig. 199) (which is much less common) is uncertain, but it appears that they represent the serpent element in a feline-serpent combination, since they often appear with feline spot designs.

The feline and serpent effigies provide some confirmation of the symbolism of these conventional designs. The feline figures (e.g., 10/4.51, fig. 61) have unconnected diamond-shaped areas with spots in resist. The serpents (e.g., 10/4.58, fig. 57) have zigzag designs on their bodies. The feline serpents have stripes on the serpent body and a checkerboard on the feline head (10/4.56, fig. 59) or zigzags and step frets on the serpent body and a plain color on the feline head (10/4.55, fig. 55). The use of chained diamonds or zigzags to identify pit vipers (fer-de-lance or bushmaster) may have begun in the Chorrera art of Ecuador, where they were employed on modeled vessels representing those snakes (Lathrap, Collier, and Chandra 1975: cat. nos. 375–377, 441).

197. Pedestal cup with conventional designs referring to the snake.
Black and cream resist with red wash on one side.
8.3 cm. high. 12/7.75.

198. *Above: S-curve and cross designs of the Yaiá phase from Cut 3 and (upper right) Cut 1.*

199. *Below: framed crosses, curling frames, and squares on Yaiá phase pottery.*

The whirling design seems to have been particularly related to the feline; it alternates with a conventional feline design on an offering vessel (fig. 200). This design is part of another continuum from the purely graphic painted design to a low relief depiction of a whirling cross (fig. 201) to designs actually *produced* by rotation, such as the eyes of a feline relief (fig. 162) and the eyes of two owl tenoned heads (fig. 187). Rotation was the subject of all these designs and was the technique by which some of them were produced, and rotation itself was evidently symbolic of power and energy. There are no surviving accounts of the symbolism of rotation, but one can perhaps imagine the kind of image this was from modern Jivaro accounts of encounters with *arutam*, " 'ancient specter' souls," which may appear as a pair of fighting jaguars rolling over and over toward the vision seeker, or as a pair of anacondas locked in battle rolling toward the visionary (Harner 1972: 138).

Although about half of the design vocabulary of Pashash artists was inherited from earlier periods, it was completely unified by the Recuay style. The consistency of the style and the design vocabulary is expressive of a coherent system of thought.

200. *Whirling design, spotted diamonds, and a step border on a jar with a neck flange (Form D-2).*
18 cm. high. 10/4.65.

201. *Stone relief with whirling cross design,*
one of seven with this motif.
40 by 40 cm.
Collection of the church, Cabana.

10.
Society and Symbolism in Ancient Pashash

The burial and its building and offerings are un-usually interesting because they give us infor-mation about one of the extremes in the ancient society of Pashash. Everything in the burial area was surplus in the economy. Although the offer-ings contained objects which have conventional value in our culture and no doubt were valu-able in the same sense when they were buried, the greatest intrinsic value in the offerings is labor. Virtually everything associated with the burial is unusual in its category for its high qual-ity. The offerings are of things a modern economist would call labor-intensive.

The products of surplus labor could have made no improvement in the standard of living of the average citizen of Pashash except as they might have offered paid employment to the land-less unemployed. It is probably safe to conclude that such was not the case and that the actual function of the offerings was to manifest the consumption of labor. Conspicuous consump-tion is a prerogative of an elite class; such a class was evidently dominant at Pashash, with a class of laborers beneath it. The skills of the laboring class as well as the ideas and taste of the elite are revealed by the offerings.

Assuming that the spindle whorls and the pins correctly identify the buried person as a woman, it is noteworthy that so much labor could be commanded in a woman's name. It is not easy to judge the place of women in ancient Andean societies, but they appear to have rarely ruled in their own names, legends of Amazons notwithstanding. The women rulers of the Chira Valley in the sixteenth century seem to have been described because the case was unusual (Lizárraga 1946: chap. 8). The Inca emperor's inheritance was as much through his mother as through his father, they being siblings, but no daughter ever ruled alone. Applying the Inca model to Pashash would suggest that the woman was a noblewoman buried by a reigning male, very likely a husband or a son to judge from the impressive location of the burial. Im-portant burial was partly a family duty, but it must also have reinforced the commanding position of the elite class.

The Recuay style in its particular manifesta-tion at Pashash is very unified. It is difficult to pick out the work of any individual artist. Even works in such different mediums as metal and stone are often so similar in style that one could

imagine that they were the work of a single artist, which was clearly not the case, the amount
of work and the span of time opposing that idea.
It is the nature of art to be expressive of the
personality of the artist. To discipline the expression of artists to the point that individual
personality is indistinguishable in their work requires considerable coercive power. Style is a
manifestation of order, or one may say a low
entropy product, which requires pressure for its
maintenance. The unity of the Recuay style is
the result of pressure sufficient to blot out nearly
all individuality in the expressive products. Social pressure is another energy-consuming activity, apart from the material products which
express it, of the ruling elite.

The offerings thus manifested and thereby
reinforced the power of the elite to command
labor for their own glorification. The art in the
offerings showed the power of the elite to control
the personal expression of skilled artists and to
use it to express their own interests and personalities. Style is a medium of communication
within the group which uses it, and it has always been obvious to authorities that control of
communication is essential to the maintenance
of authority. Art patronage is thus a prerogative
of the ruling classes; what continues to be made
without their patronage we call folk art. The art
in the offerings at Pashash was an intragroup
communication system under elite control. The
unity of the style and its use in funerary offerings for members of the ruling class were the
primary messages transmitted, apart from any
representational content. But the representational content of subjects and their meanings is also present in the art, and we may in-
quire what kinds of messages the members of
the ruling class were disseminating within their
group and to their people.

The ancient foundation on which the Recuay
style was built was the Chavín style. The great
ceremonial center of Chavín de Huantar itself
was occupied by people using the Recuay style,
building their houses within the once sacred
courtyards. The great temple at Chavín de
Huantar is still impressive to modern eyes; it is
hard to imagine its importance at a time when it
was unrivaled. The tenoned heads were still in
place, and no doubt many of the relief plaques
were still to be seen. Pottery and metal objects
were surely known to have been deposited in

subterranean galleries. Feline, bird, and serpent
images were still seen, and the rather limited
range of Chavín conventional designs was still
visible and no doubt still interpretable.

The breakdown of Chavín authority evident in
the disappearance of its style left a power vac-
uum in the ancient Chavín heartland. The absence of decorative motifs on pottery of the
Quinú period at Pashash is a minor datum point-
ing to the recession of Chavín style. The estab-
lishment of a new order is revealed by the presence of the new style. The new elite inherited a
language of power from the Chavín style, a language whose form was stone buildings ornamented with stone tenoned heads and relief
sculptures, with pottery and metal ritual deposits bearing sacred designs. Those elements
were retained by the new patrons as an assertion
of their position as heirs to the Chavín power.
The renewal of coercive power was evident in
the renewal of the tradition of public art in the
forms associated with power in ancient times.
This phenomenon is well known in our own
Western culture.

Chavín traditions remained alive among the
people in quite a different way. The basic forms
of pots for cooking and storage—the bowl with a
flat base and the neckless olla—were retained
throughout the Recuay period. It is significant
that these forms did not need to be revived since
they had not died out. The folk arts and crafts
lived on independent of elite art, responding to
social pressures just as coercive but more widely
diffused and for that reason less vulnerable to
change. This phenomenon occurred again in
the sixteenth century, when elite art was taken
over by the Spanish conquerors but folk arts and
crafts carried on many traditional forms.

Although the new elite adopted many of the
ancient Chavín forms—which were as remote
from them as Roman imperial art was from fif-
teenth-century Italians, who revived the ancient
style in many similar ways—the Recuay elite
changed the revived forms and added expressions of their own concerns. The construction of a burial temple dedicated to an individual
and the deposit of personal jewelry in the offering seem to be new elements. The depiction of
helmeted warriors, who may have been identifiable as individuals, departs from the Chavín
tradition of tenoned heads and relief panels. The
helmeted and armed warriors so often painted

on Recuay pottery show a common concern for the representation of military figures, only a minor theme in Chavín art.

Recuay representations of birds, mammals, and reptiles show this tendency to retain forms and change their content. Felines and owls began to be represented on stone tenons in the Recuay style, although Chavín artists had not depicted any identifiable bird or animal on tenons. In Chavín stone sculpture birds are represented on reliefs, and only hawks and eagles appear (Rowe 1962a: 18). In Recuay art hawks and eagles are replaced by owls and condors or vultures. It is noteworthy that all these birds are meateaters, a factor which must have been important in their use as symbols. In a Peruvian myth recorded in the sixteenth century, in which the birds and animals were divided into those favored by and those cursed by Cuniraya Viracocha, the condor was the first to appear. The god blessed the old condor with long life and the right to eat the meat of all wild animals when they die, and he ordained death to anyone who kills the condor. In the myth the other two creatures favored by Cuniraya Viracocha are the puma and the falcon, both of whom were blessed with their heads being worn by men in their headdresses at fiestas (Avila 1966: 25–27). This myth may preserve the favored position that the condor symbol was given during the Early Intermediate period.

Recuay ceremonial pottery is a mixture of old and new elements in the same way as the sculpture. The old elements derive from the Paracas style of the south coast, a style which grew out of Chavín but was in all respects an independent regional style. Pashash Recuay pottery bears somewhat the same relation to Paracas that Paracas bears to Chavín. One of the most characteristic Recuay forms—the handled bowl—is found as early as Paracas Phase 3 (Menzel, Rowe, and Dawson 1964: 23, fig. 10, g). Pashash potters changed the rim from incurved to expanded and flat. The resist technique was widely used in the New World, but in Peru the Paracas region was the earliest to use it. In the Paracas style, resist decoration developed from dot and crosshatch designs to birds, fish, and monkeys in its last phase, ending about A.D. 150 (ibid., p. 232, fig. 64). Not only a vessel form and a decorative technique but also several motifs used on Paracas pottery were re-

tained by Pashash potters. Step designs, which play an important part in Pashash imagery, seem to originate in Paracas Phase 3 (ibid., fig. 27, g.). The double feline-headed serpent is common in Paracas art in both ceramic effigies and flat designs from Ocucaje and Callango (Sawyer 1966: 80–81, 86, 118, nos. 107, 108, 115, 194, 195). The representation of feline spots as diamonds is also found in Paracas decoration (ibid., p. 95, no. 129). The top-view feline head (ibid., p. 90, no. 120) used as an appendage on serpentiform rays and bands is "a peculiar Phase 9 innovation which has no antecedents in pottery designs of the Ocucaje tradition. . . . it is exceedingly common in Phase 9" (Menzel, Rowe, and Dawson 1964: 199, where it is called a serpent head). All these motifs are important in Recuay pottery, especially at Pashash, which is closer to the Paracas style than are the other variants of the Recuay style. A hypothesis worth examination is that a small late Chavinoid settlement at Pashash was taken over by an elite class from a region of Paracas culture about the third century. The closer similarity of Pashash Recuay than of the other Recuay variants to Paracas pottery suggests that Pashash was an early center for the dissemination of the new style. Continued connections between Pashash and the Paracas-Nasca-Wari region are indicated by the anticipation of Wari style traits in Recuay pottery at Pashash, in particular by the shift to positive polychrome painting, especially by dark bands ornamented with white dots.

The independence of the Recuay pottery style is evident when it is compared with Nasca pottery, which shares the Paracas ancestry and ends with Wari influence. Nasca became colorful as Recuay developed resist; in Nasca human actors perform a variety of roles (dancing, playing musical instruments, fishing), while in Recuay only warriors and officials are represented. Despite many common features, the comparison throws into relief the narrow concentration on religious symbolism and war in Pashash Recuay.

The representational standards for Pashash Recuay ceramic painting and figurines were not set by a pottery style but by Pashash stone sculpture, of which the official class was a major subject. The round head, blocky nose, round eyes, and slash mouth found in the painted and modeled heads owe their form to stone tenoned heads. The designs on metal jewelry are similarly dependent on stone tenoned heads and relief plaques. The major role of stone sculpture in the Recuay style is an important factor in accounting for the difference between Recuay and Nasca, and it places Recuay firmly among the highland traditions, which preferred stone for their monumental art.

The dominant role of stone sculpture helps explain the adaptation of rotary tools used for stone to the making of pottery cups. The most distinctive new element in Pashash Recuay style is the emphasis on rotation and circularity and the use of tools to make circles. This was one aspect of an overriding fascination with geometry whose foundations can be traced back into the middle of the Chavín period, but which came into full flower in classic Tiahuanaco, with which Pashash is approximately contemporary. As Pashash experimented with circles and rotation, Tiahuanaco concentrated on the problems of measurement and angularity. Those two sites, so different in their geography, were led, one might say by a *genius loci*, to probe opposite aspects of natural experience, for there was wide use of circles to symbolize the heavens and quadrangles to represent the earth in ancient cultures. Tiahuanaco sits in a high wide valley, sheltered by low rolling hills, with distant peaks in view. Earth forms dominate, as if the earth had taken over part of the sky with its mass. At Pashash, on its high ridge, the sky has invaded the earth, penetrating in vast chasms into the dissected plateau. The ancient inhabitants looked out from La Capilla Hill into a surrounding sky animated by the circling lights of the heavens.

Is there any way in which twentieth-century scholarship can penetrate the expressions of meaning in the conventional symbols of an extinct society? Two methods for the analysis of ancient symbols have been devised by modern scholars: the configurational method, which formed the basis of the discussion of imagery in chapter 9, and the ethnological method (Grieder 1975). Is there any ethnological material which can provide models for the verbalization of Pashash symbols?

It is not the individual images of warriors or birds which seem to require verbal interpretation but, rather, the more complex designs in which a relationship is presented which does not simply represent a visual stimulus. A design such as that on a handled bottle (10/4.64, pl. 2)—its circular face with feline serpents emerging from the ears against a half-cream half-black background in a rectangular frame—implies a set of concepts shared by artist, patron, and audience.

Although the Pashash offerings are unusual in their richness, in many respects they are typical of ancient American thought and practice. To take a single example, the fragments of rock crystal in the burial offering (12/8.8) are symbolic objects in other American societies. The Desana of eastern Colombia, for example, consider rock crystals symbols of the semen of the divine sun and believe they are to be found where lightning—"the ejaculation of the Sun that can fertilize the land"—has struck (Reichel-Dolmatoff 1971: 48–49). Rock crystals have various symbolic meanings and uses in American cultures (Métraux in Steward 1963: vol. 5, p. 360), but they are always part of the symbolism of a religious system defined as shamanism. Although the Andean cultures are considered to have developed beyond shamanism to priestly religions, it is certain that shamanic ritual, belief, and symbolism survived in regions of ancient high culture (Tschopik 1951; Sharon in Furst 1972). The situation is summarized by Wilbert as "an archaic shamanistic substratum underlying and to some extent uniting all or most aboriginal American Indian cultures" (in Furst 1972: 83). Rock crystals were used as sacred symbols in regions beyond the American continent. Eliade notes that their use as symbols of divine power "is one of the most striking characteristics of South American shamanism," but they also "play an essential role in Australian magic and religion, and they are no less important throughout Oceania and the two Americas" (1964: 52, 139). Clearly we are dealing with a religious movement on the scale of Christianity, Islam, or Buddhism, but one whose roots lie in the Paleolithic period.

A tiny pyrite mirror with red cuprite spots, set into a gilt copper frame pierced for suspension (fig. 202), is another item which suggests shamanism. The mirror was presumably attached to clothing or hung from the neck. Among the Catio of the Cauca Valley of Colombia, "the mirror which every shaman carries around his neck" was an insignia of the office

202. Above: mirror face of iron pyrite with red
cuprite spots;
below: copper back of mirror with an engraved
design of a double feline.
2.2 by 3.3 cm. 12/8.7.

(Hernández de Alba in Steward 1963: vol. 4, p. 325). An Olmec figurine represents a woman wearing a small hematite mirror at her neck, as one might imagine the Pashash example to have been worn (Willey 1966: 99, fig. 3-24). There are several other representations in the art of La Venta and Tlatilco of mirrors worn suspended from the necks of seated crosslegged figures; the mirrors found in La Venta Offerings 9 and 11 were perforated, presumably for such suspension, a tradition we find carried on in classic Veracruz stone mirror backs (Drucker, Heizer, and Squier 1959: 181, 203; Covarrubias 1957: pl. 44, top and lower left). As in the case of rock crystals, there are parallels for the shamanic use of the mirror in Asia, where, for example, the Buryat shaman had a copper mirror hung on his chest or back (Eliade 1964: 151–152; Eliade accepts a Sino-Manchurian or Lamaist origin for Siberian shamans' mirrors [pp. 154, 498], but the trait is more widely spread and surely older than such an origin would allow). It might be noted that the Inca high priest used a concave metal mirror worn on a bracelet to kindle the new annual fire as part of the Intip Raimi festival (Garcilaso de la Vega 1966: bk. 6, chap. 22). The little mirror at Pashash easily convinces a modern observer of its mystic nature: the blood red spots marring the surface inspire reflections on mortality and the spiritual.

If we are to seek the rationale of social life in ancient Pashash, this mirror and these crystals are clues that it is in the ideology and practice of shamanism that we will find parallels and models for verbalization. Are there *shamanic* explanations for such complex designs as those on the handled bottle?

Shamanic beliefs include a cosmology in which the universe is conceived as having three levels: sky, earth, and underworld, linked by an axis (Eliade 1964: 259). Shamanism is based on belief in the possibility of human communication between these cosmic levels, especially in the possibility of communication with spirits in the sky and the underworld. The axis symbolizes such communication and may be represented as a tree, a mountain, and so on. There are well-known examples of such symbolism in ancient America: the World Tree among the Maya (Thompson 1950: 71) and the artificial mountain rising from an underworld cave at Teotihuacan (Heyden 1975). The name for the

creator god among the Desana carries the connotation "creative bone," implying his centrality, his axiality, and his being a hollow channel of fertilization between the cosmic levels (Reichel-Dolmatoff 1971: 48–49).

As typified at Teotihuacan, the cosmic mountain is conceived as quadrangular in shamanic thought. This ancient and widely held idea (see Zimmer 1955: 47–48) accounts for the use of the square or quadrangle to represent the ideal of terrestrial occupation or "the imagined shape of the world" (Rowland 1953: 154). The shamanic conception of the organization of the cosmos survived in the plan of Cuzco and the administrative organization of the Inca Empire—Tahuantinsuyu, literally the "Four Quarters of the World" (Garcilaso de la Vega 1966: bk. 1, chap. 5). It is hard to believe that the Inca invented this design, since it follows so closely designs developed by the high-culture heirs of the shamanic tradition in Asia. The Shang kingdom in China in the second millennium before Christ had "the capital and its environs at the center, surrounded by the Four Districts named after the cardinal points of the compass," and the two most ancient documents on city planning in India and China recommend a square plan with nine divisions (Wheatley 1971: 411–414, 423, 425).

In ancient America the divinely inhabited underworld was more important than the surface, where human life takes place, and thus the underworld tended to usurp the terrestrial property of directionality. To the Desana the surface of the earth is transparent, "like a large cobweb," and the directions have special significance in the underworld (Reichel-Dolmatoff 1971: 24–25).

The celestial level in Desana cosmology "has the shape of a large disk, an immense round plate" (ibid., p. 24). The celestial level is represented as circular wherever the shamanic cosmology has been influential (e.g., see Rowland 1953: 249).

The two symbols—the quadrangle for the earth and the circle for the heavens—may easily have originated in natural observation. The only part of nature which is easily seen to rotate by even casual observers is the night sky. The center of that rotation, the North Star, has been taken by many peoples as the point of support or the sacred center of the heavens (Eliade 1964:

260 ff.). The North Star also establishes one of the directions, two more being defined by the celestial passage of the sun, moon, and planets. Neither the observation of these phenomena nor their representation in circles and squares is confined to a single religious tradition, but their organization into a coherent system is a cultural achievement which distinguishes separate traditions. That the cultural distinctions occur rather late in this process is demonstrated by the symbolism of the four directions, which, like the center, are widely held to be points of contact between cosmic levels. John, in Revelations 7: 1, speaks of four angels standing at the four corners of the earth, an image given artistic form in many Christian manuscripts. An Eastern cognate appears in an eleventh-century Chinese armillary sphere clock, which had four dragons rising from the corners of its base to support a sphere (Needham, Ling, and Solla Price 1960: 30, fig. 6). The concept rests on the observation of natural phenomena; its expression varies with cultural tradition. Personifications of the four cardinal directions played an important role in several ancient American cosmologies (e.g., Thompson 1950: 10 for the Maya; Wilbert in Furst 1972: 61 for the Warao).

At this point we may return to the handled bottle (pl. 2) to ask what an observer versed in shamanic symbolism and cosmology might make of it. At the center is a circular orange face with the eyes and toothy mouth emphasized. A cream square on the forehead represents the nose, but it also reminds us that both the circle and the square appear in the central face. The large earplugs flanking the face are marked with a cross, suggesting the four directions, and with dots, reminiscent of the dotted night sky or the spotted pelt of a jaguar. The face is the center of a rectangular framed area divided in half, the left side painted black, the right side cream; one might think of night and day, the face representing the personified sun. Emerging from the earplugs of the solar face are four red bands which curl back to the middle of the top and bottom and join in top-view feline heads. From their mouths come four more bands, red on the cream background, cream on the black, which end again in feline heads. All the bands are marked with a fringe element suggestive of radiance. The bands can be identified as feline serpents, and they may be imagined to represent

the four directions as well as up and down. A space was saved on the cream side for a small conventional profile feline with a feline-serpent crest, its body marked with a cross. Profile figures commonly rank lower than comparable frontal figures, and the small scale of the feline and its eccentric position confirm its subordination to the central face, which ranks as a cult image (Kubler 1967: 5–7). The small feline might represent the shaman who is the intermediary between this world and the god or, perhaps, the god's active representative in the world.

A fine stone relief (fig. 203) representing a circular head, with four feline serpents emerging from its earplugs, within a quadrangular frame employs the same fundamental elements: the circular image of the heavens, here epitomized by a personified circle which may represent the sun, with the four directions symbolized by dragonlike monsters, all set within the shape of the earth. That the directional beasts emerge from the circle rather than from the square implies that the heavens have the superior reality and that the earth is in some sense supported from the heavens.

Granting the drift of symbolic meanings over the centuries, the fact remains that the art of Pashash becomes a coherent expression when interpreted on the basis of the cosmology of shamanism. The symbolism of the principal elements and relationships can be verbalized in shamanic terms without conspicuous omissions, but we must recognize the limitations of this explanation. The art of Pashash had a vast reservoir of symbolic meaning which was its particular cultural achievement, which distinguished it from its neighbors and from its predecessors and successors. We have a fragmentary visual record, but the narratives, music, and dances which amplified these images are unrecoverable. An attempt to verbalize the individual characteristics of Pashash art would result in another work of art with a merely conjectural relation to the ancient inspiration. Only the basic tradition, which was widely shared, can be analyzed objectively. Set in the broad tradition of shamanic religious expression, the uniqueness of the particular expression of Pashash art becomes clearer.

The recovery in the doorway offering of a large number of symbolic works of art set in their orig-

203. *Stone relief of a head with emanations.*
55 cm. high, 60.5 cm. wide.
Collection of the church, Cabana.

inal pattern provides an unusual opportunity to
consider the expression of the individual pieces
in relation to the total plan. At the top in the
center was a red stone cup (pl. 4), its redness
reinforced by iron red paint, which in Desana
terms is "the color of fecundity and of the blood
of living beings" (Reichel-Dolmatoff 1971: 24).
By analogy with the handled bottle and the
stone relief, we may interpret the images it bears
as the cult image of the personified heavens or
perhaps specifically as the sun accompanied by
its active terrestrial representative, the jaguar
(fig. 156). The red color implies the god's role as
creator.

Beside and below the red cup were four rep-

licas of it in unfired clay, two of them of yellow
clay, the color the Desana identify with the
"dwelling place of the Sun" (ibid.). The number
of unfired cups suggests that they signified the
god's presence at the four corners as well as at
the center.

The large group of lathe- and wheel-made
cups of stone and pottery surrounded the center
at a slightly lower level and may have represented the rotating celestial circle. The outer
and lowest ring consisted of various vessel
forms, all decorated with feline, snake, bird, and
rotary designs, as well as the bottle with the sun
face mentioned above. Notable were pairs of
effigy vessels representing jaguars and feline-

headed snakes and five (or perhaps six) feline serpents. The number of images in the outer ring does not seem to have been significant, but the general character of the ring appears to have emphasized the creator's active agents in the world of human experience as well as the monsters which symbolized the points of contact between the cosmic levels.

The central figure on the red stone cup has three attributes: the gesture of apparition, manifesting a divine presence; the stepped crown; and the tunic ornamented with the step design. The step design, as noted earlier, has connections with the serpent motif, but as it is represented here the effect is that of a stacked checkerboard, which is a jaguar design. On the other hand, by analogy with the design on the Sun Gate at Tiahuanaco, one might suggest that the design represents the cosmic mountain. I suspect that all these implications were present, but as minor themes. The mountain is divided and double, not the single form suggestive of a cosmic axis, and the characteristics of both the serpent and the jaguar designs have been merged. Tunics bearing this design are known in contemporary Moche art, and an actual Inca poncho bearing the design survives (Bennett 1954: fig. 118). The design appears to have been carefully calculated to embody characteristics of all the more specific designs, to be in fact a kind of universal symbol implying the jaguar serpents of the four directions and the mountain of the center of the cosmos. The rigid pose and the raised hands imply a central position which the design amplifies.

The appearance of the creator sun as a young man tells us that divine power can be invested in the human form, that the appearance of humanity is not inconsistent with immortality. That some kind of spiritual immortality was within the reach even of earthly people is shown by the offerings which accompanied the dead person. Perched on its high ridge behind its massive walls, Pashash is a dramatic image of insecurity. The militaristic foreign elite who ruled there asserted their right by an art style which manifested their alliance with the divine powers that rule the cosmos. Mortality, the ultimate insecurity, inspired the greatest outpouring of ritual power to maintain the stability of the earthly order by an access of divine energy.

Appendix 1. Radiocarbon Tests

Ten specimens of charcoal collected in the excavations were submitted to the Radiocarbon Laboratory of the University of Texas at Austin, under the direction of Dr. E. Mott Davis. The assay of age was calculated from a half life of 5,568 years, based on NBS oxalic acid 95% activity. A secondary standard was based on tree rings from a log from the Greenwade House identifying the years 1830 to 1835.

The radiocarbon ages and the associations of the specimens are listed below in age order, beginning with the earliest period. All the specimens were collected by me unless otherwise indicated. They were collected in various parts of the site; only Tx-1329 and Tx-1824 refer directly to the La Capilla burial and its offerings.

Specimen number: Tx-944
Age before present (1950): 1640±80
Associations: Cut 4, Level 4, 220 centimeters
Period (A.D.): 230–390
Comments: This sample was in the fill above the earliest Recuay period floor on the south terrace of La Capilla Hill. The floor sealed a pure Quinú period level. Only six potsherds were in Level 4. The test suggests late third century or early fourth century for the floor.

Specimen number: Tx-1332
Age before present (1950): 1610±170
Associations: Cut 9, Level 4, 170–210 centimeters
Period (A.D.): 170–510
Comments: The level in which this specimen was found consisted of stone fill laid in preparation for construction. The 137 potsherds in the level indicate early Recuay period in the ceramic sequence with some late Quinú, including white on red decoration, mixed in the fill. Early fourth century seems the probable period. The specimen was collected by John W. Smith.

Specimen number: Tx-1824
Age before present (1950): 1590±60
Associations: Cut 12, Level 4, 215 centimeters
Period (A.D.): 300–420
Comments: The specimen was charcoal in the earth fill over the La Capilla burial, found in soft grainy brown earth in the northeast corner of the excavation. From the style of the offerings the date can fall no later than the end of the Recuay Yaiá phase, and the charcoal may have been old when deposited. The last half of the fourth century is the probable period for the burning of the charcoal, which should fall in the earlier part of the Recuay period.

Specimen number: Tx-942
Age before present (1950): 1580±70
Associations: Cut 3, Level 2, 130–150 centimeters
Period (A.D.): 300–440
Comments: This level consisted of alluvium full of Recuay period potsherds. The charcoal probably dates the same as the potsherds, in a period centering on the middle of the fourth century. The specimen was collected by Hermilio Rosas.

Specimen number: Tx-940
Age before present (1950): 1500±90
Associations: Cut 3, Level 2, 100 centimeters
Period (A.D.): 360–540
Comments: The specimen was found slightly higher in the same level as Tx-942 but tested as younger, giving a period centering on the middle of the fifth century. That still associates plausibly with the Recuay period pottery in the level, which was alluvium collected on an old surface. It appears to be the mixed collection of debris one would expect in that situation. The specimen was collected by Hermilio Rosas.

Specimen number: Tx-941
Age before present (1950): 1490±70
Associations: Cut 4, Level 2, 160 centimeters
Period (A.D.): 390–530
Comments: The specimen was charcoal from logs about 10 centimeters in diameter, which probably served as rafters. Level 2 contained the remains of a burned roof of a Recuay period house, probably from the late fifth or early sixth century. The pottery is Recuay Huacohú phase.

Specimen number: Tx-1329
Age before present (1950): 1400±60
Associations: Cut 10, Level 4, 260 centimeters
Period (A.D.): 490–610
Comments: The specimen was charcoal in the fill dirt covering the doorway offering, associated with the elite burial in Cut 12, Level 6. The charcoal does not appear to have been offering material itself and thus may be older than the offering, but the offering cannot be older than the burning of the charcoal. This test must be compared with Tx-1824. At 1-sigma the dates do not overlap; at 2-sigma they overlap 430–480. Judging by the style of the offerings, which are mid-Recuay, a date at the end of the fifth or beginning of the sixth century is plausible, which suggests that this specimen was burnt about the time the offering was being assembled and that Tx-1824 was already old when deposited in the fill.

Specimen number: Tx-943
Age before present (1950): 1380±100
Associations: Cut 3, Level 4, 200–235 centimeters
Period (A.D.): 470–670
Comments: This level consisted of alluvium deposited over small stone walls, probably of domestic constructions built subsequent to El Caserón, against which this cut was set. This specimen should be compared with Tx-940 and 942 from Level 2 of the same cut, which tested as older despite their position nearer the surface. That may be an indication that erosion of primary deposits higher up the hill was resulting in inverted secondary deposition at this spot. The abundant potsherds—1,747 of which were recovered—are mostly Recuay Yaiá phase types. The specimen was collected by Hermilio Rosas.

Specimen number: Tx-1331
Age before present (1950): 1110±270
Associations: Cut 9, Level 3, 120 centimeters
Period (A.D.): 570–1110
Comments: The specimen consisted of powder and chips of charcoal which required cleaning before testing. It was part of the fill just under the latest floor built in the small house on the west edge of the top of La Capilla Hill. Judging by the associated pottery, the house was built at the beginning of the last phase—Huacohú—of the Recuay period, which may be plausibly dated at the end of the sixth century or perhaps the earliest years of the seventh. The specimen was collected by John W. Smith.

Specimen number: Tx-1330
Age before present (1950): 420±80
Associations: Cut 7, Level 4, 205 centimeters
Period (A.D.): 1450–1610
Comments: The cut was made to reveal the foundation of a large wall in the hope of determining its date or period. The sample was collected at the base of the wall on sterile soil. The very recent period indicated by the test shows that the wall was still clear of debris about the beginning of the colonial period and that recent farming of the site has produced the deep accumulation of debris from erosion.

Appendix 2. Catalog of the Contents of the La Capilla Burial Temple

All the objects listed here are deposited with the National Government of the Republic of Peru, in storage at the Museum of Pachacamac unless otherwise noted. Several items were deposited in the Artisans' Center in Cabana at the insistence of the local authorities. The items listed as "missing 8/6/75" or "8/7/75" were probably missing already by the evening of July 30, 1973, when all the excavated material was stolen from the locked storeroom of the Artisans' Center. A complete inventory of all the recovered material was never achieved until the field season of 1975.

The metal items are reproduced here on a scale of 1:1.05. The scale for the stone, wood, and bone items is 1:1.67. The other items, including all the ceramics, are reproduced on a scale of 1:2.08.

Items are numbered consecutively through all materials in each level or sector. Individual items are referred to by cut, level, and catalog numbers: for example 10/2.7, or catalog number 7 in Level 2 of Cut 10. The numbering order does not indicate the order in which items were discovered but, rather, tries to group items by material and form. Besides abbreviations for units of measurement, the following abbreviations are used: approx./approximately; diam./diameter; ext./exterior; fig./figure; int./interior; no./number; and pl./plate. Potsherds for each level are totaled at the end of that level.

For assistance in the identification of materials, I am indebted to many experts, among them Dr. Ernest Lundelius, Dr. Edward Jonas, Dr. Earl Ingerson, and Don Hamilton of the University of Texas; Dr. E. Mott Davis of the Radiocarbon Laboratory, the University of Texas; and the U.S. Department of Agriculture, Forest Products Laboratory.

Cut 10: La Capilla Temple

Level 1

Sector A. Area 1.6 x 1 m. outside the north wall of the temple chamber.

Stone
1. Drilled slate circle, approx. 8.7 to 7.3 x 1.2 cm.
2. Stone mortar, approx. 10 cm. high, 22 x 25 cm., irregular. See also fig. 80.
3. Granite stone, rounded, about 9.7 x 6.9 x 5.5 cm., probably a pestle.
4. Granite stone, rounded, probably a pestle.

Ceramics
5. Fragments of large Pashash Orange Plain jars and basins (Forms B-3 and E-4).

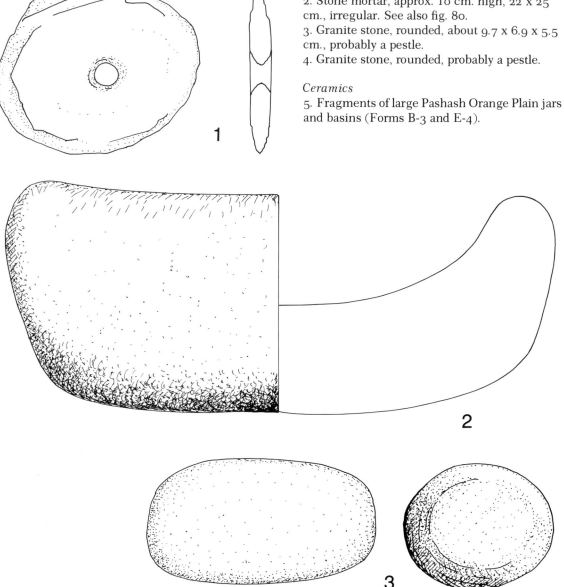

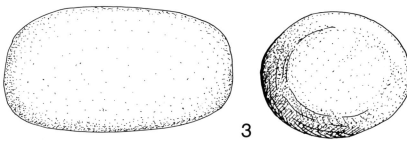

Sector B. Interior of the temple chamber, 4 x 4.3
m. The actual thickness of the earth deposit in
this level varied from 125 cm. at the east wall,
whose top was considered the zero point for all
measurements in this cut, to 50 cm. at the
doorway in the west wall.

Stone
1. Green stone cup, 6.8 cm. high x 6.8 cm. wide.
A hooded face is carved on one side; the other
half is missing. See also fig. 98.
2. Green stone cup, two fragments. The larger,
6.7 x 5.1 cm., has a carved "ear" or handle; the
smaller, 3 x 3.5 cm., has a rim. 5 mm. maximum
wall thickness. See also fig. 99.
3. Four fragments (three of which fit together)
of a red stone cup, base and about half the rim
missing. About 10 cm. diam., 6 cm. wall height.
Wall thins to 1 mm. at base.
4. Block, 16 x 9 x 12.5 cm. One face 9 x 16 cm.
incised with a three-part fret pattern.
Deposited in the Artisans' Center, Cabana.

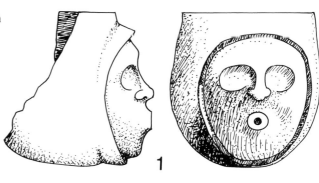

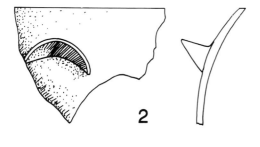

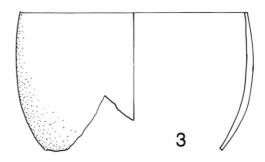

5. Mortar, granite, half of top broken away. Approx. 18 cm. high, 18 cm. diam. See also fig. 80.
6. Polished granitic stone carved to represent an animal, probably a guinea pig, 13.8 x 9 x 5 cm. See also fig. 100.
7. Polished stone, 3 x 3.3 cm.
8. Half of a doughnut-shaped stone, probably a club head, 12.7 cm. diam. Deposited in the Artisans' Center, Cabana.
9. Fragment of a rough stone bowl, 6 cm. diam.
10. Fragment of a rough stone bowl, 8 cm. diam.
11. Four pieces of stone showing human work. Left in the Artisans' Center, Cabana.

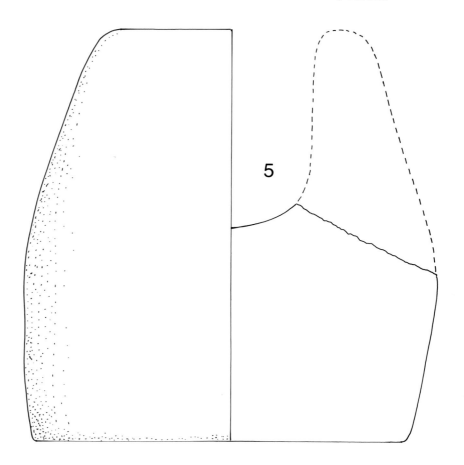

5

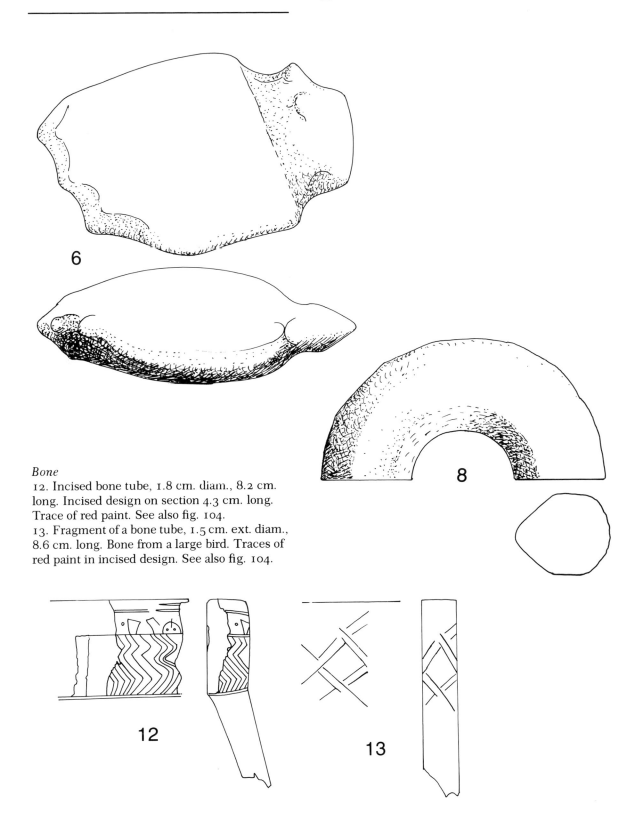

Bone

12. Incised bone tube, 1.8 cm. diam., 8.2 cm. long. Incised design on section 4.3 cm. long. Trace of red paint. See also fig. 104.

13. Fragment of a bone tube, 1.5 cm. ext. diam., 8.6 cm. long. Bone from a large bird. Traces of red paint in incised design. See also fig. 104.

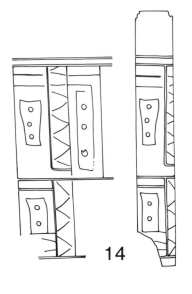

14. Bone tube, complete except for small piece broken from one end. 1.6 cm. diam., 11.2 cm. long. Incised design, red paint. See also fig. 104.
15. Fragmentary bone tube, 8.2 cm. long. Bone of a large mammal, possibly human. Drilled pits, incised lines, and excised areas, with many traces of red paint. See also fig. 105.
16. Fragmentary bone tube, 9 cm. long. Large mammal (llama, deer, puma, jaguar, or possibly human). Incised design of four connected diamonds, traces of red paint. See also fig. 106.
17. Bone pendant, 10 cm. long. Biconical suspension hole at one end, with some lateral incised lines. See also fig. 104.

14

15

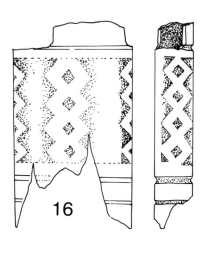

16

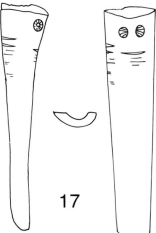

17

Metal

18. Cover from the end of a staff or shaft, made of sheet copper. Forged rectangular nail in place. Cover 2.5 cm. diam., 4 cm. long, open at both ends. Fragments of wood identified as hardwood of the Dicotyledoneae group. See also fig. 129.

Ceramics

19. Solid humanlike effigy head, 4.3 cm. relief, 3.5 x 3.3 cm. Appears to have projected from the shoulder of a vessel. Clay is crude ware, probably imported. See also fig. 45.

20. Hollow head, probably of a guinea pig, 5 cm. relief, 8 x 8 cm. Pashash Orange Plain with traces of white slip. Appears to have projected from the shoulder of a large vessel. See also fig. 44.

21. Four-legged animal with a tail, 6.5 cm. long, 4 cm. high. Pashash Orange Plain.

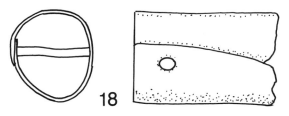

18

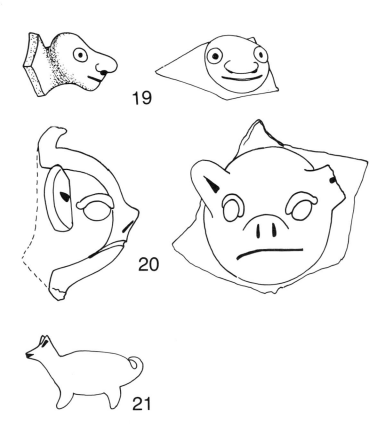

19

20

21

Sector C. 1 m. wide by 3 m. along the outside of the west, or front, wall of the temple chamber, infringing on the doorway. There was only about 50 cm. of soil in this sector. The stone cups and whole ceramic vessels may have been associated with the burial represented by the human bones.

Bone
1. Disarticulated bones of an adult human. The burial had been disturbed and partially eroded out of the ground. The bones were located directly against the outside of the left side of the doorway. Vertebrae, part of the lower jaw, ribs, and long bones were represented.

Stone
2. Fragments of a green stone cup, pedestal base 3.8 cm. diam.
3. Fragments of a green stone cup, pedestal base 4.5 cm. diam.
4. Yellow brown mottled stone pedestal cup, restored, with two sections missing. 7.1 cm. high, 10.6 cm. diam., 4.28 cm. diam. of pedestal base.

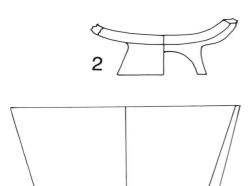

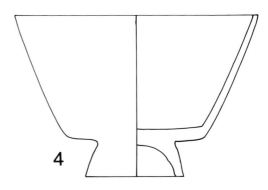

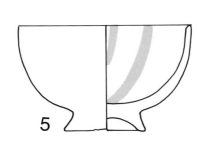

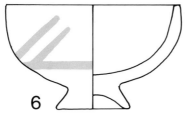

Ceramics
5. Pashash Orange Painted pedestal cup, 5.8 cm. high, 9.5 cm. diam. Red cross painted on int. Irregular. See also fig. 39.
6. Pashash Orange Painted pedestal cup, approx. 5.8 cm. x 9.5 cm. diam. Red lines on ext.
7. Pashash Orange Painted pedestal cup, approx. 5.8 cm. x 9.5 cm. diam. Red line on int. See also fig. 39.
8. Pashash Orange Painted pedestal cup, approx. 5 cm. high x 8.5 cm. diam. Cream slip, red diagonal lines on ext. Red line on int. See also fig. 39.

9. Pashash Orange Painted pedestal cup, approx. 4.8 cm. high x 7 cm. diam. Two pale black bands around ext. Red line in int. See also fig. 39.

10. Pashash Orange Painted pedestal cup, 4.5 cm. high, 8.9 cm. diam. Red lines on int. and ext. Broken in half. See also fig. 39.

11. Pashash Orange Painted pedestal cup, 5 cm. high, 8.2 cm. rim diam. Pairs of red lines on ext., red line on int. See also fig. 39.

12–19. Pashash Orange Painted pedestal cups, crude ware with casual red lines as the only decoration.

20. Fragments of Pashash Orange Plain cup (Form F-4).

21. Lower half of Pashash Orange Plain cup (Form F-4).

22. Pashash Orange Painted jar (Form K), 11 cm. high, 7 cm. diam. Cream slip. Badly cracked. See also fig. 39.

23–26. Fragments representing four small jars (Form K) and one complete vessel (Form K) in Pashash Orange Plain.

27. Pashash Orange Painted jar (Form K). Red lines. Broken. See fig. 51.

28. Caserón Orange Painted handled bowl (Form H-2), 5.5 cm. high, 12 cm. diam. White slip, painted int. and ext. except handle and base. Int. floor: warrior head in helmet. Int. walls: crested feline serpents, double-headed, with four-part design in circle. Ext. walls: birds with large beaks. Repaired. See fig. 137.

29. Total potsherds in Level 1: 4,868
Pashash Orange Plain: 2,726
   Painted: 115
Vista Brown Plain: 328
   Red-slipped: 7
Caserón Orange Plain: 598
   Painted: 362
   Resist: 84
Cabana Cream Plain: 322
   Painted: 202
   Resist: 64
Horno Black: 22
Horno Buff Plain: 22
   Painted: 9
Unclassified (trade wares?): 7

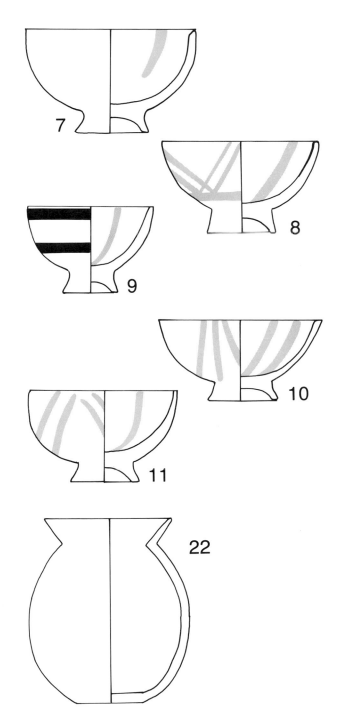

Level 2

Bone

1. Three small fitting fragments of carved mammal bone. Traces of red paint. See also fig. 108.
2. Ulna of a condor, carved and painted red; restored and nearly complete. About 11 cm. long. See also fig. 109.
3. Bird bone, 9.1 cm. long, 2.2 cm. diam. Rings incised around ends. Two painted red, the other black. See also fig. 107.

Stone

6. Game board of architectural model (?), 23.5 x 20 x 9.8 cm. There are twenty-one sunken compartments in diagonal symmetry on one 23.5 x 20 cm. surface (the top); the bottom is plain. Conventional Recuay feline designs are incised on the 9.8 x 23.5 cm. sides. See also figs. 28, 96.

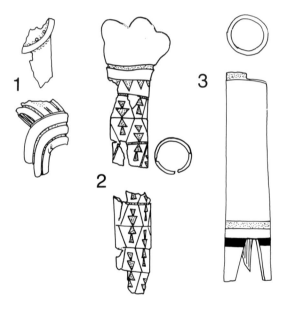

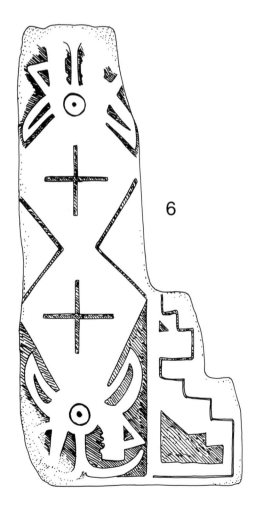

Metal

4. Copper strip, 1.8 x 5 cm. x 1 mm. thick, with five diamond-shaped holes pierced through it. See also fig. 110.
5. Fragments of copper wire about 1 mm. thick in curls about 5 cm. diam. See fig. 110.

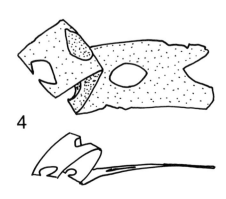

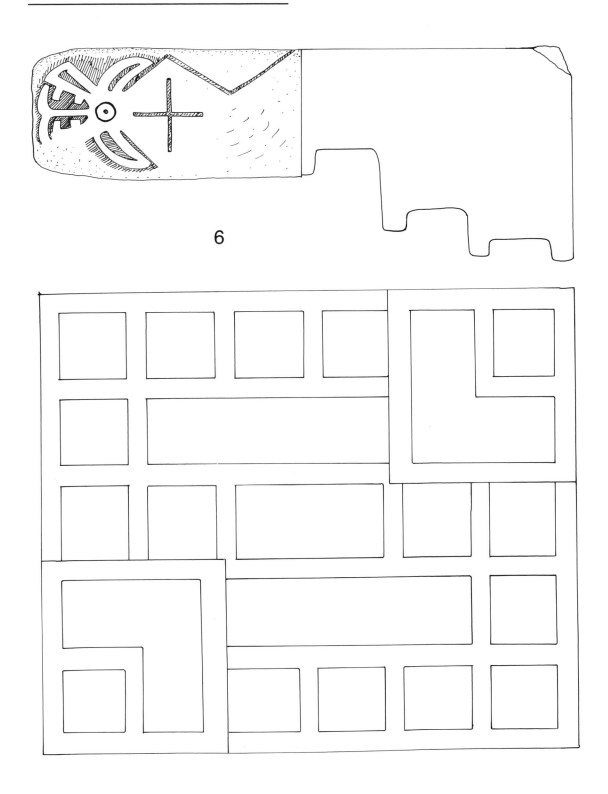

6

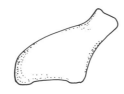

7

7. Polished black granitic stone in the form of an animal, probably a guinea pig, 4.3 x 3.4 x 1.4 cm. See also fig. 101.
8. White coral, 6 cm. long. See fig. 83.
9. White coral, 4.5 cm. long. See fig. 83.
10. Three small pieces of stone showing human work. Left in the Artisans' Center, Cabana.

Ceramics
11. Total potsherds in Level 2: 1,246
Pashash Orange Plain: 745
  Painted: 39
Vista Brown: 36
Caserón Orange Plain: 150
  Painted: 101
  Resist: 12
Cabana Cream Plain: 76
  Painted: 67
  Resist: 12
Horno Black: 4
Horno Buff: 2
Unclassified (trade wares?): 2 (from one vessel)

Level 3

Stone

1. Pierced stone, 17.5 x 7.5 x 4 cm., with a sub-rectangular hole 4.3 x 3.5 cm., 6 cm. from one end. Use unknown.
2. Rim fragment of black stone bowl. Other fragments of the same vessel appear in Level 4.
3. Red stone in the form of a grasshopper, 5 x 2.3 x 1.4 cm. See also fig. 102.
4. Irregularly shaped white stone, 5.5 x 4.8 x 2.5 cm. See also fig. 103.

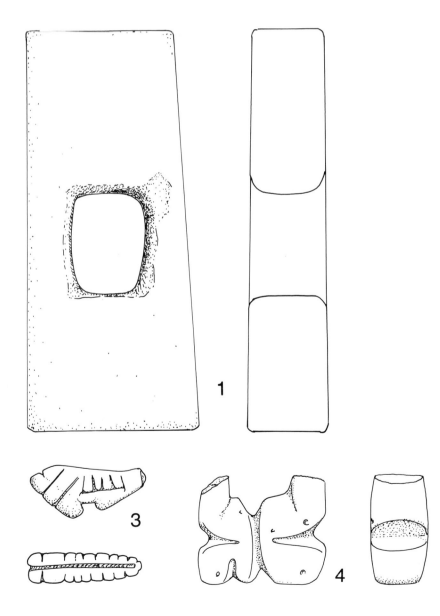

Ceramics

5. Fragments of about half of a large basin, approx. 68 cm. diam., 40 cm. base diam., 27 cm. high. A few pieces of this vessel were also found in Level 4. The vessel was broken and its pieces scattered throughout the last layer of fill. Caserón Orange Painted, walls 7 mm. thick, orange slip, red paint, and thin red wash. Int. floor: organic cross with double-hook ends. Int. walls: framed panels of smiling heads with emanations, alternating with crested felines. Ext.: plain. See fig. 136.

6. Horno Black bowl (Form F-4), about one-third of wall. Original size about 7 cm. high, 11.6 cm. diam. Engraved design. Two more sherds of this vessel were found in 4.50.

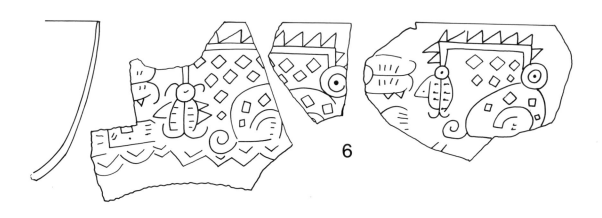

6

7. Total potsherds in Level 3: 1,129
Pashash Orange Plain: 551
   Painted: 24
Vista Brown Plain: 76
   Red-slipped: 8
Caserón Orange Plain: 147
   Painted: 101
   Resist: 22
Cabana Cream Plain: 58
   Painted: 59
   Resist: 63
Horno Black: 11 (two are pedestal bases)
Horno Buff: 7
Unclassified (trade wares?): 2

Level 4

Stone

1. Red stone pedestal cup (Form G), 7.3 cm. high, 10.5 cm. diam., with two relief figures of a crowned frontal god alternating with two profile rampant jaguars. Green stone inlays in gods' eyes and crowns, jaguar pelage spots. About half of the inlays are missing. Traces of iron red paint. See also figs. 31, 87, 156, pl. 4.

2. Black stone pedestal cup (Form G), 7.9 cm. high, 10.26 cm. diam. Break in rim. See also figs. 31, 87, 89, 91.

3. Green stone pedestal cup, 7.3 cm. high. 11.15 cm. diam. All the green stones are silicified clastic iron-rich volcanic rock. See also figs. 31, 87, 90, 92.

4. Green stone pedestal cup, restored fragments. 7.5 cm. high, 10.2 cm. diam. See also figs. 31, 87.

5. Green stone pedestal cup, fragments. Base originally about 4.2 cm. diam. See fig. 31.

6. Green stone pedestal cup, fragments. See fig. 31.

7. Red stone pedestal cup, fragments. See fig. 31.

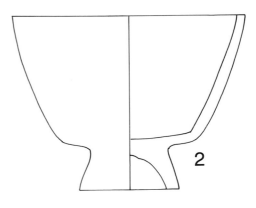

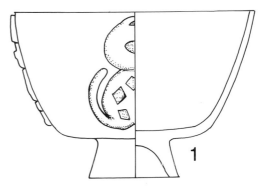

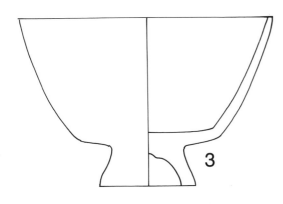

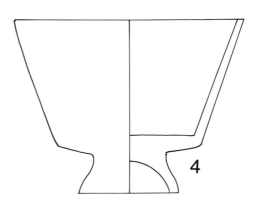

8. Black stone pedestal cup, fragment with rim and base. 7.3 cm. high, 4.6 cm. base diam. A rim fragment of this vessel was found in Level 3 (no. 2). Rim approx. 11 cm. diam. See also figs. 31, 87.

9. Black stone pedestal cup, five fitting fragments, one side of rim missing. 6.2 cm. high, 9.3 cm. diam., 4.9 cm. base diam. See also figs. 31, 87.

10. Black and tan stone cup (Form F-4), six fitting fragments. 4.23 cm. high, 10 cm. diam. Smooth base, but had a glued-on pedestal base, the mark of which is still visible. Part of wall and rim missing. See also figs. 31, 87.

11. Irregular rectangular pierced stone. One side tapers from 23 cm. to 20.5 cm., another from 26 cm. to 25.3 cm. 6.5 cm. thick. Hole is 8.4 x 9 cm. Deposited in the Artisans' Center, Cabana. See also figs. 31, 80.

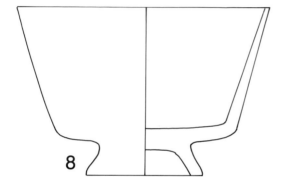

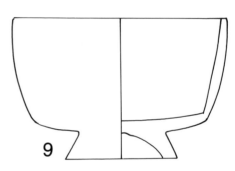

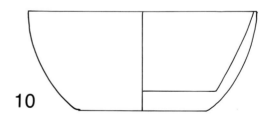

Unfired clay

12. Red pedestal cup, fragments. Alternating reliefs of crowned gods and rampant feline with turquoise inlays. See fig. 31.

13. Brown pedestal cup, fragment preserved. Reliefs as in no. 12. See fig. 31.

14. Yellow pedestal cup, fragment preserved. Reliefs as in no. 12. Diam. about 12 cm. See figs. 31, 77.

15. Yellow pedestal cup. Reliefs as in no. 12. See figs. 31, 77–79.

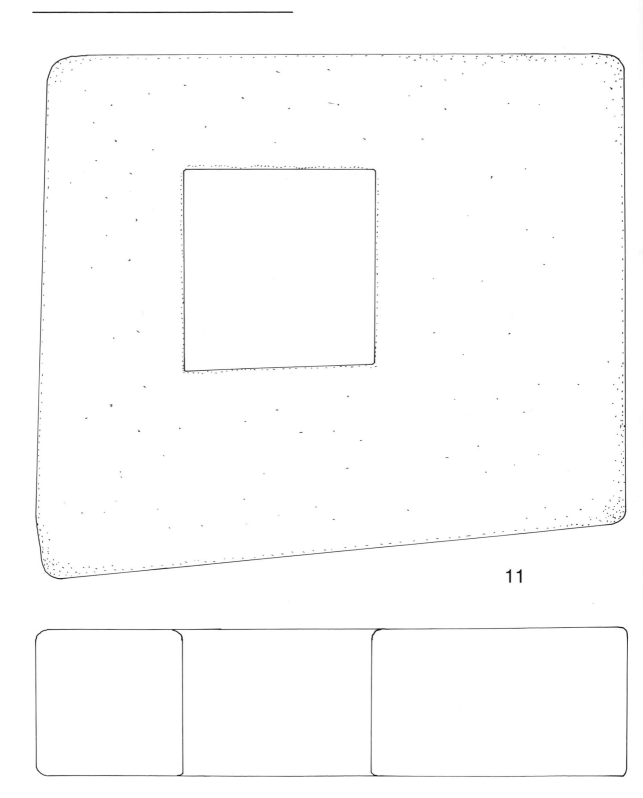

11

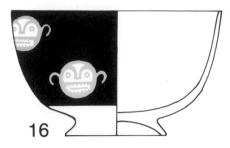

16

17

18

Ceramics

Nos. 16–41 are Cabana Cream Resist pedestal cups. They were made in sets designated by capital letters F–K, with three unique vessels (nos. 39, 40, 41) not assigned to a set. Sets G, J, and K appear to be the work of individual artists. Sets J and K include vessels in Cut 12 (see chap. 5), and those artists have been given nicknames, J being called the Vulture Painter from his special subject and K being called Red Football from his signature on vessels in Cut 12.

The other sets are evidently the work of several artists, each one usually making two similar vessels. Set I, for example, includes eight vessels which fall into subject pairs designated by lowercase letters a–d, each pair probably decorated by a single painter. The signature, an incised cross, on nos. 30 and 31 and the different frontal faces on nos. 34 and 35 imply different artists, despite the great similarities. The social and technical meanings of the sets are uncertain: they may identify artists, studio workshops, or patrons' requirements.

16. Pedestal cup, Cabana Cream Resist. 6.9 cm. high, 10.6 cm. diam. Ext.: two registers of frontal faces, red on cream, black background. Complete except for break in rim. Int.: plain. Set F. See also figs. 31, 72, 138.

17. Pedestal cup, Cabana Cream Resist. 6.9 cm. high, 11.4 cm. diam. Ext.: black with two registers of frontal faces, red on cream, four faces to each register. Int.: plain, red stain. One wall broken, otherwise complete. Set F. See also fig. 31.

18. Pedestal cup, Cabana Cream Resist. Approx. 7 cm. high, 10.6 cm. diam. Ext.: black with two registers of red on cream frontal faces. Int.: plain. In fragments, not reconstructed. Set F. See also fig. 31.

19. Pedestal cup, Cabana Cream Resist. 7 cm. high, 11 cm. diam. Ext.: six felines, cream on black background, alternating tongues up and down ending in feline heads. Int.: plain. One wall broken. Set G. See also fig. 31.

20. Pedestal cup, Cabana Cream Resist. 6.7 cm. high, 11.7 cm. diam. Ext.: nine cream felines on black, feline-headed tongues alternately up and down. Int.: four frontal warriors, full-figure, wearing two-lobed headdresses, red on cream. Broken, not restored. Set G. See also figs. 31, 152.

21. Pedestal cup, Cabana Cream Resist. Approx. 6.9 cm. high, 11 cm. diam. Ext.: cream felines with feline-headed tongues, alternately up and down, on black. Int.: plain. In fragments, not reconstructed. Set G. See also figs. 31, 163.

22. Pedestal cup, Cabana Cream Resist. Approx. 7 cm. high, 11 cm. diam. Ext.: felines with feline-headed tongues, alternately up and down, cream on black. Int.: plain. In fragments, not reconstructed. Set G. See also fig. 31.

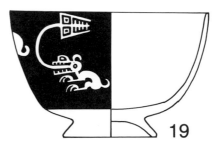

19

20

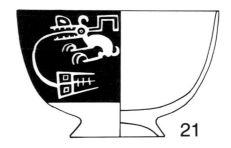

21

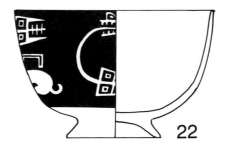

22

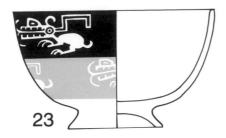

23

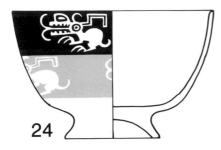

24

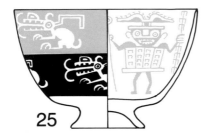

25

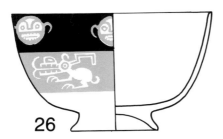

26

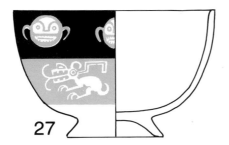

27

23. Pedestal cup, Cabana Cream Resist. 6.5 cm. high, 11.1 cm. diam. Ext.: two registers—upper cream felines on black, lower cream felines on red. Int.: plain. Restored. Set H. See also figs. 31, 76, 161.

24. Pedestal cup, Cabana Cream Resist. Approx. 7 cm. high, 11 cm. diam. Ext.: two registers—upper cream felines on black, lower cream felines on red. Int.: plain. Partially restored. Set H. See also fig. 31.

25. Pedestal cup, Cabana Cream Resist. 6.6 cm. high, 10 cm. diam. Ext.: two registers—upper cream felines on red, lower cream felines on black. Int.: four full-figure frontal warriors, red on cream. Reconstructed except for base. Set H. See also figs. 31, 152.

26. Pedestal cup, Cabana Cream Resist. 6.5 cm. high, 11 cm. diam. Ext.: two registers—upper red on cream frontal faces on black, lower cream felines on red. Int.: plain. Complete. Set H. See also figs. 31, 160.

27. Pedestal cup, Cabana Cream Resist. Approx. 7 cm. high, 11 cm. diam. Ext.: two registers—upper red on cream frontal faces on black, lower cream felines on red. Int.: plain. In fragments, not reconstructed. Set H. See also fig. 31.

28. Pedestal cup, Cabana Cream Resist. 6.9 cm. high, 11.1 cm. diam. Ext.: black background, upper register red on cream frontal faces, lower register cream felines. Int.: plain. Slight restorations. Set I, a. See also fig. 31.

29. Pedestal cup, Cabana Cream Resist. 7 cm. high, 10.3 cm. diam. Ext.: black background with red and cream frontal faces alternating with cream felines in two registers. Int.: plain. Complete except for half of base. Set I, a. See also fig. 31.

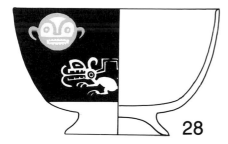 

30. Pedestal cup, Cabana Cream Resist. 7 cm. high, 11 cm. diam. Ext.: black background, three registers—top and bottom alternating frontal faces in red on cream with cream felines, middle feline serpents in cream. Int.: plain. Cross incised in base. Reconstructed. Set I, b. See also figs. 31, 173.

31. Pedestal cup, Cabana Cream Resist. Approx. 7 cm. high, 11 cm. diam. Ext.: black background with two registers of alternating red and cream frontal faces and cream felines. Int.: plain. Cross incised in base. In fragments, not reconstructed. Set I, b. See also fig. 31.

 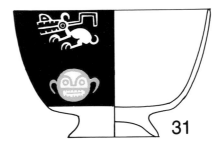

32. Pedestal cup, Cabana Cream Resist. Approx. 7 cm. high, 11 cm. diam. Ext.: black background with two registers alternating red on cream frontal faces and felines with feline-headed tongues. Int.: plain. In fragments, not reconstructed. Set I, c. See also fig. 31.

33. Pedestal cup, Cabana Cream Resist. Approx. 7 cm. high, 11 cm. diam. Ext.: black background with two registers alternating red on cream frontal faces and felines with feline-headed tongues in cream. Int.: plain. In fragments, not reconstructed. Set I, c. See also fig. 31.

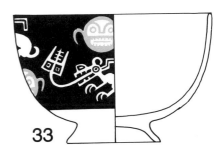

34. Pedestal cup, Cabana Cream Resist. Approx. 6.6 cm. high, 10.4 cm. diam. Ext.: black background, two registers alternating red on cream frontal faces with rectangular noses and cream felines without crests. Int.: plain. In fragments, not reconstructed. Set I, d. See also fig. 31.

35. Pedestal cup, Cabana Cream Resist. Approx. 7 cm. high, 11 cm. diam. Ext.: black background, two registers alternating red on cream frontal faces with rectangular noses and cream felines with crests. Int.: plain. In fragments, not reconstructed. Set I, d. See also fig. 31.

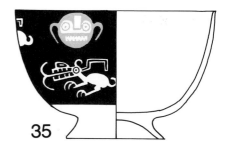

36. Pedestal cup, Cabana Cream Resist. 7 cm.
high, 10.7 cm. diam. Ext.: black background
with cream condors or vultures and felines. Int.:
plain. Reconstructed. Set J, the Vulture Painter.
See also figs. 31, 67.

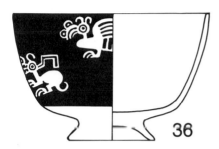

37. Pedestal cup, Cabana Cream Resist. 7 cm.
high, 10 cm. diam. Ext.: black background with
six cream felines with feline-headed tongues
and crests of chained loops. Int.: plain. Reconstructed; surface chipped. Set K, Red Football.
See also figs. 31, 70.
38. Pedestal cup, Cabana Cream Resist. Approx.
7.8 cm. high, 12 cm. diam. Ext.: black background, three registers of cream felines, their
tongues forming next feline. Int.: plain. Partially
reconstructed. Set K, Red Football. See also figs.
31, 70–71.

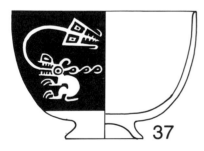

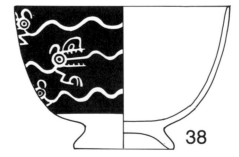

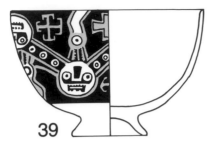

39

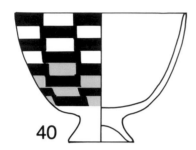

40

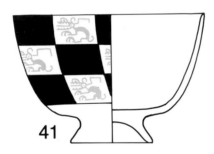

41

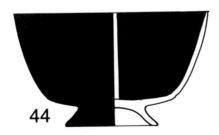

44

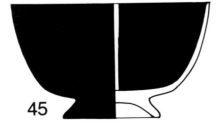

45

39. Pedestal cup, Cabana Cream Resist. 7 cm. high, 10.5 cm. diam. Ext.: zigzag-linked frontal faces with crosses and feline serpents in red, cream, and black. Int.: plain. Reconstructed. See also figs. 31, 47.

40. Pedestal cup, Cabana Cream Resist. 7 cm. high, 9.2 cm. diam. Ext.: in two levels—upper black and cream checkerboard, lower black and red checkerboard. Int.: plain. Restored. See also fig. 31.

41. Pedestal cup, Cabana Cream Resist. Approx. 7 cm. high, 10.5 cm. diam. Ext.: three registers checkerboard; black squares and red felines on cream. Int.: plain. Partially restored, except base. See also fig. 31.

42. Pedestal base, Cabana Cream Plain.

43. Pedestal base fragment, Cabana Cream Painted. Red paint on ext.

44. Pedestal cup, Horno Black. 6.1 cm. high, 10.7 cm. diam. Complete except for chipped rim.

45. Pedestal cup, Horno Black. 6.3 cm. high, 11 cm. diam. Broken, not reconstructed.

46. Pedestal base, Horno Black.

47. Pedestal base, Horno Black. Good wheel marks.

48. Pedestal base, Horno Black. Fragment. Wheel marks.

49. Pedestal cup, Horno Black. Fragment of base and floor.

50. Fragment of bowl (probably Form F-4), Horno Black. Originally 7 cm. high, 11.6 cm. diam. Engraved design. 10/3.6 is another sherd from this vessel.

51. Feline effigy, Cabana Cream Resist. 13 cm.
high, 13 cm. long. Pedestal base. Diamond
spots, tail curls to spout. Restored. See also figs.
31, 61.

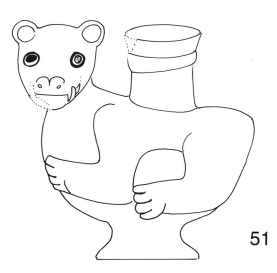

51

52. Feline effigy, Cabana Cream Resist. 13 cm.
high, 13 cm. long. Pedestal base. Diamond spots
in cream resist on black, red on belly. Part of
spout missing. Restored. See also figs. 31,
62–63.

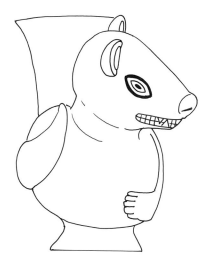

52

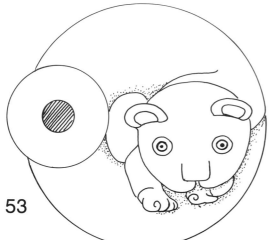

53

53. Feline-headed serpent-bodied effigy, Cabana Cream Resist. 13.5 cm. diam. Buff slip, alternate panels of resist on black and white designs on red. Large "smiling" mouth. Complete. See also figs. 31, 60.

54. Serpent-bodied effigy, Cabana Cream Resist. 20 cm. diam. Feline (?) head broken off; originally about 14 cm. high; now 10 cm. high. Humanlike arms grasp head of naked human male. Serpent body decorated with interlocking triangles in black on cream resist and red stripe on faded resist step-fret pattern. Partly restored. See also figs. 31, 54.

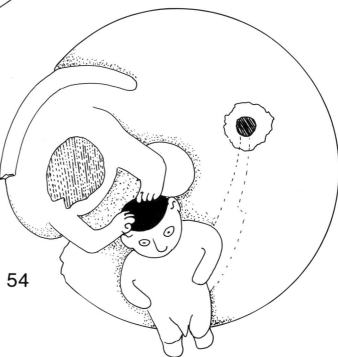

54

55. Feline-headed serpent-bodied effigy, Cabana Cream Resist. 15 cm. diam., 14 cm. high. Eyes are blank (faded), pairs of fangs on each side of open mouth. Arms missing. Black on cream resist interlocking triangles on body and red, black, and cream step-fret. Partly restored. See also figs. 31, 55.

56. Serpent-bodied effigy with feline head, Cabana Cream Resist. 12 cm. diam., 9.5 cm. high. Black on cream checkerboard on back of head; black stripes on face; red, black, and cream stripes on body. Restored. See also figs. 31, 59, pl. 5.

57. Serpent effigy with feline head, Cabana Cream Resist. 21 x 16 cm., 10.7 cm. high. Black on cream resist and red paint; red spots on ears. Restored. See also figs. 31, 56.

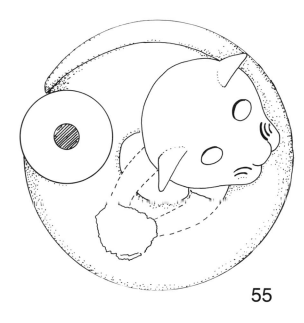

55

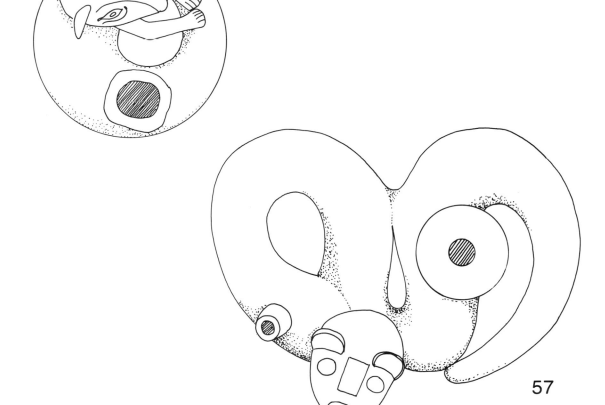

56

57

58. Serpent effigy with feline head, Caserón Orange Resist. About 20 cm. diam., 10.5 cm. high. N-curve to body. Diamond chain pattern on body. Restored, but parts missing on right side of head. See also figs. 31, 57.

59. Feline-headed serpent-bodied effigy, Cabana Cream Resist. About 12 cm. diam. Arms rest on tail. Bands of black whiskers flank nose. In fragments, unreconstructed. See also figs. 31, 58.

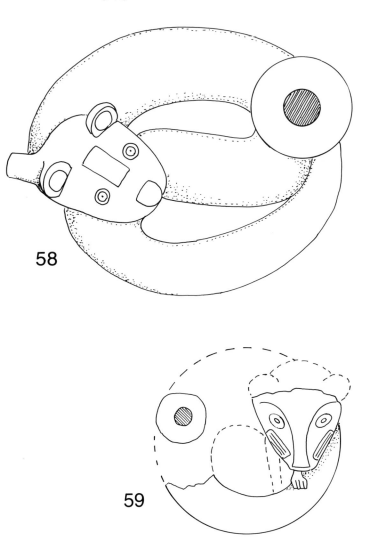

58

59

60. Spouted basin (Form I), Caserón Orange
Painted. Approx. 13.5 cm. high, 20 cm. diam.
Fragments found in Levels 2–5 of Cut 10. Ext.:
white with framed panels of red birds and black
steps, border of step and curl. Int.: S-curves
with crosses, step border. Partially reconstructed. See also figs. 31, 182.
61. Bowl (Form F-1), Cabana Cream Painted.
13 cm. diam. Ext.: plain. Int.: red on cream;
border of step and angular linear fret, wall of
alternating serpent-crested feline and double-
headed crested feline in red-framed panels. Delicate linear style. Restored. See also fig. 31.
62. Bowl (Form F-1), Cabana Cream Resist. 6.5
cm. high, 14 cm. diam. Ext.: black on cream
step border, black crosses and diagonal crosshatching in alternating panels. Int.: plain. Restored. See also fig. 31.

60

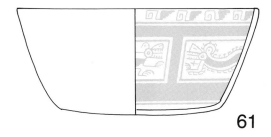

61

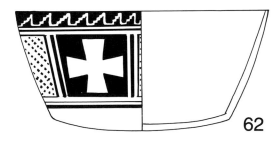

62

63. Bowl (Form F-1), Cabana Cream Resist. Exact duplicate of no. 62. Restored, parts still missing. See fig. 31.

64. Spout-handled vessel (Form N), Cabana Cream Resist. 23.5 cm. high. Top is orange. Front has head with emanations and a feline in red, orange, and resist black in a red frame. Back has black resist double-headed feline monster, vertical. Restored. See also fig. 31, pl. 2.

65. Jar with neck flange (Form D-2), Cabana Cream Resist. About 18 cm. high, 19 cm. diam. Ext.: panels black on cream resist with pale orange of crested feline, whirling design, spotted diamonds; shoulder border of stepped triangles. Int.: plain. Partially reconstructed. See also figs. 31, 200.

66. Large vessel, form uncertain, Cabana Cream Resist. Fragment 16 cm. high. Original vessel diam. over 20 cm. Ext.: red, cream, and black cross with hooked ends as feline heads in one panel, another panel of double-headed crested feline with tongues as crested felines.

64

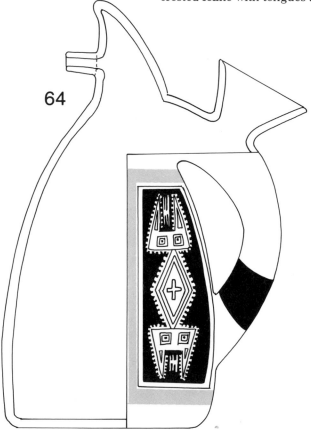

65

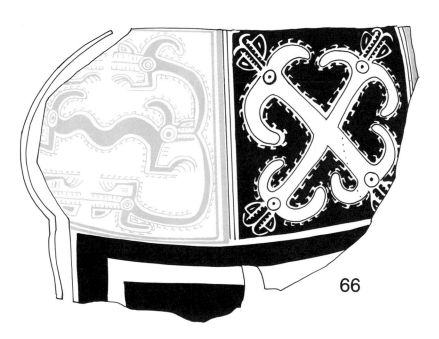

66

67. Jar (Form B-5), Cabana Cream Resist. 29 cm. high, 13 cm. diam. Pinkish paste, cream slip. Serpent body in effigy around shoulder of vessel, feline head in relief, red, black, and cream resist. Restored; sherds scattered through levels 4 and 5.

68. Total potsherds in Level 4 not definitely part of offering vessels: 680
Pashash Orange Plain: 396
   Painted: 37
Vista Brown: 6
Caserón Orange Plain: 62
   Painted: 50
   Resist: 14
Cabana Cream Plain: 37
   Painted: 9
   Resist: 64
Horno Black: 5

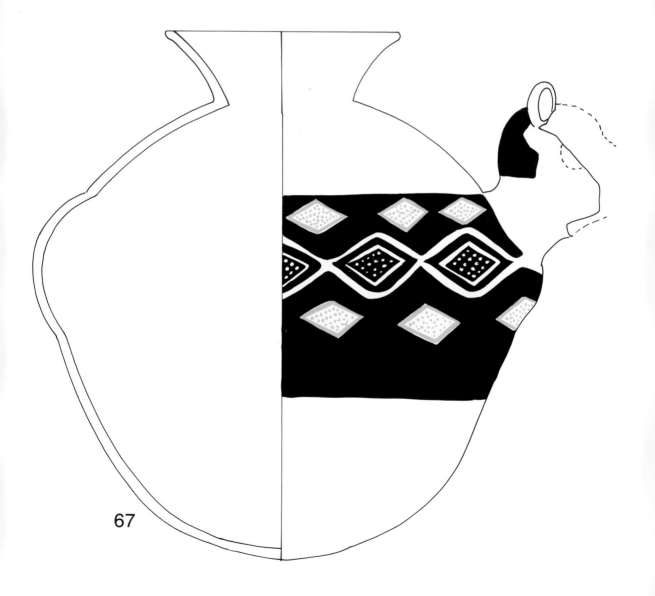

67

Level 5

Metal
1. Ten copper bells, each 5 x 5.5 x 3 cm., lying as if strung together. 315 cm. deep in the west wall of the excavation 180 to 200 cm. from the east wall. See also fig. 110.

Ceramics
2. Fragments of at least four large Pashash Orange Plain jars. One had a hollow conical handle (Form H), and one had a flange below the rim (Form D). All had round bases. They appear to have been intentionally broken and laid at the 300 to 315 cm. level just west of the offering cloth.
3. Simple bowl (Form E-2), Pashash Orange Plain with red slip. Irregular, about 20 cm. diam. Dusted with red pigment powder. This bowl was nested in nos. 4 and 5; the group was the lowest level of the offering, 345 cm. deep, lying 160 cm. west of the east wall.
4. Simple bowl (Form E-2), Pashash Orange Plain. Contained about half a cup of red pigment. Irregular, about 20 cm. diam.
5. Simple bowl (Form E-2), Pashash Orange Plain. Contained red pigment; nos. 4 and 3 nested in it. About 20 cm. diam.

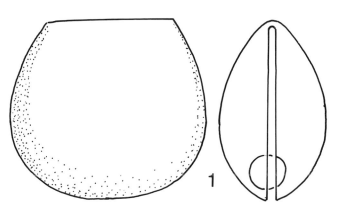

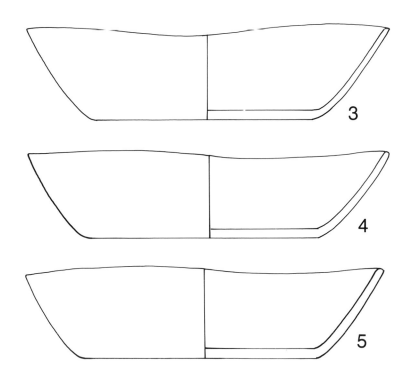

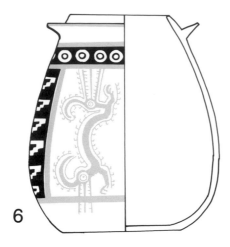

6

7

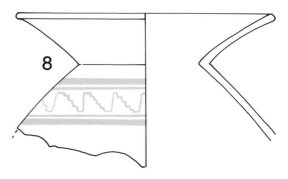

8

6. Jar with flange below rim (Form D-2), Cabana Cream Resist. About 12 cm. high, about 8 cm. rim diam. Ext.: border of cream circle-dot on black. Red framed panels, black on cream steps, and red double-headed felines. Int.: plain. Unrestored.

7. Cup (Form F-1 with flatter base), Cabana Cream Resist. About 8 cm. high. Ext.: border of cream step fret on black, red-framed panels of cream felines on black. Int.: plain. Unrestored.

8. Jar (Form B-9), Cabana Cream Painted. About 14 cm. diam. Red step patterns in borders. Int.: plain. Unrestored.

9. Total potsherds in Level 5: 112

Pashash Orange Plain: 17

Vista Brown Plain: 1
   Red-slipped: 2 (one painted)

Caserón Orange Plain: 11
   Painted: 30
   Resist: 23

Cabana Cream Plain: 4
   Painted: 12
   Resist: 12

Cut 11: La Capilla Temple

Level 2

Bone
1. Human skeleton, very badly decayed, in extended position with the head toward the east, but oriented to the building wall, not the cardinal directions. Adult.
2. Bird bone, 5.5 cm. long.

Shell
3. Four snail shells, scattered among the human bones in the area of the legs and feet.

Stone
4. Calcite concretion, stalagmite, 11 cm. long. See also fig. 84.
5. Gray slate palette, very carefully worked, 6.6 x 5 x 1.2 cm. See also fig. 85.

Ceramics
6. Total potsherds in Level 2: 323
Pashash Orange Plain: 163
  Painted: 2
Vista Brown: 14
Caserón Orange Plain: 73
  Painted: 23
  Resist: 14
Cabana Cream Plain: 9
  Painted: 9
  Resist: 14
Horno Black: 2

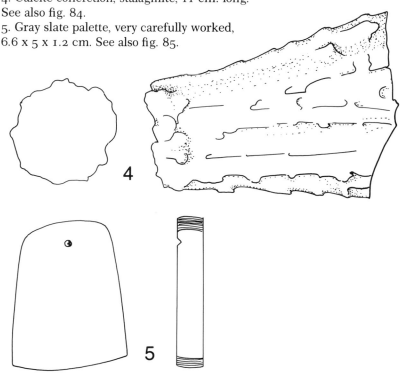

4

5

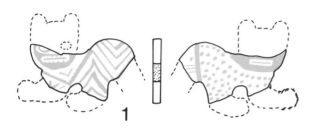

1

Level 3

Ceramics

1. Plaque, Cabana Cream Painted. 5.8 x 3.5 x .4 cm. Spotted and striped feline, conventional red designs on both sides of cut-out shape. Head missing above mouth, tail missing.

2. Double pedestal cup, Cabana Cream Resist. (Form F-5, doubled). 6.5 cm. high, each cup 10 cm. diam. Only one cup survives; the other is just a wall fragment joined at rim and by basal bridge. Another fragment of this vessel was found in Cut 12, Level 4, at the same level in the ground. Ext.: border black on cream triangles, panels of black cross on cream, crosshatch over-painted in red. Int.: red feline serpents vertical from lower border. Unrestored. See fig. 172.

3. Total potsherds in Level 3: 50
Pashash Orange Plain: 19
    Painted: 1
Cabana Cream Plain: 12
    Painted: 10
    Resist: 6
Horno Black: 2

Level 4

Ceramics

1. Total potsherds in Level 4: 91
Pashash Orange Plain: 73
    Painted: 6 (with red lines)
Caserón Orange Plain: 3
    Painted: 1
    Resist: 2
Cabana Cream Painted: 2
    Resist: 2
Horno Black: 2

Level 5

Ceramics

1. Total potsherds in Level 5: 26
Pashash Orange Plain: 16
    Painted: 1
Vista Brown: 1
Caserón Orange Plain: 2
    Painted: 1
    Resist: 1
Cabana Cream Plain: 1
    Painted: 2
    Resist: 1

Cut 12: La Capilla Temple Inner Chamber

Level 1

Bone
1. Leg bone of a small mammal.

Ceramics
2. Total potsherds in Level 1: 255
Pashash Orange Plain: 95
   Painted: 2
Vista Brown: 4
Caserón Orange Plain: 25
   Painted: 38
   Resist: 8
Cabana Cream Plain: 36
   Painted: 22
   Resist: 22
Horno Black: 3

Level 2

Ceramics
1. Handled bowl, Cabana Cream Painted. 5 cm. high, 11.8 cm. diam. Rim 1.3 cm. wide, relief snakes, red step fret. Ext.: crosshatch panels. 16.3 cm. long with handle. Restored; parts lost.
2. Pedestal cup, Cabana Cream Resist. 8.5 cm. high, 12.2 cm. diam. Ext.: panels 5.5 cm. high alternating profile and frontal feline monsters. Int.: four panels of owls, profile body, frontal face, in red; no border. Restored from five fragments; some fragments missing. See also figs. 170, 188.
3. Necked jar, Pashash Orange Painted. 13.3 cm. high, 7.3 cm. diam. Ext.: two red lines on shoulder in two places. Int.: plain. Some fragments missing from base.

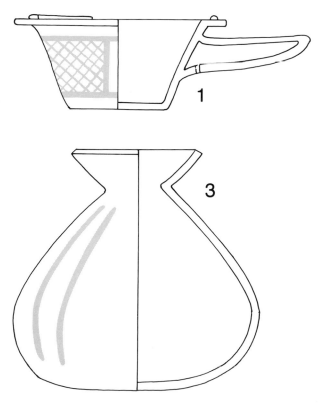

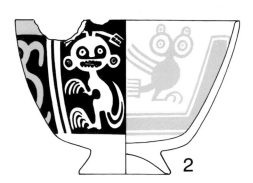

4. Pedestal cup, Cabana Cream Painted. 5 cm. high, 7.2 cm. diam. Red on cream. Ext.: chain border, eight panels alternating cross and crosshatch. Int.: plain. One section of wall missing.
5. Total potsherds in Level 2: 497
Pashash Orange Plain: 261
   Painted: 1
   Resist: 3
Vista Brown: 2
Caserón Orange Plain: 72
   Painted: 37
   Resist: 25
Cabana Cream Plain: 31
   Painted: 37
   Resist: 27
Horno Black: 1

Level 3

Stone
1. Gray granite ax head, abraded for hafting, 8.5 x 7.3 x 3.1 cm. See also fig. 82.
2. Circular flattened granite pebble, indentation pecked in one side, 3.8 cm. diam., 1.8 cm. thick.

Ceramics
3. Handled bowl (Form H-2), Cabana Cream Resist. 5.6 cm. high, 15.4 cm. diam. Rim 1.5 cm. wide; applied snakes (heads missing), red step fret. Ext.: three panels red crosshatch. Int.: plain. Breaks in rim and base.
4. Effigy head of man, Caserón Orange Resist. 9 cm. high, 8 cm. headdress diam. Spout on front of headdress. Cream slip, red face, black and cream resist details. Broken off at neck. See also pl. 3.
5. Handled bowl (Form H-2), Cabana Cream Resist. 5.5 cm. high, 13.4 cm. diam. Rim 1.2 cm. wide; two applied snakes with punched design, red step fret. Ext.: alternate crosshatching and rows of resist dots or "beans" (three joined dots) in black, orange, and cream. Int.: plain. Black stripe around base of handle. Pieces broken from base and tip of handle, rim chipped.
6. Half of rim flange and one wall of bowl (probably Form H-2), Cabana Cream Resist. Rim diam. 17.5 cm., 2.1 cm. wide. Two male heads 2.2 cm. high modeled on rim; with red faces, earplugs. One applied snake on rim, panels of painted felines in red. Ext.: alternating panels of black on cream resist design and red on cream head with emanations. Int.: plain. See also fig. 133.

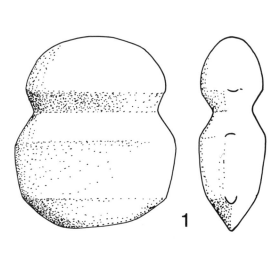

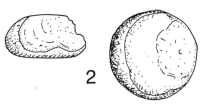

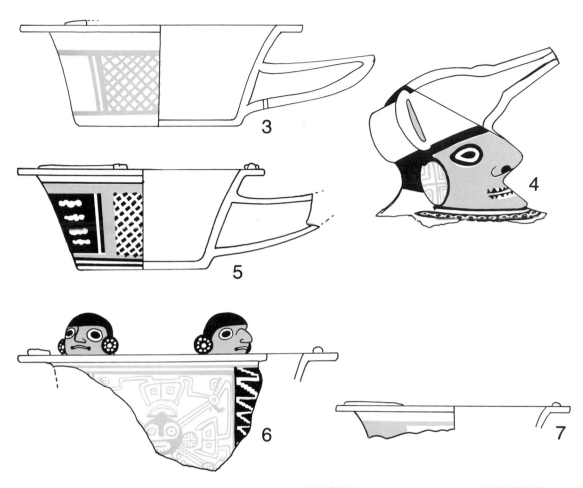

7. Complete rim of bowl (Form H-2), Caserón Orange Painted. 12.9 cm. diam. Rim 1.3 cm. wide, two applied snakes, red on cream step fret. Ext.: orange on cream panels. Int.: plain. Body, base, and handle lost.

8. Half of simple bowl (Form F-1), Cabana Cream Resist. 6.1 cm. high, 13.3 cm. diam. Ext.: S-border, alternate panels of bird and feline designs, black on cream resist with alternate panels given red wash. Int.: three (two extant) frontal warrior heads with rays emanating from four points of each head, black on cream resist.

9. Pedestal cup, Cabana Cream Resist. 7.1 cm. high, 12.7 cm. diam. Ext.: border of frets, resist panels of spotted feline serpents. Int.: nine panels of spinning circles, all spinning left; border of hollow circles. Complete except for chipped rim. See also fig. 171.

10. Half of pedestal cup (Form G), Pashash Orange Plain. 8.5 cm. high, 17 cm. diam. Flared wall.

11. Half of pedestal cup (Form G), Pashash Orange Resist. Base lost. 4.4 cm. high, 10 cm. diam. Ext.: black, resist crosses, red triangular frames. Int.: plain.

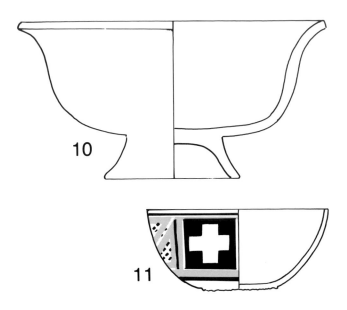

12. Miniature pedestal cup, Cabana Cream Painted. Triangular rim 4.1 cm. on side. 3.2 cm. high. Ext.: double zigzag line of white dots on red. Int.: plain. Complete.

13. Miniature pedestal cup, Cabana Cream Painted. Triangular rim 3.8 cm. on side. 2.6 cm. high. Ext.: white dots on red. Int.: plain. Two chips in rim.

14. Miniature pedestal cup, Cabana Cream Plain. 2.5 cm. high, 3.4 cm. diam. Complete.

15. Miniature pedestal cup, Cabana Cream Painted. 2.9 cm. high, 3.6 cm. diam. Ext.: double line white dots on red in zigzag. Int.: plain. Complete.

16. Miniature jar, Cabana Cream Painted. 3.1 cm. high, 2.3 cm. rim diam. Neck pierced for suspension, red band on shoulder.

17. Whistle, Cabana Cream Painted. 4.7 cm. long. Lower part is red-painted human face 2.2 cm. high. Right earplug lost. Back plain. Complete.

18. Whistle, Cabana Cream Painted. 3.6 cm. long. Lower part is bat face. Back plain. Small break at mouthpiece.

19. Whistle, Cabana Cream Painted. 3 cm. long. Bird with mouthpiece in tail. Brown paint on wings. Head lost.

20. Spindle whorl, Cabana Cream Painted. Truncated cone 2.5 cm. high, 3.5 cm. diam. Solid with hole through it. Step design on sides and base, red paint in incised line. See also fig. 27.

21. Spindle whorl, Pashash Orange Painted. Truncated cone 2.1 cm. high, 2.7 cm. diam. Incised lines and zigzag, black paint. See also fig. 27.

22. Spindle whorl, Cabana Cream Painted. Truncated cone 2.1 cm. high, 2.8 cm. diam. Red on cream, incised zigzag. See also fig. 27.

23. Total potsherds in Level 3: 1,511
Pashash Orange Plain: 586
   Painted: 3
   Resist: 8
Vista Brown: 5
Caserón Orange Plain: 203
   Painted: 102
   Resist: 129
Cabana Cream Plain: 264
   Painted: 56
   Resist: 143
Horno Black: 12

Level 4

Metal

1. Copper pin with feline head, 8 cm. long. Hole below head. Point nearly broken. Lost-wax casting. See fig. 111.

2. Copper pin with feline head, 9.5 cm. long. Hole below head. Lost-wax casting. See fig. 111.

3. Six forged copper nails: 7.6 cm.; 1.7 cm.; 2.5 cm. shaft; 12.1 cm. with head .9 cm. diam.; 13.2 cm. with head 1.1 cm.; head 1 cm. See fig. 112.

4. Straight pin, 9 cm. long, 4.4 mm. thick. Copper core, gold leaf mostly lost. Head lost.

5. Straight pin fragment, 6.3 cm. long, broken at both ends. Copper core, gold leaf.

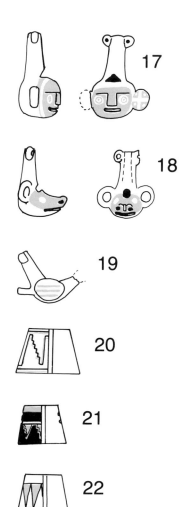

6

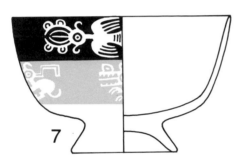

7

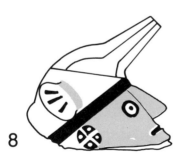

8

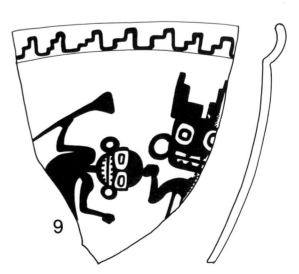

9

Stone

6. Rim fragment of black stone bowl, 4.8 cm. high, 8.1 cm. along rim, .5 cm. thick. Originally about 14 cm. diam. Ext.: plano-relief, step-fret border, two framed panels with facing crested felines. Traces of red in background. Int.: plain. See also fig. 166.

Ceramics

7. Pedestal cup, Cabana Cream Resist. 7.5 cm. high, 12 cm. diam. Ext.: two registers—upper birds in black on cream resist; lower felines in cream on red. Two sections of wall lost. See also fig. 68.

8. Head of a man, Caserón Orange Resist. 7.4 cm. high. Spout in headdress, red face, black on cream resist details. Left earplug missing, head broken off at neck.

9. Rim fragment of large vessel (probably Form I-2), Horno Black. Fragment 13 cm. high, 12.5 cm. along rim, .6 cm. thick. Ext.: plain. Int.: cupped rim with step design in shiny black on dull black; wall has two warriors, one in stepped crown holding other by hair, painted in shiny black on dull black. Original rim diam. about 47 cm. See also fig. 130.

10. Total potsherds in Level 4: 191
Pashash Orange Plain: 34
   Resist: 1
Caserón Orange Plain: 35
   Painted: 16
   Resist: 22
Cabana Cream Plain: 38
   Painted: 16
   Resist: 29

Level 5

Stone

1. Five fragments of pedestal cup of soft red stone, about 8 cm. high, 11 cm. diam., base diam. 3.6 cm. Ext.: reliefs of two rampant felines, one with inlaid turquoise eye, and the feet of two human figures. Other fragments are the base and a rim fragment. The bodies of the felines are excised for diamond-shaped inlays.
2. Fragment of pedestal cup of soft red stone, floor and base, 2.2 cm. high, 6.2 cm. wide.
3. Slate, rough piece 4.3 x 3.1 x .7 cm., red paint on one side and edge.

Ceramics

4. Pedestal cup, Cabana Cream Resist. 5.1 cm. high, 8.2 cm. diam. Ext.: border of two zigzag lines cream resist on black, wall of step fret and chain. Restored from three pieces; rim chipped and one piece lost.
5. Pedestal cup, Caserón Orange Resist. 6.4 cm. high, 11 cm. diam. Ext.: black on pale orange resist—cross, step, and "bean." Int.: plain cream slip. One side lost.
6. Miniature pedestal cup, Cabana Cream Plain. 3.9 cm. high, 5.3 cm. diam. Complete.
7. Spouted bowl (Form I-1), Cabana Cream Resist. 5.4 cm. high, 14.5 cm. diam. Ext.: step border, cross, crosshatch. Int.: three warrior heads. Break in rim.
8. Total potsherds in Level 5: 1,119
Pashash Orange Plain: 358
   Painted: 22
   Resist: 5
Vista Brown: 8
Caserón Orange Plain: 98
   Painted: 39
   Resist: 59
Cabana Cream Plain: 215
   Painted: 124
   Resist: 182
Horno Black: 9

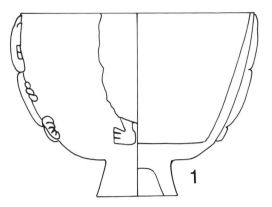

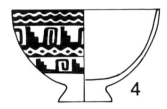

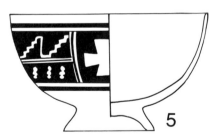

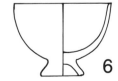

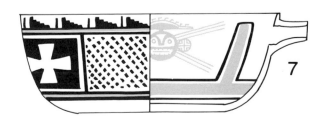

Level 6
Burial chamber with skeletal material.

Level 7

Metal
1. Pin, complete head and curved shaft, 11.2 cm. long. Hollow head. Copper core, gold leaf. Deposited in the Artisans' Center, Cabana. See also fig. 113.
2. Pin, hollow cast head, curved shaft, 11.9 cm. top to curve. Head 3 cm. diam. Copper core, gold leaf. Top: frontal feline head. Sides: three framed panels of feline-crested felines. Smooth pin, pierced. Ten pieces of fringe lost from head. See also fig. 113.
3. Pin, hollow cast head, curved shaft, 11.9 cm. top to curve. Head 3.2 cm. diam. Copper core, gold leaf. Top: frontal male face with turban and earrings. Sides: three framed panels with crested felines, mouth incised, eyes hollow circles once inlaid. Shaft had sixteen diamond-shaped inlays, now lost. End of shaft and eight pieces of fringe lost. See also figs. 115, 123.
4. Pin, hollow cast head, 11.9 cm. top to curve. Head 3.1 cm. diam. Copper core, gold leaf. Top: frontal male face, turban, earrings. Sides: three framed felines with hollow eyes. Shaft smooth, curved to point. Missing 8/7/75. See also fig. 114.
5. Pin, solid head, curved shaft, 9.8 cm. top to curve. Head 2 cm. diam. Copper core, gold leaf. Top: feline in 2.5 mm. relief, four incised diamond spots on body, humanlike frontal face, turban, feline ears. Sides plain, shaft plain, pierced. See also fig. 158.

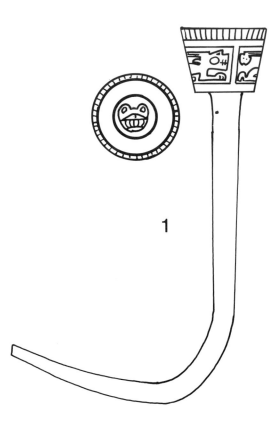

1

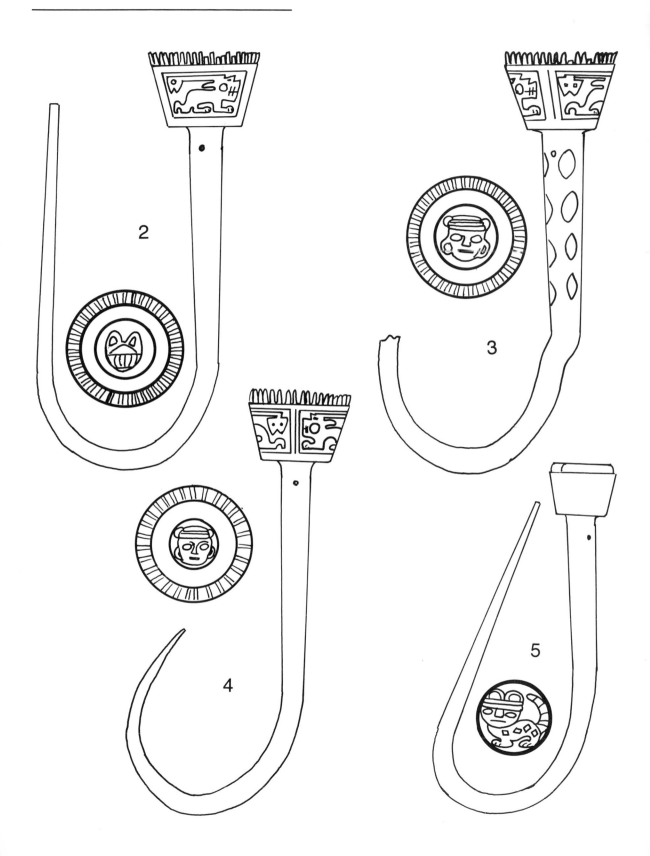

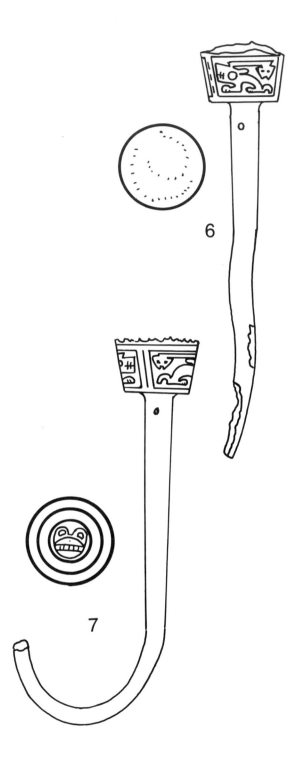

6. Pin, solid head, straight shaft, 11.4 cm. long. Head 2.1 cm. diam. Copper core, gold leaf. Top has lost its decoration, which may have been no. 31. Sides: three framed panels of left-facing crested felines, inlays lost from eyes. Incised mouths. Shaft plain, pierced, point lost. See also fig. 119.

7. Pin, solid head, curved shaft, 10.7 cm. top to curve. Head 2.3 cm. diam. Copper core, gold leaf. Top: frontal feline head. Sides: three panels of crested felines. Shaft plain, pierced. Point of shaft and all fringe on top lost. See also pl. 7.

8. Pin, solid head, curved shaft, 11 cm. top to curve. Head 2.8 cm. diam. Copper core, gold leaf. Top: projecting frame for inlay of frontal head, all inlay missing. Sides: two panels of framing for inlay. Ten pieces of green stone remain in place. Many inlay stones have tiny hole through center. Shaft had relief animal facing point, front half of animal lost; rear half 3.3 cm. long. Shaft broken 1 cm. from head, where pierced. Eleven pieces of fringe lost from top. See also fig. 124.

9. Pin, solid head, straight shaft, 22 cm. long. Head 2.8 cm. diam. Copper core, gold leaf. Top: owl, frontal head, profile body, inlays lost from eyes. Sides: three framed panels of crested felines, incised circle eyes, excised eyes in crest. Shaft has four feline-headed serpents spiraling around it. Shaft broken 1.6 cm. from head, where pierced, point lost. See also figs. 116, 118, pl. 7.

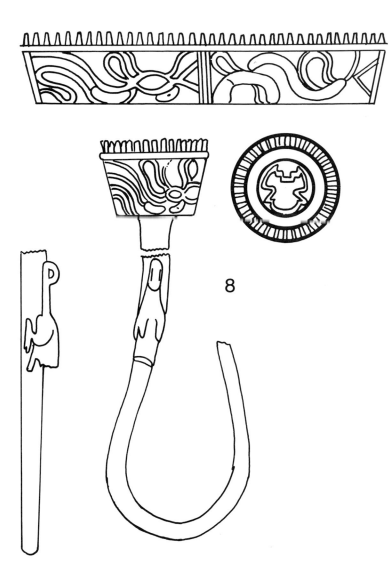

8

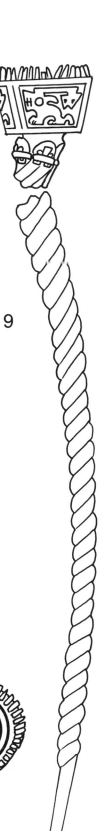

9

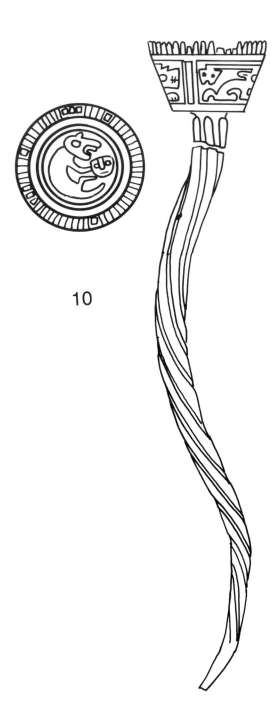

10

10. Pin, solid head, irregularly curved shaft, 17.5 cm. long. Head 3.5 cm. diam. Copper core, gold leaf. Top: rampant feline holding frontal human head. Inlaid eye of feline lost. Sides: three framed panels of crested felines, eyes inlaid with green stone. Shaft has five relief strips spiraling around it. Shaft broken .8 cm. below head, where pierced. See also figs. 121, 131, pl. 7.

11. Pinhead, hollow cast, 3.3 cm. diam., 2.3 cm. wall. Copper core, gold leaf. Metal about .8 mm. thick. Top: frontal male head in turban and earrings, 1.2 cm. chin to turban. Sides: three panels of crested felines. Inlaid eyes of felines missing. Shaft lost, wide hole in base of head. Six pieces of fringe missing from top.

12. Pinhead, hollow cast, 3 cm. diam., 2 cm. wall. Copper core, gold leaf. Top: frontal feline head with large ears, large mouth with teeth. Sides: three framed panels of crested felines with incised eyes, mouths. Shaft lost, hole in base.

13. Pinhead, hollow cast, 2.9 cm. diam. 2 cm. wall. Copper core, gold leaf. Top: frontal feline head, large ears and mouth with teeth. Sides: three framed panels of crested felines with incised eyes, mouths. Shaft lost, large break in base of head, sprue in place on int. See also fig. 117.

14. Pinhead, hollow cast, 3.1 cm. diam., 2.3 cm. wall. Copper core, gold leaf. Top: frontal feline head, large ears and mouth with teeth. Sides: three panels of crested felines with incised eyes, mouths. Shaft broken 1 cm. from head, at perforation. Large "exploded" break in wall and base.

15. Pinhead, hollow cast, 2.9 cm. diam., 2 cm. wall. Copper core, gold leaf. Top: owl, frontal head, eyes inlaid with green stone, black pupils, "ears" inlaid with black. Sides: three framed panels of crested felines, details incised, circular eyes incised. Fringe lost except one piece; shaft broken off at base of head. See also fig. 189, pl. 7.

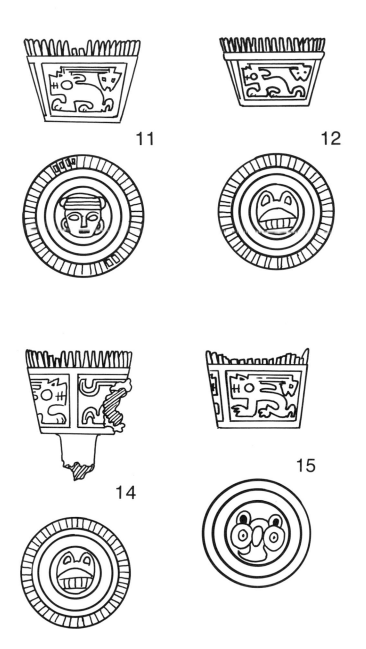

11

12

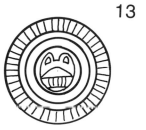

13

14

15

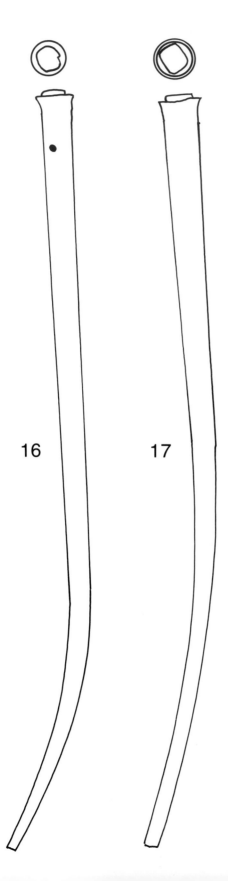

16

17

16. Pin shaft, straight, 20.8 cm. long, .8 cm. thick at perforation, which is 1.6 cm. from top. Copper core, gold leaf. Head lost, point lost. (Head may be no. 10, 11, or 12.)

17. Pin shaft, straight, 20.7 cm. long, .85 cm. thick at perforation, which is 1.6 cm. from top. Copper core, gold leaf. Circular top or rivet was inside head. Head lost (may have been no. 10, 11, or 12); point lost.

18. Pin shaft, curved, 8 cm. top to curve, 1 cm. thick at perforation. Copper core, gold leaf. Sixteen diamond-shaped pits (four rows of four) for inlays (lost). Perforation through one inlay pit. Head lost (may have been no. 10, 11, or 12); point lost.

19. Pin shaft, curved, 9.5 cm. long top to curve, .9 cm. thick at perforation 1.7 cm. below top. Copper core, gold leaf. Top has rectangular butt of rivet which was inside the lost head. Sideward twist to point, which is broken. (Head may have been no. 10, 11, or 12.)

20. Pin shaft, straight, 11.2 cm. long, .74 cm. thick. Copper core, gold leaf. Broken at both ends, head lost (may have been no. 10, 11, or 12).

21. Pin shaft, straight, 12 cm. long, .6 cm. thick. Copper core, gold leaf. Head lost, point lost.

22. Pin shaft fragment, copper with gold leaf, 5.8 cm. long. This was probably part of one shaft, along with nos. 23–26.

23. Pin shaft fragment, copper core, gold leaf, 3.8 cm. long.

24. Pin shaft fragment, copper core, gold leaf, 3.6 cm. long.

25. Pin shaft fragment, copper core, gold leaf, 2.5 cm. long.

26. Pin shaft fragment, copper core, gold leaf, 2.2 cm. long.

27. Pin shaft, twisted, 7.5 cm. long, .5 cm. thick. Copper core, gold leaf. Head and point lost.

28. Pin shaft, straight, 3.4 cm. long, .7 cm. thick. Copper core, gold leaf. Four twist relief elements. Part of nos. 29 and 30, broken at both ends, head lost.

29. Pin shaft, straight, 2.4 cm. long, .72 cm. thick. Copper core, gold leaf. Four twist relief elements. Part of nos. 28 and 30, broken at both ends, head lost.

30. Top of pin shaft, straight, 1.9 cm. long, 1.25 cm. thick. Copper core, gold leaf. Four frontal feline faces on spiraling snake bodies. Broken from head and at perforation. Part of nos. 28 and 29. See also pl. 7.

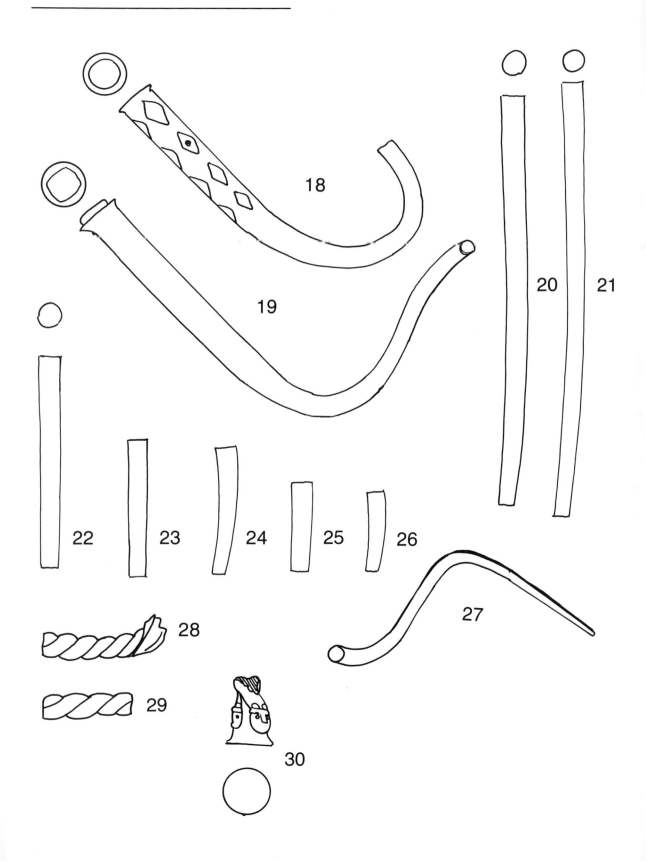

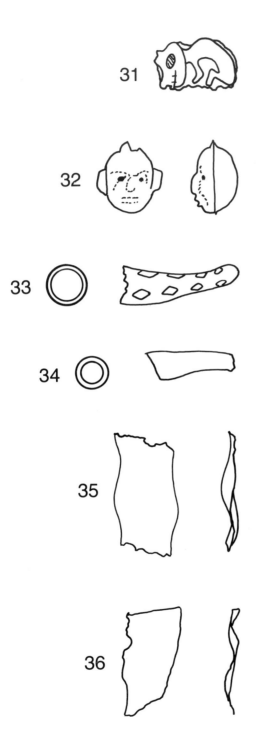

31. Relief of rampant feline, 2.1 cm. long. Copper core, gold leaf. Inlaid eye lost. This may have been the top of no. 6.

32. Bead, hollow, formed of two sheets of gold, 1.7 cm. high. Represents a human head, holes at eyes, small break behind right ear. Formed by repoussé and soldering. See also fig. 122, pl. 7.

33. Hollow cast gold form, 3.2 cm. long, .9 cm. diam. Shallow diamond-shaped inlays of copper. Broken at one end; tail of an animal figurine? See also fig. 122.

34. Gold tube, hollow, curving, 2.3 cm. long, .8 cm. diam. Metal is .7 mm. thick. Plain surface. Broken ends. See also fig. 122.

35. Sheet gold fragment, 3.5 x 1.7 cm., 1.2 mm. thick. Plain. All edges broken.

36. Sheet gold fragment, 2.9 x 1.5 cm., 1.2 mm. thick. Plain. All edges broken.

37. Pin, solid cast, 2.5 cm. long, head .9 cm. diam. Copper, no gold extant. Top: feline, head frontal. Shaft pierced 1 mm. below head. Point lost.

38. Pin shaft, curved, 11 cm. top to curve. Copper, golf leaf. Broken at perforation, head lost. Plain surface.

39. Pin shaft, curved, 11 cm. long top to curve. Copper and gold leaf. Five-element twist in relief from top to bend, remaining length plain. Broken at perforation, head lost.

40. Pin, solid cast, 10 cm. long, curved shaft. No gold extant. Head is 1.6 cm. diam., 1 cm. wall. Top: feline, frontal face, crested, pressed-in dots on body, 4 mm. high relief. Sides: three panels of incised profile felines. Shaft perforated .8 cm. below head.

41–42. Two fragments of hollow cast pinhead, 1.4 cm. wall height. 2.3 cm. longest measure. Copper core, gold leaf. Top: frontal feline. Sides: framed panels. See also fig. 120.

43. Pin shaft, curved, 11.8 cm. long. Copper core, gold leaf. Square butt of pin in top. Head lost.

44. Two fragments of pin shaft with copper core, gold leaf: (a) 6.3 cm. long, (b) 8.25 cm. long, gold lost.

45. Pinhead, solid cast, 1 cm. long, .8 cm. diam. Copper, no gold leaf extant. Top: left profile feline. Shaft broken off at perforation.

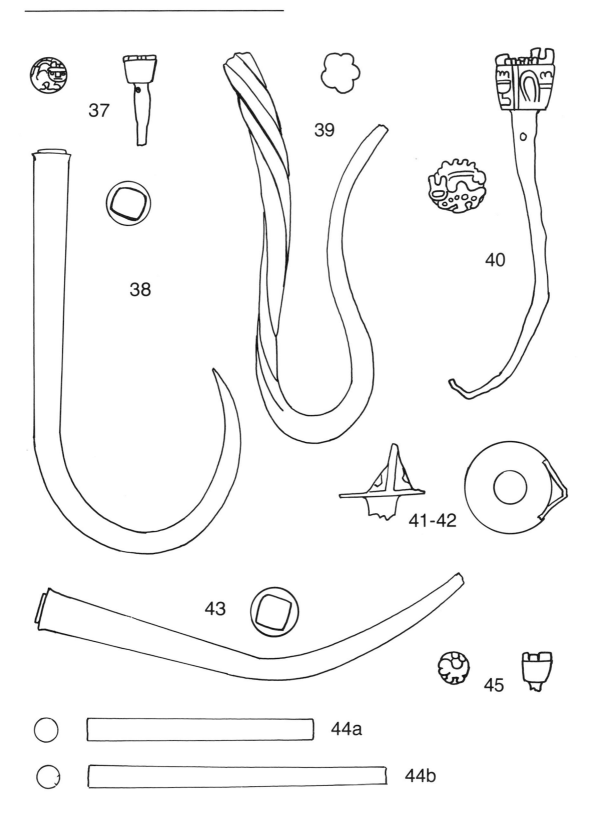

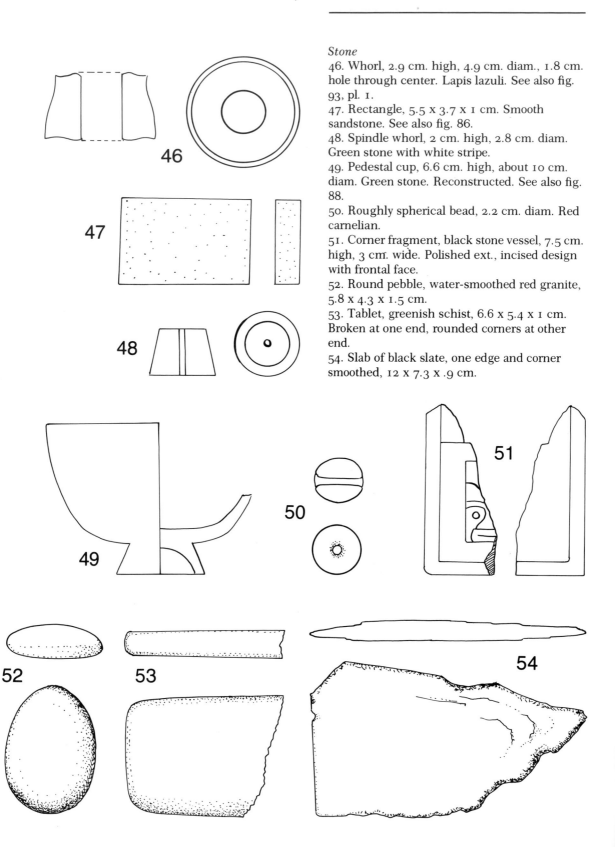

Stone
46. Whorl, 2.9 cm. high, 4.9 cm. diam., 1.8 cm. hole through center. Lapis lazuli. See also fig. 93, pl. 1.
47. Rectangle, 5.5 x 3.7 x 1 cm. Smooth sandstone. See also fig. 86.
48. Spindle whorl, 2 cm. high, 2.8 cm. diam. Green stone with white stripe.
49. Pedestal cup, 6.6 cm. high, about 10 cm. diam. Green stone. Reconstructed. See also fig. 88.
50. Roughly spherical bead, 2.2 cm. diam. Red carnelian.
51. Corner fragment, black stone vessel, 7.5 cm. high, 3 cm. wide. Polished ext., incised design with frontal face.
52. Round pebble, water-smoothed red granite, 5.8 x 4.3 x 1.5 cm.
53. Tablet, greenish schist, 6.6 x 5.4 x 1 cm. Broken at one end, rounded corners at other end.
54. Slab of black slate, one edge and corner smoothed, 12 x 7.3 x .9 cm.

Ceramics

55. Jar (Form D, unpierced flange at rim),
Cabana Cream Resist. 28 cm. high, body cir-
cumference 73 cm. Lid (Form F-4), Cabana
Cream Plain, rests on rim flange. Ext.: two
panels double-headed feline serpent on black
and cream resist crosshatch. Three borders:
step fret, chain, white stepped zigzag on black.
Int.: plain. See also fig. 64.

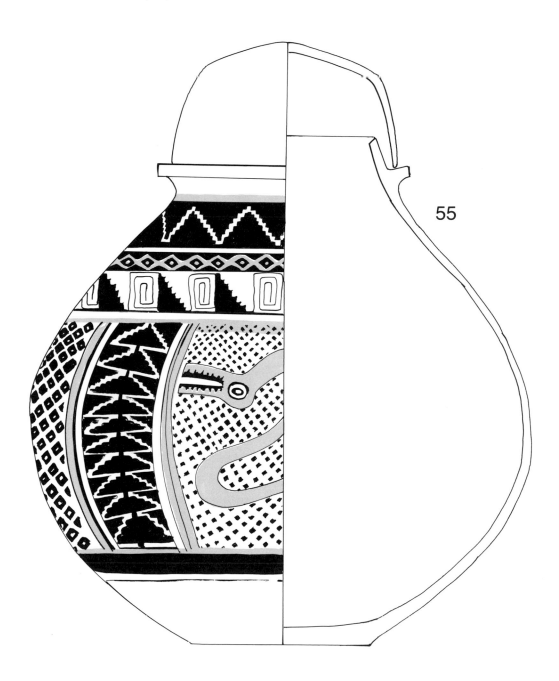

55

56

57

58

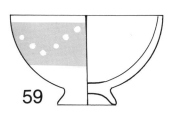

59

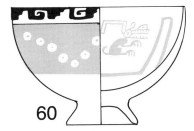

60

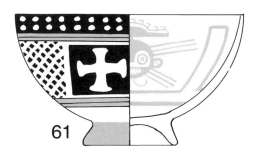

61

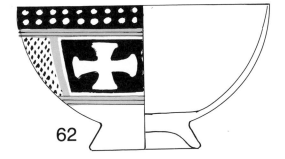

62

56. Pedestal cup, Cabana Cream Resist. 7 cm. high, 10.5 cm. diam. Ext.: panels of cross and crosshatch. Int.: plain. Missing 8/6/75. See also pl. 6.

57. Pedestal cup. Cabana Cream Resist. 8 cm. high, 13 cm. diam. Ext.: red and cream resist birds, felines, frontal heads on black. Int.: plain. Wheel-thrown; exceptionally fine vessel. Missing 8/6/75. See also fig. 66.

58. Pedestal cup, Cabana Cream Painted. 5.3 cm. high, 8.5 cm. diam. Ext.: three bands of step designs. Int.: crested felines in panels, red on cream. Missing 8/6/75.

59. Pedestal cup, Cabana Cream Painted. 4.9 cm. high, 8.5 cm. diam. Ext.: red dots on orange band. Int.: plain. Red pigment powder inside.

60. Pedestal cup, Cabana Cream Resist. 6.5 cm. high, 9.5 cm. diam. Ext.: step-fret border in black on cream, red band with opaque white dot and circle. Int.: three panels crested felines red on cream. Restored from three sherds; one side missing.

61. Pedestal cup, Cabana Cream Resist. 7.3 cm. high, 12.5 cm. diam. Ext.: four resist crosses, panels black crosshatch, border of double row of cream dots on black. Int.: three red warrior heads with rays. See also fig. 141, pl. 6.

62. Pedestal cup, Cabana Cream Resist. 8 cm. high, 14 cm. diam. Ext.: two resist crosses between panels of red crosshatch, border of two rows of cream dots on black. Int.: plain. Missing 8/6/75.

63. Pedestal cup, Cabana Cream Resist. 7.5 cm. high, 12.2 cm. diam. Ext.: two rows cream dots on black, two crosses separated by panels of red crosshatch, step, "beans." Int.: plain. Missing 8/6/75.

64. Pedestal cup, Cabana Cream Painted. 4 cm. high, 6.7 cm. diam. Ext.: red dots on cream. Int.: plain. See also fig. 192.

65. Pedestal cup, Cabana Cream Resist. 6.4 cm. high, 10.8 cm. diam. Ext.: cross and crosshatch panels, step-fret border. Int.: three red felines in fringed frames. Base: two red lines, like ||, at edge.

66. Pedestal cup, Cabana Cream Painted. 5.9 cm. high, 9 cm. diam. Ext.: plain. Int.: red felines on cream. Missing 8/6/75.

67. Pedestal cup, Cabana Cream Resist. 7.7 cm. high, 12.7 cm. diam. Ext.: chained loop border, four panels of crosses and crosshatch. Int.: three red felines in framed panels. Base: red spot. See also fig. 70.

68. Pedestal cup, Cabana Cream Resist. Base lost, wall 5 cm. high, 9.7 cm. diam. Ext.: chain border, four panels of crosses alternating with crosshatch. Int.: three red felines. One side lost.

69. Pedestal cup, Cabana Cream Resist. 6.2 cm. high, 8.2 cm. diam. Ext.: four crosses and panels of crosshatch, step-fret border. Int.: red crested felines in fringed frames. Missing 8/6/75.

70. Pedestal cup, Cabana Cream Resist. 6.8 cm. high, 10.2 cm. diam. Ext.: step-fret border, four panels of crosses and crosshatch. Int.: panels of red felines. Chipped rim.

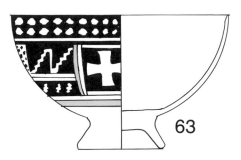

63

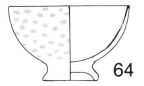

64

65

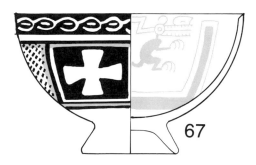

67

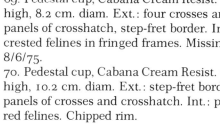

66

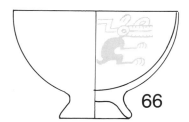

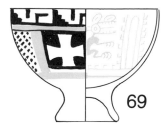

69

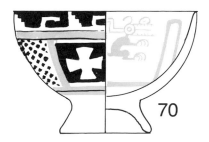

70

68

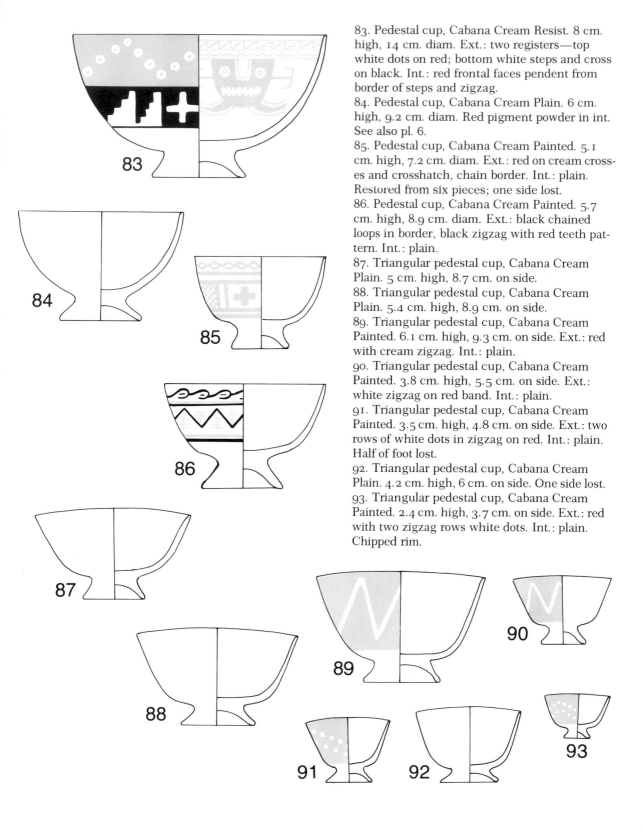

83. Pedestal cup, Cabana Cream Resist. 8 cm. high, 14 cm. diam. Ext.: two registers—top white dots on red; bottom white steps and cross on black. Int.: red frontal faces pendent from border of steps and zigzag.

84. Pedestal cup, Cabana Cream Plain. 6 cm. high, 9.2 cm. diam. Red pigment powder in int. See also pl. 6.

85. Pedestal cup, Cabana Cream Painted. 5.1 cm. high, 7.2 cm. diam. Ext.: red on cream crosses and crosshatch, chain border. Int.: plain. Restored from six pieces; one side lost.

86. Pedestal cup, Cabana Cream Painted. 5.7 cm. high, 8.9 cm. diam. Ext.: black chained loops in border, black zigzag with red teeth pattern. Int.: plain.

87. Triangular pedestal cup, Cabana Cream Plain. 5 cm. high, 8.7 cm. on side.

88. Triangular pedestal cup, Cabana Cream Plain. 5.4 cm. high, 8.9 cm. on side.

89. Triangular pedestal cup, Cabana Cream Painted. 6.1 cm. high, 9.3 cm. on side. Ext.: red with cream zigzag. Int.: plain.

90. Triangular pedestal cup, Cabana Cream Painted. 3.8 cm. high, 5.5 cm. on side. Ext.: white zigzag on red band. Int.: plain.

91. Triangular pedestal cup, Cabana Cream Painted. 3.5 cm. high, 4.8 cm. on side. Ext.: two rows of white dots in zigzag on red. Int.: plain. Half of foot lost.

92. Triangular pedestal cup, Cabana Cream Plain. 4.2 cm. high, 6 cm. on side. One side lost.

93. Triangular pedestal cup, Cabana Cream Painted. 2.4 cm. high, 3.7 cm. on side. Ext.: red with two zigzag rows white dots. Int.: plain. Chipped rim.

94. Triangular pedestal cup, Cabana Cream Plain. 4.5 cm. high, 7.5 cm. on side.

95. Triangular pedestal cup, Cabana Cream Painted. 5.3 cm. high, 7.3 cm. on side. Ext.: red bands on cream. Int.: plain. Restored from three pieces, one corner lost.

96. Pedestal cup, Cabana Cream Resist. 7 cm. high, 10 cm. diam. Ext.: black and cream step border, white circle in zigzag on red band. Int.: unframed felines with feline-headed crests in red. See also fig. 168, pl. 6.

97. Triangular pedestal cup, Cabana Cream Painted. 4 cm. high, 7.5 cm. on side. Ext.: red step pattern. Int.: plain.

98. Triangular pedestal cup, Cabana Cream Painted. 4.3 cm. high, 6.5 cm. on side. Ext.: red and cream diamonds in chain. Int.: plain. Fragmentary: only base and one half.

99. Pedestal cup, Cabana Cream Plain. 2.4 cm. high, 3.4 cm. diam.

100. Pedestal cup, Cabana Cream Painted. 2.9 cm. high, 3.7 cm. diam. Ext.: red with two zig-zag rows of white dots. Int.: plain.

101. Pedestal cup, Caserón Orange Plain. 4.5 cm. high, 6.2 cm. diam. Cream slip.

102. Pedestal cup, Caserón Orange Painted. 4.5 cm. high, 7.1 cm. diam. Cream slip. Ext.: two red stripes. Int.: plain.

103. Pedestal cup, Caserón Orange Painted. 5.4 cm. high, 7.8 cm. diam. Ext.: large red checkerboard. Int.: plain. Thick walled, coarsely painted. Chip in rim.

104. Pedestal cup and lid, Cabana Cream Plain. Cup 3.4 cm. high; both cup and lid 4.6 cm. diam. Lid has nubbin handle.

105. Pedestal cup, Cabana Cream Painted. 3.5 cm. high, 3.7 cm. diam. Ext.: red with two zig-zag rows of white dots. Int.: plain. Rim chipped.

106. Pedestal cup, Cabana Cream Painted. 3.7 cm. high, 4.2 cm. diam. Ext.: red with two zig-zag rows of white dots. Int.: plain. Rim distorted but not triangular.

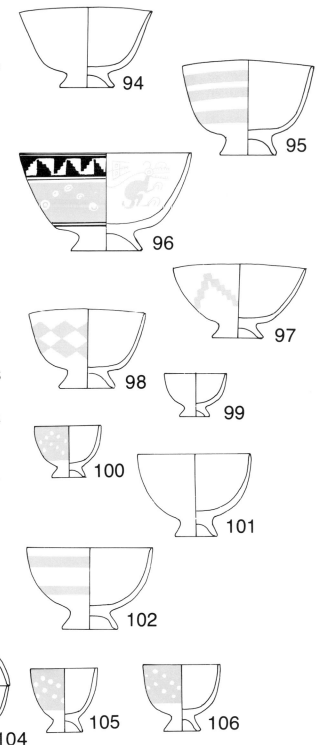

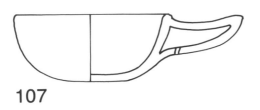

107

107. Handled bowl (Form H-1), Caserón Orange Painted. 3.8 cm. high, 8.4 cm. diam. Int.: cream slip. Missing 8/7/75.
108. Handled bowl (Form H-2), Caserón Orange Painted. 7.3 cm. high, 18.2 cm. diam. Ext.: three red lines. Int.: plain. Rim: red zigzag and red areas.

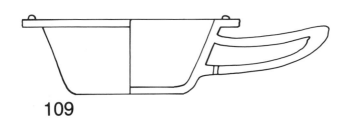

108

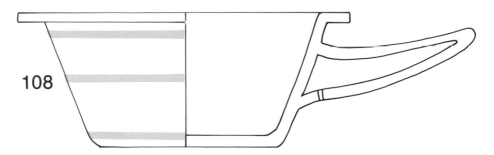

109

109. Handled bowl (Form H-2), Cabana Cream Painted. 4.1 cm. high, 12 cm. diam., 16.9 cm. length with handle, rim 1.3 cm. wide. Rim: applied snakes (lost), red concentric circles. Rest plain.
110. Handled bowl (Form H-2), Caserón Orange Painted. 4.3 cm. high, 12.8 cm. diam. Rim 1.5 cm. wide, red and black step fret. Ext.: linear cross and crosshatch panels. Int.: plain.

110

111

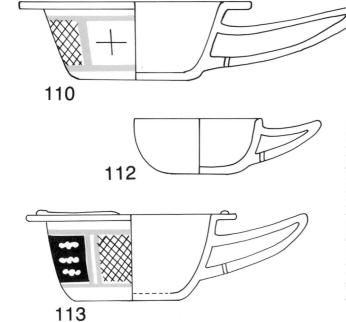

112

113

111. Handled bowl (Form H-1), Cabana Cream Painted. 3.8 cm. high, 7.8 cm. diam., 11.5 cm. length with handle. Penetration through wall opposite handle. Ext.: red areas and red rim.
112. Handled bowl (Form H-1), Cabana Cream Plain. 3 cm. high, 7 cm. diam., about 10 cm. long with handle. Unrestored fragment.
113. Handled bowl (Form H-2), Caserón Orange Resist. 4.7 cm. high, 11.5 cm. diam. Ext.: red and black resist on cream slip, crosshatch and "bean" panels. Int.: plain. Rim: red step frets. Handle orange. Floor broken, wall cracked.

114. Handled bowl (Form H-1), Caserón
Orange Plain. 4.2 cm. high, 7.7 cm. diam., 11.5
cm. long with handle. Thin cream slip.
115. Bowl (Form I-1), Caserón Orange Resist.
15.5 cm. high, irregular ovoid rim 14.8 to 29 cm.
diam. Ext.: black and cream resist bands, lat-
ticed areas holding "beans" and crosses, red,
black, and cream. Int.: red and brown lines,
steps. Spout broken off. Reconstructed. See also
fig. 190.

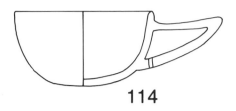

114

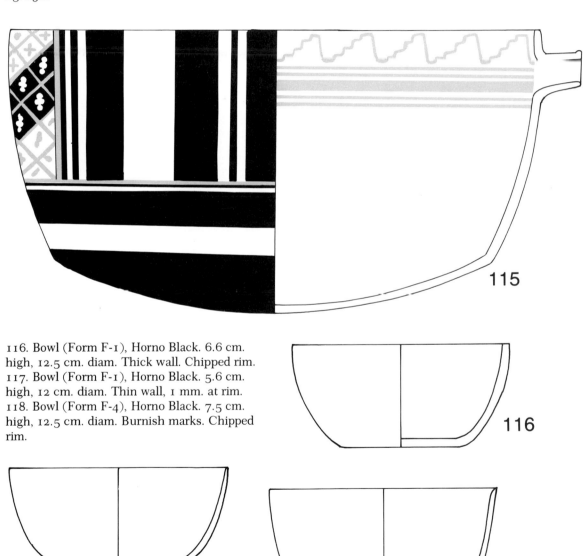

115

116. Bowl (Form F-1), Horno Black. 6.6 cm.
high, 12.5 cm. diam. Thick wall. Chipped rim.
117. Bowl (Form F-1), Horno Black. 5.6 cm.
high, 12 cm. diam. Thin wall, 1 mm. at rim.
118. Bowl (Form F-4), Horno Black. 7.5 cm.
high, 12.5 cm. diam. Burnish marks. Chipped
rim.

116

117

118

119. Spouted basin, Cabana Cream Resist. 12 cm. high, 19 cm. diam. Ext.: step-fret border, crosses, and crosshatch. Int.: red on cream framed panels of crested felines, step border. Restored, part of floor, wall, and spout broken.

120. Bowl (Form F-4), Cabana Cream Resist. 5.3 cm. high, 12.4 cm. diam. Ext.: framed panels of steps and crosses, border of steps and whirl. Int.: four red warrior heads in frame.

121. Bowl (Form F-4), Cabana Cream Resist. 5.2 cm. high, 12.2 cm. diam. Ext.: feline, head on tongue, in black and cream resist. Int.: plain. Very thin walls. See also fig. 165.

122. Jar (Form D), Pashash Orange Plain. 14.5 cm. high, 9 cm. diam., 4 mm. wall thickness. Yellow pigment powder on int. Shoulder flange lost.

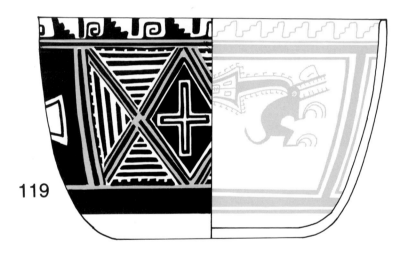

119

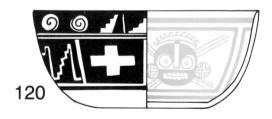

120

121

123. Jar (Form B-4), Cabana Cream Painted. 2.6 cm. high, 1.3 cm. diam. Ext.: lower half red slip. Int.: plain. Missing 8/7/75.

124. Jar (Form B-4), Cabana Cream Painted. 4.9 cm. high, 1.8 cm. diam. Ext.: upper half red slip to rim. Int.: plain. Missing 8/7/75.

125. Jar (Form B-4), Cabana Cream Painted. 4.8 cm. high, 2.2 cm. diam. Ext.: upper half red slip to rim. Int.: plain. Missing 8/7/75.

126. Spouted jar, Cabana Cream Resist. 3.3 cm. high, 1.3 cm. diam., 5 cm. length with spout. Ext.: concentric circles in red, cream, and black on walls. Int.: plain. Missing 8/7/75.

127. Jar (Form B-4), Cabana Cream Painted. 3 cm. high. Ext.: red band. Int.: plain. Missing 8/7/75.

128. Jar (Form D), Cabana Cream Resist. 14 cm. high, 11.5 cm. flange diam. Ext.: double-headed feline serpents, steps, concentric rectangles, red, black, and cream resist. Int.: plain. Restored, a few fragments missing. Flange at rim. See also fig. 65.

129. Figurine, Cabana Cream Painted. 7.8 cm. high. Man, probably a chief. Winged headdress, plain cream circle eye, cream step design on red tunic. Broken on right side. Missing 8/7/75. See also fig. 140.

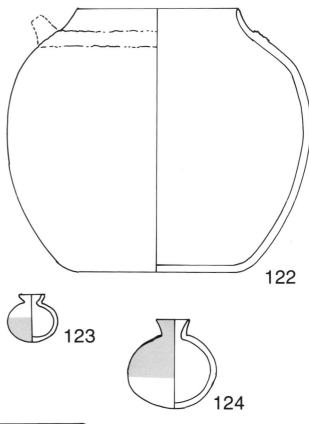

122

123

124

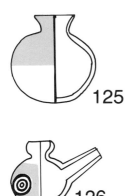

125

126

127

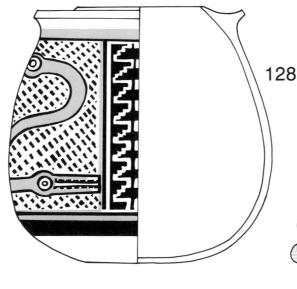

128

129

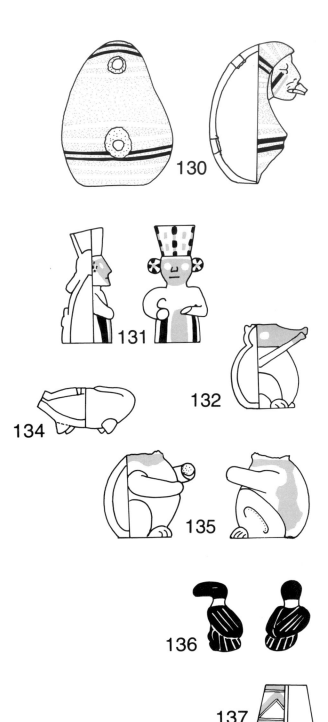

130. Effigy vessel, unclassified ware, dark red orange, probably imported. 8 cm. high. Two holes 1 cm. wide in back. Human figure, probably with hand touching mouth, blanket over head, face looks moldmade. Half of vessel broken away, lost. Wall 4 mm. thick. Face has red and black paint on orange slip. Back has pairs of black and pairs of white horizontal stripes on orange slip. See also figs. 41–42.

131. Figurine, Cabana Cream Painted. 6.3 cm. high. Male figure in tall hat. Red and brownish black on cream. Hands lost. Missing 8/7/75. See also figs. 154–155.

132. Figurine, Cabana Cream Painted. 4.6 cm. high. Small animal with long nose, thin front legs to nose. Red brown paint on head.

133. Figurine, Cabana Cream Painted. 4.5 cm. high. Animal and the legs of a lost human figure. Red on cream.

134. Figurine, Cabana Cream Painted. 4.5 cm. high. Animal. Head and left front paw lost. Red brown paint on neck.

135. Figurine, Caserón Orange Painted. 2.5 cm. high. Animal. Head lost. Red paint on neck and side.

136. Figurine, Cabana Cream Painted. 3.8 cm. high. Bird with large beak, black except for cream ring around neck. Break at feet. See also fig. 185.

137. Spindle whorl, Cabana Cream Painted. 3 cm. diam., 2.3 cm. high. Incised zigzag line, red lines. See also fig. 27.

138. Spindle whorl, Cabana Cream Painted. 2 cm. high, 2.7 cm. diam. Incised zigzag line, red lines. See also fig. 27.

139. Total potsherds in Level 7: 248
Pashash Orange Plain: 111
    Painted: 7
Caserón Orange Plain: 18
    Painted: 24
    Resist: 25
Cabana Cream Plain: 30
    Painted: 5
    Resist: 28

Level 8

Metal

1. Hollow cone, 2.6 cm. high, .5 cm. opening. Sheet gold. Tight joint, probably soldered. Repoussé indented grooves around cone. Flattened.

2. Eight identical ear spools, 2.5 cm. diam., 1.2 cm. deep, 1.6 cm. opening. Gold, with irregular corroded copper alloys. Two are broken. See fig. 125.

3. Flanged edge of wooden disk, 3.4 cm. diam., 5 mm. wide, rim 1 mm. wide. Gold. See fig. 126.

4. Flanged edge of wooden disk, 3.4 cm. diam., 5 mm. wide, rim 1 mm. wide. Gold. Traces of wood in channel. Identical to no. 3. See fig. 126.

5. Danglers. Four folded double circles, each circle 1.9 cm. diam. Very thin sheet copper, badly corroded. These were lying in triangular pedestal cup no. 25 below.

6. Pin shaft, curved, 10.9 cm. top to curve. Copper core, gold leaf. Head lost.

7. Mirror, 2.2 x 3.3 x .6 cm. Irregularly rounded shape, flat front and back. Face is polished iron pyrite with red cuprite spots. Edges and back are copper container with gold leaf (extant only in incisions). Back engraved with double-headed feline. Edge pierced for suspension. See fig. 202.

Stone

8. Three small pieces of rock crystal, largest 3.6 x 2 x .8 cm. Irregular chips.

9. Five white quartz pebbles, worn smooth by water, largest about 4 cm. diam.

10. Inlaid disk, 4.1 cm. diam., 1 mm. thick. Gray, perfect circle, material uncertain. Traces of yellow adhesive, inlays lost. Probably earplug ornament. See also fig. 127.

11. Disk, 2.3 cm. diam., less than 1 mm. thick. Traces of yellow adhesive. Probably earplug ornament.

12. Disk, 2.3 cm. diam. Porous adhesive on one side, greenish polished stone inlays in five-pointed star pattern. See also fig. 128.

13. Disk, 2.5 cm. diam. Traces of adhesive on one side.

14. Disk, 2.5 cm. diam. Five-pointed star of polished greenish stone attached with adhesive.

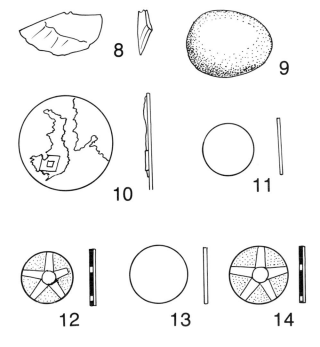

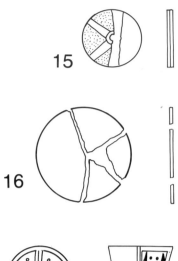

15

16

17

18

15. Two halves of disk with center hole. 2.6 cm. diam. Traces of five-pointed star inlay.

16. Four fragments of one disk, or parts of more. About 4.2 cm. diam. Traces of inlay attached with adhesive on one fragment.

17. Shiny black stone spindle whorl, 2.85 cm. base diam., 2 cm. top diam., 1.7 cm. high, 1.8 cm. on wall. Four jaguar-head designs on base and four on wall. Traces of red paint in excised areas. Hole .5 cm. diam. See also fig. 27.

18. Red stone spindle whorl, bell-shaped, 2.7 cm. base diam., 1.8 cm. top diam., 1.7 cm. high. Half of top broken off. Incised circle and dot on wall. Trace of red paint in incision. See also fig. 27.

Stucco

19. About half a cup of white stucco with red paint on smooth curved surfaces. No restorable form.

Wood

20. Two pieces of brown wood in good condition. Both 4.2 cm. long, 1.6 cm. diam. Smooth rounded ends. These may have been parts of earplugs.

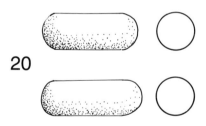

20

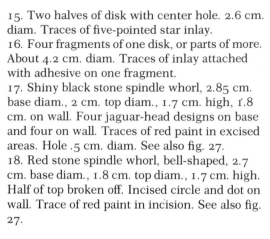

Ceramics

21. Pedestal cup, Cabana Cream Resist. 7.3 cm.
high, 13.4 cm. diam. Ext.: panels of cross and
crosshatch in black and cream (four crosses),
zigzag border. Int.: three feline serpents, looking somewhat like birds, in red on cream. See
also fig. 70.

22. Pedestal cup, Cabana Cream Resist. 5.8 cm.
high, 9.2 cm. diam. Ext.: crosses and crosshatch
in black and cream resist. Int.: red trophy heads.
Base: two red lines, like ||.

23. Pedestal cup, Cabana Cream Painted. 5.4
cm. high, 8.1 cm. diam. Ext.: red frames on
cream. Int.: red felines in frame. Base: two red
lines, like ||.

24. Triangular pedestal cup, Cabana Cream
Plain. 5.4 cm. high, 9.4 cm. on side. Red pigment powder in int.

25. Triangular pedestal cup, Cabana Cream
Painted. 6 cm. high, 8.8 cm. on side. Ext.: upper
half positive cream step on orange band. Int.:
plain. This contained no. 5 above.

26. Spindle whorl, Cabana Cream Painted with
incision. 2.7 cm. base diam., 2.1 cm. top diam.,
1.5 cm. high, 1.6 cm. along wall slant. Zigzag
designs on base and wall, red paint and incised
line.

27. Total potsherds in Level 8: 5
Pashash Orange Plain: 1
   Red-slipped: 4

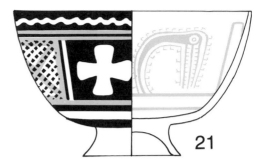

21

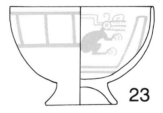

22

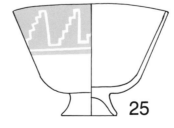

23

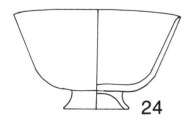

24

25

Bibliography

Alvarez-Brun, Félix
  1970 *Ancash: Una historia regional peruana.*
        Lima: Villanueva.
Arnheim, Rudolf
  1957 "Accident and the Necessity of Art." *Journal
        of Aesthetics and Art Criticism* 16 (Sep-
        tember). Reprinted in *Art History: An An-
        thology of Modern Criticism,* by Wylie
        Sypher, pp. 411–428. New York: Vintage,
        1963.
  1964 *Art and Visual Perception.* Berkeley & Los
        Angeles: University of California Press.
  1969 *Visual Thinking.* Berkeley & Los Angeles:
        University of California Press.
Avila, Francisco de
  1966 *Dioses y hombres de Huarochiri.* Translated
        by J. M. Arguedas. Bibliographical study by
        P. Duviols. Lima.
Bennett, Wendell C.
  1939 *Archaeology of the North Coast of Peru.*
        Anthropological Papers of the American
        Museum of Natural History 37, pt. 1. New
        York.
  1944 *The North Highlands of Peru: Excavations in
        the Callejón de Huaylas and at Chavín de
        Huantar.* Anthropological Papers of the
        American Museum of Natural History 39, pt.
        1. New York.

  1950 *The Gallinazo Group, Virú Valley, Peru.* Yale
        University Publications in Anthropology 43.
        New Haven: Yale University Press.
  1954 *Ancient Arts of the Andes.* New York:
        Museum of Modern Art.
Benson, Elizabeth P.
  1972 *The Mochica: A Culture of Peru.* New York:
        Praeger.
Covarrubias, Miguel
  1957 *Indian Art of Mexico and Central America.*
        New York: Alfred A. Knopf.
Disselhoff, Hans D.
  1971 *Vicus.* Berlin: Gebr. Mann Verlag.
Donnan, Christopher B.
  1971 "Ancient Peruvian Potters' Marks and Their
        Interpretation through Ethnographic Anal-
        ogy." *American Antiquity* 36, no. 4 (Oc-
        tober): 460–466.
  1973 *The Moche Occupation of the Santa Valley,
        Peru.* University of California Publications in
        Anthropology 8. Berkeley & Los Angeles:
        University of California Press.
Drucker, Philip, Robert F. Heizer, and Robert J.
Squier
  1959 *Excavations at La Venta, Tabasco, 1955.*
        Smithsonian Institution, Bureau of American
        Ethnology, bulletin 170. Washington, D.C.

Earle, Timothy K.
 1972 "Lurin Valley, Peru: Early Intermediate
   Period Settlement Development." *American
   Antiquity* 37, no. 4 (October): 467–477.
Easby, Elizabeth K.
 1968 *Pre-Columbian Jade from Costa Rica*. New
   York: André Emmerich.
Eliade, Mircea
 1964 *Shamanism: Archaic Techniques of Ecstasy*.
   Translated by Willard R. Trask. Bollingen
   Series 76. Princeton: Princeton University
   Press.
Emmerich, André
 1968 *Art of Ancient Peru: An Exhibition Or-
   ganized in Cooperation with Alan C. Lapiner*.
   December 7, 1968, to January 9, 1969. New
   York.
 1969 *Sun Gods and Saints. Art of Pre-Columbian
   and Colonial Peru: An Exhibition Organized
   in Cooperation with Alan C. Lapiner*. De-
   cember 6 to 13, 1969. New York.
Engel, Frederic
 1966 *Paracas: Cien siglos de cultura peruana*.
   Lima: Juan Mejía Baca.
Ford, James A., and Gordon R. Willey
 1949 *Surface Survey of the Virú Valley, Peru*.
   Anthropological Papers of the American
   Museum of Natural History 43. New York.
Foster, George M.
 1955 *Contemporary Pottery Techniques in South-
   ern and Central Mexico*. Middle American
   Research Institute 22. New Orleans: Tulane
   University.
Furst, Peter T.
 1968 "The Olmec Were-Jaguar Motif in the Light
   of Ethnographic Reality." In *Dumbarton
   Oaks Conference on the Olmec*, edited by
   Elizabeth P. Benson, pp. 143–174.
   Washington, D.C.: Dumbarton Oaks.
 1972 Editor. *Flesh of the Gods: The Ritual Use of
   Hallucinogens*. New York: Praeger.
Garcilaso de la Vega
 1966 *Royal Commentaries of the Incas and Gen-
   eral History of Peru*. Translated by Harold V.
   Livermore. 2 vols. Austin: University of
   Texas Press.
Grieder, Terence
 1975 "The Interpretation of Ancient Symbols."
   American Anthropologist 77, no. 4 (De-
   cember): 849–855.
Harner, Michael J.
 1972 *The Jivaro: People of the Sacred Waterfalls*.
   Garden City, N.Y.: Doubleday.
Heyden, Doris
 1975 "An Interpretation of the Cave underneath
   the Pyramid of the Sun in Teotihuacan,
   Mexico." *American Antiquity* 40, no. 2
   (April): 131–147.

Izumi, Seiichi, and Toshihiko Sono
 1963 *Andes 2: Excavations at Kotosh, Peru*.
   Tokyo: Kadokawa.
Kano, Chiaki
 1972 "Pre-Chavín Cultures in the Central High-
   lands of Peru: New Evidence from Shillacoto,
   Huánuco." In *The Cult of the Feline*, edited
   by Elizabeth P. Benson. Washington, D.C.:
   Dumbarton Oaks Research Library and Col-
   lection, Trustees for Harvard University.
Kauffmann Doig, Federico
 1973 *Manual de arqueología peruana*. 5th ed.
   Lima: Ediciones Peisa.
Kosok, Paul
 1965 *Life, Land, and Water in Ancient Peru*. New
   York: Long Island University Press.
Kubler, George
 1962 *Art and Architecture of Ancient America*.
   Pelican History of Art. Baltimore: Penguin.
 1967 *The Iconography of the Art of Teotihuacan*.
   Washington, D.C.: Dumbarton Oaks.
Lagunas R., Zaíd
 1975 "La determinación sexual en mandíbulas por
   medio de las funciones discriminantes."
   *Anales del Instituto Nacional de
   Antropología e Historia, 1972–1973*,
   época 7a, vol. 4. Mexico City.
Larco Hoyle, Rafael
 1945a *La cultura Virú*. Lima.
 1945b *Los Mochicas*. 2 vols. Lima.
 1960? *Escultura lítica del Perú pre-colombino*.
   Lima: Instituto de Arte Contemporáneo.
 1965? *La cultura Santa*. Lima: Museo Rafael
   Larco Herrera.
 1966 *Archaeologia Mundi: Peru*. Cleveland: World.
Lathrap, Donald W., Donald Collier, and Helen
Chandra
 1975 *Ancient Ecuador: Culture, Clay, and Creativ-
   ity, 3000–300 B.C.* Chicago: Field Museum
   of Natural History.
Lechtman, Heather
 1973 "The Gilding of Metals in Pre-Columbian
   Peru." In *The Application of Science in the
   Examination of Works of Art*, edited by William J. Young, pp. 31–37. Boston: Museum of
   Fine Arts.
———, Lee A. Parsons, and William J. Young
 1975 "Siete jaguares de oro del Horizonte Tem-
   prano." *Revista del Museo Nacional* 41:
   277–310. Lima.
Lizárraga, Fray Reginaldo de
 1946 *Descripción de las Indias*. Lima: F. A.
   Loayza.
Lumbreras, Luis G.
 1959 "Esquema arqueológica de la sierra central
   del Perú." *Revista del Museo Nacional* 28.
   Lima.